Parliament and the Church, 1529–1960

Parliament and the Church, 1529–1960

Edited by
J.P. Parry
Pembroke College, Cambridge

and
Stephen Taylor
University of Reading

Edinburgh University Press
for
The Parliamentary History Yearbook Trust

© 2000 Edinburgh University Press

Edinburgh University Press
22 George Square
Edinburgh

Typeset in Bembo by WestKey Limited, Falmouth, Cornwall and
printed and bound in Great Britain by Page Bros Ltd, Norwich

A CIP record for this title is available from the British Library

ISBN 0 7486 1445 1

CONTENTS

PREFACE

This present collection of essays on *Parliament and the Church, 1529–1960* is the sixth in a series of special volumes sponsored by the journal *Parliamentary History*, and published by Edinburgh University Press for The Parliamentary History Yearbook Trust. The series consists of volumes on particular topics (like the present one) as well as collections of essays covering specific periods. The seventh in the series to be published in 2001 will be on Ireland and parliament.

Clyve Jones

General Editor

Versions of all the papers in this volume, except the introduction, were first given at the fifth *Parliamentary History* Conference, held at the Institute of Historical Research, London, on 15 July 1998. As the organisers of that conference, we are very grateful to the staff of the Institute of Historical Research for their help on the day, and especially to Bridget Taylor. Linda Clark, David Hayton and Clyve Jones all contributed greatly to the success of the event, as did the chairmen of the four sessions, who in addition to one of the editors, were John Morrill, Julian Hoppit and David Cannadine. Eleven of the 12 papers presented then are reproduced here; in revised form the twelfth (by Stephen Taylor) will appear in *Parliamentary History*, XIX (2000). We would like to thank the contributors for their co-operation, and Alasdair Hawkyard who compiled the index. We are also grateful to Arthur Burns, John Morrill and Brian Watchorn for very helpful comments on a draft of the introduction, and to Gerald Bray for valuable assistance on specific points therein.

Our intention in planning the conference was always to concentrate on relations between parliament and the Church of England. However, we did not wish to exclude discussion of the dissenting sects, and indeed of religious issues in politics in general. In the event, two of the papers focused on dissent. Both dealt with broad issues, clearly relevant to the Church of England's relationship with the political world, and it is appropriate that both should be included in this volume. It has recently been decided to devote a future *Parliamentary History* conference to the theme of parliament and dissent.

In the footnotes the place of publication is London unless otherwise stated.

J.P. Parry
Stephen Taylor

Editors

LIST OF CONTRIBUTORS

Clyde Binfield is professor associate in history at the University of Sheffield. He is the author of *George Williams and the Y.M.C.A.* (1973), *So Down to Prayers* (1977) and *Pastors and People* (1984), and a co-editor of the *History of the City of Sheffield* (3 vols., 1993). He has also written many papers in journals and collected volumes on his main research area, the architectural, cultural and ecclesiastical context of English nonconformity.

Arthur Burns is lecturer in Modern British History at King's College London. He is the author of *The Diocesan Revival in the Church of England, 1800–75* (1999). He has also written on the legitimation of Church reform and has edited W. J. Conybeare's *Church Parties* for the Church of England Record Society.

Patrick Carter was a research fellow at McMaster University and a temporary lecturer at the University of St Andrews. He is the author of several articles on clerical taxation and finances in early modern England.

Matthew Cragoe is currently senior lecturer in British history at the University of Hertfordshire. His publications include *An Anglican Aristocracy. The Moral Economy of the Landed Estate in Carmarthenshire, 1832–95* (1996), and several articles on mid-Victorian Welsh politics. He is currently engaged in writing a study entitled *Culture, Politics and the Rise of National Identity in Wales, 1832–95*.

G.M. Ditchfield is reader in eighteenth-century history at University of Kent at Canterbury. He is co-editor of *British Parliamentary Lists, 1660–1800* (1995), and author of *The Evangelical Revival* (1998) and many essays and articles on eighteenth-century British political and religious history.

S.J.D. Green is extraordinary research fellow of All Souls College, Oxford, and senior lecturer in history at the University of Leeds. He is author of *Religion in the Age of Decline. Organisation and Experience in Industrial Yorkshire, 1870–1920* (1996) and editor (with R.C. Whiting) of *The Boundaries of the State in Modern Britain* (1996). He is the co-editor of *Northern History*.

Colin Haydon is principal lecturer in history at King Alfred's College, Winchester. He is the author of *Anti-Catholicism in Eighteenth-Century England, c. 1714–80. A Political and Social Study* (1993). He has also edited (with John Walsh and Stephen Taylor) *The Church of England, c. 1689–1833. From Toleration to Tractarianism* (1993) and (with William Doyle) *Robespierre* (1999).

G.I.T. Machin is professor of British history at the University of Dundee. He has written various books on British churches in relation to political and social developments, including *Politics and the Churches in Great Britain, 1832 to 1868* (1977), *Politics* and the Churches in Great Britain, 1869 to 1921 (1987), and *Churches and Social Issues in Twentieth-Century Britain* (1998).

J.P. Parry is lecturer in history at the University of Cambridge and a fellow and director of studies at Pembroke College. His books include *Democracy and Religion. Gladstone and the Liberal Party 1867–1875* (Cambridge, 1986) and *The Rise and Fall of Liberal Government in Victorian Britain* (New Haven, 1993).

Conrad Russell has held posts at Bedford College London (1960–79), Yale (1979–84) and University College London (1984–90). Since 1990 he has been professor of British history at King's College London. He is the author of *Parliaments and English Politics 1621–1629* (1979), *The Causes of the English Civil War* (1990), *The Fall of the British Monarchies 1637–42* (1991) and other works. He has also been a practising parliamentarian in the house of lords since 1988.

David L. Smith is fellow, director of studies in history and admissions tutor at Selwyn College, Cambridge. His publications include *Oliver Cromwell* (1991), *Louis XIV* (1992), *Constitutional Royalism and the Search for Settlement, c. 1640–49* (1994), *The Theatrical City. Culture, Theatre and Politics in London, 1576–1649* (co-edited with Richard Strier and David Bevington, 1995), *A History of the Modern British Isles, 1603–1707. The Double Crown* (1998), and *The Stuart Parliaments, 1603–1689* (1999).

Stephen Taylor is reader in history at the University of Reading. He has published numerous articles on politics and religion in the early eighteenth century. Most recently he has edited (with Richard Connors and Clyve Jones) *Hanoverian Britain and Empire. Essays in Memory of Philip Lawson* (1998) and *From Cranmer to Davidson. A Church of England Miscellany* (1999).

Allen Warren has been a member of the history department at the University of York since 1971. He is presently head of department and also provost of Vanbrugh College. His research interests are centred on nineteenth-century British and Irish politics and the history of youth in Britain, on which he has written many articles.

Introduction: Parliament and the Church of England from the Reformation to the Twentieth Century

J.P. PARRY

and

STEPHEN TAYLOR

The histories of the Church of England and of parliament are inextricably linked. The English Reformation may have had its origins in Henry VIII's desire for a divorce from Catherine of Aragon, but the break with Rome was effected between 1529 and 1536 by a series of statutes passed by the king in parliament.[1] This had profound constitutional implications, affecting both parliament and the Church. On the one hand, although parliament was to remain a spasmodic event in the English political calendar for another 150 years, the legislation passed by the Reformation Parliament between 1529 and 1536 did much to secure the primacy of statute in English law. On the other hand, the Church which emerged from the burst of Reformation law making was, in many respects, a parliamentary Church. The role assumed by parliament in matters of religion was revealed most clearly by the Acts of Uniformity of 1549, 1552, 1559 and 1662, establishing successive Books of Common Prayer as the only legal form of worship.[2] Not only was the Church's liturgy being imposed by parliamentary statute; that body was also, in effect, implementing changes in religious doctrine. Even during the interregnum, when the Church of England had been dismantled, parliament assumed that it had the right to mould the religious settlement, as David Smith shows in his essay in this volume. What is more, Oliver Cromwell, despite being deeply at odds with the first protectorate parliament over its opposition to the promotion of liberty of conscience, did not attempt to challenge that right.

The role of parliament in religious affairs was not, however, clearly defined. The legislative legacy of the Reformation was very ambiguous, and consequently the relationship between Church and state was a matter of considerable controversy in the sixteenth and seventeenth centuries. One debate concerned the nature of the royal supremacy: was it personal or did it reside in the monarch in parliament?[3] Under Henry VIII it was clearly regarded as essentially personal. After all, the Act of Supremacy of 1534 had not claimed to be conferring new powers upon the king; it had merely recognized and confirmed that he was supreme head of the Church in England, entitled to exercise

---

[1] *Documents of the English Reformation*, ed. Gerald Bray (Minneapolis, 1994), pp. 41–117; Stanford E. Lehmberg, *The Reformation Parliament 1529–1536* (Cambridge, 1970).

[2] *Documents of the English Reformation*, ed. Bray, pp. 266–71, 281–3, 329–34, 546–59.

[3] On the royal supremacy, see Claire Cross, *The Royal Supremacy in the Elizabethan Church* (1969), p. 23; D. M. Loades, *The Oxford Martyrs* (1970), ch. 2.

powers which had always belonged to the crown. The 1559 Act of Supremacy, however, was more open to other interpretations. In part, this was because Elizabeth, by choosing to style herself supreme governor rather than supreme head 'renounced the semi-ecclesiastical', Constantinian aspect of the Henrician supremacy.[4] But it was also because the act restored the royal supremacy 'by the authority' of parliament. Elizabeth clearly believed that her supremacy was essentially personal and tried to exclude parliament from a role in Church affairs. But many parliamentarians, lawyers and even churchmen contested this interpretation, insisting that it should be exercised through the queen in parliament.

This issue was a major source of tension between crown and parliament throughout the late sixteenth and early seventeenth centuries. An early cause of conflict was Elizabeth's refusal between 1563 and 1571 to allow parliament to consider and confirm the 39 articles – the formulation of articles of faith was, she maintained, an issue for her and convocation. More controversial, perhaps, was the long running debate over the powers of the court of high commission, established in the early 1560s and grounded on section 8 of the 1559 Act of Supremacy, which explicitly granted to the queen the authority to delegate her ecclesiastical jurisdiction to others. In particular, attention focused on the claim by the court to exercise powers, such as the *ex officio* oath, not available at common law, an issue which provoked fierce attacks on the court by parliamentarians and common lawyers, in 1593 and again in 1610. In 1641 they won an important victory, securing the abolition of the court, when section 8 was repealed. Despite this, the controversy refused to disappear, rumbling on until 1689, when the establishment by James II of a commission for ecclesiastical causes was declared illegal by the Bill of Rights.[5]

Another area of ambiguity in the Reformation settlement, discussed in the first two chapters of this volume, concerned the legislative power and independence of the Church. As Conrad Russell's contribution reminds us, the Act in Restraint of Appeals (1533) offered a definition of the body politic which could be used by churchmen and ecclesiastical lawyers to assert the independence of the spiritual jurisdiction. By contrast, the Act for the Submission of the Clergy (1534) enabled common lawyers and others to claim that that jurisdiction was inferior to the temporal, limited not only by the royal supremacy but also by the force of parliamentary statute. The debate between these con-flicting conceptions of the constitution focused on the power and role of two institutions: the ecclesiastical courts and convocation, the Church's legislative body.[6] Controversy was particularly heated in the decades before the outbreak of the civil war. Lawyers, such as Sir Edward Coke, tried to assert the supremacy of the common law courts over the ecclesiastical, while parliamentarians contested the independent powers of convocation. In 1604 James I's approval of a new set of canons provoked protests that, without parliamentary approval, they could not apply to the laity. But the right of convocation to pass legislation in ecclesiastical matters was only one element in the

---

[4] Cross, *The Royal Supremacy*, p. 23.

[5] J. P. Kenyon, 'The Commission for Ecclesiastical Causes 1686–1688: A Reconsideration', *Historical Journal*, XXXIV (1991), 727–36.

[6] On the ecclesiastical courts see *The Anglican Canons 1529–1947*, ed. Gerald Bray (Woodbridge, 1998), pp. xcii–cxii. In the absence of any modern study, Thomas Lathbury, *A History of the Convocation of the Church of England* (2nd edn., 1853), remains useful.

broader debate. As Patrick Carter's essay reveals, in the early seventeenth century there was also parliamentary concern about the power of convocation to grant clerical subsidies to the crown. In the constitutional crisis of 1640–1 these two issues were closely linked. When convocation continued to sit after the dissolution of the Short Parliament in order to approve a subsidy and to frame further canons, controversy was inevitable, and both actions were among the grievances complained of by the Commons in the 'grand remonstrance' of November 1641.

In 1660 the pre-civil war ecclesiastical constitution was restored intact, leaving this debate, like so many others concerning the powers of parliament, unresolved. Churchmen were, however, fighting a losing battle. Archbishop Sheldon's agreement of 1664 that the clergy should surrender the power to tax themselves was, as Carter notes, fatal to the power of convocation. Between then and 1717 that body met to do business in only 16 years and failed to pass any new canons; after 1717 it did not meet to do business for almost a century and a half.[7] Vigorous defenders of the legislative independence of the Church could still be found in the early eighteenth century. Anticlerical initiatives, such as the Ecclesiastical Courts Bill of 1733, which would have subordinated the spiritual courts to the temporal even in cases concerning morals, were fiercely resisted by churchmen.[8] Significantly, however, Lord Chief Justice Hardwicke's judgment in 1736 that the canons of 1604 did not apply to the laity provoked no *public* protests from the Church hierarchy, which recognized that the strength of opposition to Church power among the parliamentary and legal classes would have made any assertion of the principle of the independence of spiritual jurisdiction a futile and possibly counter-productive gesture.[9] The declining business of the ecclesiastical courts by the mid-eighteenth century may have made the issue less sensitive. Whatever the reason, by the 1830s the dominance of the common law tradition and the supremacy of statute were established as essential features of the English constitution. The inferiority of the spiritual jurisdiction was made explicit in 1833 by the creation of the judicial committee of the privy council as the final court of appeal in ecclesiastical causes; its procedure followed the common law, and secular judges were in a majority. This body showed its willingness to overturn rulings of the ecclesiastical courts on doctrinal issues, most famously in its Gorham judgment (1850) and the *Essays and Reviews* case (1864). Nor did the revival of convocation in 1852 imply any reassertion of the Church's claim to legislative independence, as it had been articulated in the seventeenth century. The supremacy of parliament was tacitly accepted, a fact acknowledged by the Enabling Act of 1919, which constituted the church assembly and provided for parliamentary ratification or rejection of its measures by a single vote.

---

[7] G. V. Bennett, *The Tory Crisis in Church and State 1688–1730. The Career of Francis Atterbury, Bishop of Rochester* (Oxford, 1975).

[8] Stephen Taylor, 'Whigs, Tories and Anticlericalism: Ecclesiastical Courts Legislation in 1733', *Parliamentary History*, XIX (2000). This was originally given as a paper at the 1998 *Parliamentary History* conference.

[9] In the case of *Middleton v. Crofts*. See Norman Sykes, *From Sheldon to Secker. Aspects of English Church History 1660–1768* (Cambridge, 1959), p. 203.

1

By excluding the power of the pope and establishing the royal supremacy over the Church, it was inevitable that the Reformation should have provoked debate about the constitutional position and authority of the Church of England. Neither the break with Rome nor the doctrinal changes of the next 40 years, however, challenged the idea that it was the spiritual embodiment of the nation. Towards the end of the sixteenth century Richard Hooker stressed the identity of Church and state in a christian commonwealth; the Church of England was the Church of all the English people.[10] But gradually it became apparent that the identification of Church and nation was under threat, in practice if not in theory. On the one hand, there were those who adhered to the old religion and refused to accept the Reformation. By the early years of Elizabeth's reign there had emerged a recusant community conscious of its distinctness within the nation.[11] On the other hand, there were those who sought to assert the protestant claim to the exercise of private judgment in matters of religion in ways which were unacceptable to the authorities in Church and state, who wished to push the Reformation further, and who were prepared to separate from the Church if their proposals were not accepted. Until the outbreak of the civil war protestant separatism was never more than a small problem. However, the abolition of episcopacy, the dismantling of the judicial structures of the Church, and the ensuing proliferation of sects during the 1640s and 1650s significantly and permanently changed the religious demography of England and Wales. When the Church of England was restored between 1660 and 1662, some 2,000 predominantly puritan ministers felt unable to conform to the new religious settlement.[12] From this point there was a numerous and significant body of protestant dissenters as well as catholic recusants outside the Church. The *via media* of anglicanism took on a new meaning, and increasingly in the late seventeenth and eighteenth centuries it was defined as the golden mean between the superstition of popery and the extravagancies of organized dissent. Implicitly, however, this identity involved the recognition that the Church of England no longer embraced all Englishmen.

For the first century and a half after the Reformation, parliament had tended to support the ideal of religious uniformity. Weekly attendance at church was required by the 1559 Act of Uniformity, a provision which was reinforced by a raft of Elizabethan and Jacobean statutes against popery. The Cavalier Parliament elected in 1661 proved equally hostile to the practice of religious nonconformity, enacting the repressive 'Clarendon code' in an attempt to stamp out dissent. The motivation behind this legislation was political and religious.[13] Both catholics and protestant dissenters were seen as enemies to the constitution and threats to the state, but it was also accepted that it was the duty of the civil power to promote religious truth. Adherence to true christian belief was one of the ways in which the English nation, God's chosen people, could assure itself of

[10] Richard Hooker, *Of the Laws of Ecclesiastical Polity. An Abridged Edition*, ed. A. S. McGrade and Brian Vickers (1975), pp. 339–40.

[11] John Bossy, *The English Catholic Community 1570–1850* (1975), ch. 1.

[12] Michael R. Watts, *The Dissenters from the Reformation to the French Revolution* (Oxford, 1978), p. 219.

[13] Paul Seaward, *The Cavalier Parliament and the Reconstruction of the Old Regime 1661–1667* (Cambridge, 1989), pp. 186–95.

his continued blessings. This hostility to the theory and practice of religious toleration was manifested by parliament even in the 1650s. As David Smith shows in this volume, the presbyterian majority in the first protectorate parliament supported the idea of a national ministry which should publicly profess its conformity to the doctrines of the protestant reformed religion and stubbornly sought to restrict Cromwell's efforts to promote liberty of conscience.

After the Restoration there was a variety of responses to the pluralism which was now one of the facts of English religious life.[14] Charles II seems to have favoured some kind of toleration, promising a 'liberty to tender consciences' in the declaration of Breda in 1660, reaffirming that promise in the so-called declaration of indulgence of 1663, and finally issuing a declaration of indulgence, grounded on his prerogative powers, in 1672. Moreover, there is some evidence that the king was determined that any indulgence should apply to catholics as well as protestant dissenters. Among the dissenters some – mainly presbyterians – were attracted by the idea of a comprehension, extending the Church's terms of communion so as to allow them to conform, while others – independents, baptists and quakers, as well as some presbyterians – looked for a toleration which would allow them the freedom to worship as their consciences dictated. Some of these advocates of toleration were quite happy to see it established, as in 1672, by virtue of the royal prerogative, while others were only prepared to see it secured by parliamentary statute. Within the Church, among the laity as well as the clergy, could be found supporters of both comprehension and toleration, their main concern being, most notably at the time of the exclusion crisis of 1679–81, to foster unity among English protestants of all denominations, so that they could better resist the advance of the Counter Reformation, whether at home or abroad.[15] But among the clergy the advocates of the policy of intolerance were in the ascendant, resisting both comprehension and toleration, seeking to defend the true religion and fearing the consequences of introducing schism into Church and state.[16] In the 1660s the Cavalier Parliament, many of whose members saw the catholics and particularly the dissenters as responsible for plunging the country into the chaos of the 1640s, also remained firmly committed to upholding religious uniformity by force. Indeed, on occasion it is possible to discern an alliance between parliament and the Church against the crown, as Charles II sought to advance a policy of religious toleration.[17] When the king issued his declaration of indulgence in 1672, parliament responded not only by declaring that use of his suspending power illegal but also by passing the Test Act which restricted civil and military offices to members of the established Church. However, over the next decade there were a number of indications that parliament was becoming more sympathetic to the plight of dissenters – such as the bill 'for the ease of Protestant Dissenters' introduced following the passage of the Test Act in 1673.

[14] John Spurr, 'The Church of England, Comprehension and the Toleration Act of 1689', *English Historical Review*, CIV (1989), 927–46; Roger Thomas, 'Comprehension and Indulgence', in *From Uniformity to Unity 1662–1962*, ed. Geoffrey F. Nuttall and Owen Chadwick (1962), pp. 189–253.

[15] Henry Horwitz, 'Protestant Reconciliation in the Exclusion Crisis', *Journal of Ecclesiastical History*, XV (1964), 201–17.

[16] Mark Goldie, 'The Theory of Religious Intolerance in Restoration England', in *From Persecution to Toleration. The Glorious Revolution and Religion in England*, ed. Ole Peter Grell, Jonathon I. Israel and Nicholas Tyacke (Oxford, 1991), pp. 331–68.

[17] Ronald Hutton, *The Restoration. A Political and Religious History of England and Wales 1658–1667* (1985), pp. 199–200, 213–14.

The relaxation of the laws against protestant dissenters finally occurred with the passage of the Toleration Act in 1689. In retrospect, this act appears as a landmark in the development of religious liberty in England and Wales; in fact, it was a highly contingent event, dependent on the shifting alliances of Restoration politics. The accession of William III, a Dutch calvinist sympathetic to the position of the dissenters, undoubtedly contributed to the achievement of toleration. But of far more importance was the impact of the policies of his predecessor, James II, who used his prerogative powers to issue a declaration of indulgence, granting religious freedom to catholics and protestant dissenters, in April 1687. While the declaration won the support of some dissenters, others remained suspicious of the intentions of a catholic king. James's actions also alienated the anglican hierarchy, which had been one of his strongest supports during the attempts to exclude him from the succession to the crown in the early 1680s. The bishops, in an attempt to reinforce protestant unity in the face of James's catholicizing policies, committed themselves to supporting concessions to nonconformists which would be grounded on parliamentary statutes. In the event, the 1689 act was a much more limited measure than James's declaration, its character being well illustrated by its full title: 'An act for excepting their majesties' protestant subjects dissenting from the church of England from the penalties of certain laws'. It merely granted to trinitarian nonconformists the freedom to worship publicly according to their consciences; it allowed them no civil equality.[18] Even so, many high church clergy and their tory allies continued to hanker after the authoritarian anglican regime of the past and for the next 25 years pressed for at least some limitation on the concessions granted by the Toleration Act.[19] Gradually, however, the 1689 settlement, which, it was claimed, allowed liberty to tender consciences while providing security for the established Church by means of the Test Act, came to be widely accepted by churchmen of all shades of opinion. Indeed, by the early eighteenth century toleration was seen as one of the glories of both the English constitution and the anglican Church.

Roman catholics continued to be treated differently. As Colin Haydon's article makes clear, the old penal statutes remained and some new ones were added. However, the justification for anti-catholic legislation was being placed on a narrower footing. By the early eighteenth century toleration was increasingly being supported, as John Locke had done, by an appeal to the natural rights of the subject to follow his conscience in matters of religion. Yet the concessions granted to protestant dissenters were denied to catholics, not however for their religious beliefs but rather, as Locke had also argued, for political reasons, above all because they owed their allegiance to a foreign power.[20] While this had always been one key argument in the anti-catholic case, by the mid-eighteenth century it was increasingly relied on as the only reason for the denial of toleration to catholics. In practice, their treatment, by clergy and laity alike, ensured that they enjoyed a *de facto* freedom to worship as they chose. Later in the century the decline in the threat from jacobitism in Britain and the Counter Reformation on

---

[18] *Documents of the English Reformation*, ed. Bray, pp. 570–7; W. A. Speck, *Reluctant Revolutionaries. Englishmen and the Revolution of 1688* (Oxford, 1988), ch. 8.

[19] G. V. Bennett, 'Conflict in the Church', in *Britain after the Glorious Revolution 1689–1714*, ed. Geoffrey Holmes (1969), pp. 155–75.

[20] John Locke, *A Letter Concerning Toleration*, ed. James H. Tully (Indianapolis, 1983).

the continent meant that catholics ceased to be seen as a potential fifth column and it became easier to grant legal recognition to the recusant community. The significance of the Relief Act when it finally came in 1778 was largely symbolic – in practice the few laws which it repealed had never been implemented. A similar point might be made about the change in attitudes towards protestant dissenters in the course of the eighteenth century. In theory they were excluded from most civil offices by the Test and Corporation Acts, but the Indemnity Acts, passed almost annually from 1728, rendered their prosecution very difficult. Moreover, parliament imposed no religious tests on the members of the multitude of statutory bodies established in the eighteenth century to administer enterprises such as canals and turnpikes. Thus, dissenters (and even some catholics) exercised considerable power in local government.[21] In practice, therefore, the Test Act, that great bulwark of the pre-1828 anglican constitution, was becoming of very limited significance.

Certainly, as G. M. Ditchfield reveals in his essay on ecclesiastical legislation under the Younger Pitt, by the end of the eighteenth century a significant gap was opening up between the attitudes of most of the anglican hierarchy and those expressed in parliament. William Pitt was prepared at least to contemplate the repeal of the Test and Corporation Acts, still defended by many churchmen as the guarantors of the constitutional position of the Church. Moreover, while Pitt and the ministry remained firmly committed to the idea of the Church as a national, established body, especially in the wake of the French revolution, the grounds on which that establishment was supported were subtly changing. Though there was still anxiety to uphold the Church as a divinely ordained institution responsible for the propagation of true religion, the widespread perception of political and social crisis ensured that a particular emphasis would be placed on its value as an essential spiritual, educational and charitable organization. This conception of its social function was to prove immensely valuable in defending its established status in the nineteenth century.

2

Though the repeal of the Test and Corporation Acts in 1828, the granting of catholic emancipation in 1829 and the Reform Act of 1832 were not in themselves revolutionary, each ensured that parliament could not ignore the variety of religious opinion in the nation. Their passage in quick succession stimulated a debate of unprecedented intensity about the Church's role.[22] The number of M.P.s professing non-anglican beliefs was significantly increased by the legislation of 1828 to 1832. In the 1830s, protestant dissenters lobbied for legislation to tackle six historic grievances; radicals charged that the Church establishment was a nest of 'old corruption'; O'Connell made sure that Westminster did not forget the problems of Irish catholics.[23] Anglican whigs

[21] Paul Langford, *Public Life and the Propertied Englishman 1689–1798* (Oxford, 1991), pp. 72–80.

[22] Two useful overviews of the relationship between religion and politics in the nineteenth century are David Hempton, *Religion and Political Culture in Britain and Ireland. From the Glorious Revolution to the Decline of Empire* (Cambridge, 1996), and John Wolffe, *God and Greater Britain. Religion and National Life in Britain and Ireland, 1843–1945* (1994).

[23] G. I. T. Machin, *Politics and the Churches in Great Britain 1832 to 1868* (Oxford, 1977), ch. 2.

sought to build a new political coalition on the principle of renegotiating the church-state relationship, hoping to attract but also discipline these radical groups and to shore up a reformed establishment. The compromise which emerged in the late 1830s involved a recognition of the nation's religious diversity (the legalization of civil marriage; state support for non-anglican education) and internal redistribution of Church wealth, but also a reassertion of the national and established status of the Church.[24] Moreover, leading whigs expected parliament (and the judicial committee of the privy council) to guarantee that national status against attempts by Church factions to restrict its doctrinal latitude. The controversies that developed while this compromise was being hammered out gave a boost to the development of the two-party system; committed defenders of Anglican supremacy naturally gravitated to the Conservatives and staunch critics of the ecclesiastical status quo to the Liberal coalition.[25] However, the fervour of many in both camps embarrassed their party leaders; in particular, the Conservatives' ill-fated attempt of 1843 to assert the Church's rights in the field of factory education demonstrated the counter-productiveness of an active defence strategy.[26]

Nor could the Church itself agree on such a strategy. Some churchmen sought to challenge radical claims that the Church was a mere sectional and exclusive body by reasserting its national scope as a social and spiritual force. Some (usually but not always different people) aimed to assert its independence from control by a liberal parliament and secular jurisdiction. Each instinct spawned a variety of approaches. The former group included conservatives who clung to traditional notions of Church status, but also broad churchmen who sought to use parliamentary pressure to help reform the Church in a more expansive and inclusive direction. The latter included many who hoped that steps towards self-government – such as the gradual revival of convocation from 1852 – could be taken without compensatory surrender of the Church's political privileges; but there were also some who recognized that substantial surrender might be necessary or desirable, and that this might even include established status itself.[27]

Between 1832 and 1867, most M.P.s, Conservative and Liberal, appreciated the Church's social function, were unwilling to contemplate disturbing its established status, and therefore assumed the right of parliament to legislate for it. But this made Church reform very difficult, as Arthur Burns's essay on the fate of clergy discipline legislation shows. Given the other demands on the parliamentary timetable, bishops

[24] O. Chadwick, *The Victorian Church. Part I* (1966), ch. 2; R. Brent, *Liberal Anglican Politics. Whiggery, Religion and Reform 1830–1841* (Oxford, 1987); J. P. Ellens, *Religious Routes to Gladstonian Liberalism. The Church Rate Conflict in England and Wales, 1832–1868* (University Park, PA, 1994), ch. 1.

[25] D. H. Close, 'The Formation of a Two-Party Alignment in the House of Commons between 1832 and 1841', *English Historical Review*, LXXXIV (1969), 257–77; John Wolffe, *The Protestant Crusade in Great Britain, 1829–1860* (Oxford, 1991), ch. 3.

[26] On dissenting radicals, see M. R. Watts, *The Dissenters. Volume II: The Expansion of Evangelical Nonconformity* (Oxford, 1995), ch. 4, and Ellens, *Religious Routes*, chs. 1 and 2; on 1843, see N. Gash, *Reaction and Reconstruction in English Politics 1832–1852* (Oxford, 1965), pp. 86–91, and Machin, *Politics and the Churches 1832 to 1868*, pp. 151–60.

[27] See e.g. O. Brose, *Church and Parliament. The Reshaping of the Church of England 1828–1860* (Stanford, 1959); M. A. Crowther, *Church Embattled. Religious Controversy in Mid-Victorian England* (Newton Abbot, 1970); P. A. Butler, *Gladstone: Church, State and Tractarianism. A Study of his Religious Ideas and Attitudes 1809–1859* (Oxford, 1982), ch. 5.

needed a great deal of patience. They also needed government acquiescence in their bills, so these often had to reflect whig constitutional assumptions. Parliament was also a problem, not so much because of obstruction by dissenters as because of a general radical and evangelical suspicion of bills that asserted episcopal authority, which became more marked in the 1840s and 1850s.

But, as he demonstrates, prospects for legislation were also damaged by the debates within the Church about its internal structure and its constitutional relationship with the state. The bishops were themselves divided on the issue of clergy discipline; the lower clergy, increasingly assertive about their status, were demanding more participation in Church affairs; much lay opinion was wary of excessive episcopal and clerical power and anxious for involvement.[28] In other words, the Church was exploring the degree of constitutional reform required, in the mid-nineteenth century, by an institution with pretensions to national status. This vigorous debate was enlivened further by the intense controversy over ritualism from the 1850s onwards. Ritualists were unpopular in the media; they weakened the Church's ability to project itself as a centrist national force; they demonstrated the inadequacy of episcopal authority. Many M.P.s felt that it was necessary for parliament to act against them in order to prevent the Church from narrowing its appeal. But ritualists presented attempts to discipline them as an unwarranted interference in religious affairs by a despotic secular state. To them, the 1874 Public Worship Regulation Act, a compromise between the bishops and the government, was a two-pronged erastian assault: the manner of its passing, and its proposal that a lay judge should decide cases of liturgical illegality, were equally offensive. The affair, and the subsequent support given to imprisoned ritualist martyrs, showed the impossibility of getting the Church to settle its constitutional differences.[29]

3

By the 1860s and 1870s, then, the variety of opinion about religious politics, in Church and parliament, ensured on the one hand that ecclesiastical issues played a large part in public life, and on the other that agreement on a decided religious policy was almost impossible to reach. This is shown by the fate of Disraeli's attempt to organize Conservatism around the principle of Church defence in the 1860s, analysed by Allen Warren in his article. There was widespread concern about the survival of religious values, which seemed challenged by science, by middle-class materialism and by working-class ignorance. There was also anxiety about the threats to established institutions and customs posed by assertively confident dissenters and by secular radicals, especially if these groups could harness central state power (and the newly left-leaning Gladstone) to their ends. Disraeli built on these fears with a series of Church defence speeches and initiatives. But Warren's account reveals the two great problems that this strategy

[28] On the clergy especially, see A. Burns, *The Diocesan Revival in the Church of England, 1800–1870* (Oxford, 1999).

[29] P. T. Marsh, *The Victorian Church in Decline. Archbishop Tait and the Church of England 1868–1882* (1969), chs. 5, 7; J. Bentley, *Ritualism and Politics in Victorian Britain. The Attempt to Legislate for Belief* (Oxford, 1978).

encountered – one in the Church sphere, the other in the parliamentary. The first was the diversity of opinion within the Church about its future. Disraeli could not get agreement among the Church parties, many members of which were no longer primarily interested in fighting their battles by political means. The second was that an avowed policy of 'Church defence' was no longer the only way of building a religious coalition at the parliamentary level. Gladstone, who was similarly concerned about the defence of the Church and about the challenges from modern materialism, had an alternative strategy.

Gladstone's approach was to use the language of regeneration to integrate anglicans, dissenters and Irish catholics within the Liberal party.[30] Of course he could not do this alone; Liberalism was already developing an interest in reflecting and celebrating the country's religious pluralism. In the provinces, different pressure groups were seeking the space to articulate their own political needs, encouraged by the notion that, with continued agitation, these might one day assume legislative form.[31] Matthew Cragoe's essay demonstrates the way in which activist Welsh Liberal M.P.s sought to create a new local political culture, defining Wales as (among other things) a nation of nonconformists. To this end they used a series of religious issues – opening anglican burial grounds to nonconformist services, and giving congregations powers to purchase land for schools or chapels, as well as the more well-known elementary education question. The Liberal appeal to religious and national identity in Wales, like its separate legislation for Ireland, was part of an attempt to establish an inclusive pluralist identity for the United Kingdom as a whole.

These Conservative and Liberal strategies ensured that religious issues contributed a great deal to the character of both parties in the 1860s and 1870s. But the legislative consequences of this religious partisanship were much less far-reaching than many contemporaries feared. Both parties came to appreciate the dangers of excessive religious bias in their policies, in view of the diversity of national sentiment on ecclesiastical topics. Liberals found that powerful elements of anglican and dissenting opinion reacted vehemently against their 1870 Education Act; they shied away from further major educational reform. Having observed the controversy about disestablishment in the early 1870s (stimulated by the Irish Church Act of 1869), the Liberal leadership was equally cautious about future commitments in that direction; the Church in Wales was only disestablished in 1914–20 and establishment survived in England and Scotland.[32] The Conservative government of 1874 to 1880 discovered that an aggressive defence of Church interests, whether over education, patronage or burials, had the effect of reuniting the Liberals in defence of 'toleration' or 'fairness' to minorities.[33] The upshot was that parties tried (usually but not always successfully)

[30] J. P. Parry, *Democracy and Religion. Gladstone and the Liberal Party 1867–1875* (Cambridge, 1986); D. W. Bebbington, 'Gladstone and the Nonconformists: A Religious Affinity in Politics', *Studies in Church History*, XII (1975), 369–82.

[31] On dissenting political activity, see D. A. Hamer, *The Politics of Electoral Pressure. A Study in the History of Victorian Reform Agitations* (Hassocks, 1977), W. H. Mackintosh, *Disestablishment and Liberation. The Movement for the Separation of the Anglican Church from State Control* (1972), and T. Larsen, *The Friends of Equality. Nonconformist Politics in Mid-Victorian England* (Woodbridge, 1999).

[32] P. M. H. Bell, *Disestablishment in Ireland and Wales* (1969).

[33] G. I. T. Machin, *Politics and the Churches in Great Britain 1869 to 1921* (Oxford, 1987), ch. 3.

to avoid controversial ecclesiastical proposals made by sections of their backbenchers. And, at the grass-roots level, anglicans usually voted Conservative and dissenters usually voted Liberal, not so much in the hope that their parties would advance their interests, but from a tribal antagonism to the culture of the opposing side, and an anxiety to rally to their church against the attacks that it faced in the modern world. However, the dissenting anger at some of the terms of the 1902 Education Act, resonating down to the 1906 election and beyond, showed the continuing capacity of religious issues to inflame political debate.[34]

Such anger notwithstanding, there were few successful parliamentary attempts between 1880 and 1914 to challenge the Church's major privileges. Its schools escaped political attack to a much greater degree than had seemed likely in the late 1860s.[35] And, after the failure of the Public Worship Regulation Act became apparent, governments tried to ignore occasionally intense sectional pressure to discipline ritualists further.[36] The conclusion to the Bradlaugh affair of the 1880s heightened the perception (suggested by Jewish emancipation in 1858) that parliament could no longer claim to be a christian body.[37] Church leaders sought more self-government, and the 1919 Enabling Act established a new national assembly which would shape legislative proposals for submission to parliament.

None the less, parliament not only retained the right to reject those proposals, but exercised that right swiftly, when the Commons defeated the Revised Prayer Book in 1927–8. As G. I. T. Machin shows below in discussing this crisis, some M.P.s argued that the decisions of the assembly should be respected, but these were outvoted by those who disliked the concessions to ritualists made in the new book. The affair exposed the old ambiguities in the Church-state relationship. Many M.P.s (including Scottish and Welsh ones) were determined to act to save what they saw as the inclusive national character of the Church of England from sectional extremism. And the Church itself was not united about the proposals: on some aspects, especially the reservation of the sacrament, compromise was not possible between the contending parties, thus weakening the claim that the revised version would win general consent. The result was that parliament's action did not lead to a major crisis; the Church let use of the new book become optional, alongside the old. Here was a graphic demonstration of what some saw as the lack of authority in the Church, and others as its attractive tolerance of diversity. Intentionally or not, parliament's intervention had had the effect of protecting that diversity.[38]

4

Whatever their attitudes to Church-state relations, the leaders of both major nineteenth-century political parties took care to identify with religious ideals, and this

---

[34] S. Koss, *Nonconformity in Modern British Politics* (1975), chs. 2–4.

[35] M. Cruickshank, *Church and State in English Education 1870 to the Present Day* (1963), ch. 3.

[36] Machin, *Politics and the Churches 1869 to 1921*, pp. 234–55.

[37] W. L. Arnstein, *The Bradlaugh Case. A Study in Late Victorian Opinion and Politics* (Oxford, 1965).

[38] Enoch Powell saw parliament's role in 1927–8 in terms of asserting liberty: *Great Parliamentary Occasions* (1960), p. 12. We owe this reference to Dr S. J. D. Green.

had a major impact on the tone of public life. The use of religion in twentieth-century politics has been less widespread, but by no means insignificant. Though other issues dominated political controversy in the first half of the twentieth century, religion still had a major impact in determining voting, and continued to influence the content of political rhetoric and debate.[39] Between the wars, many M.P.s expressed a real concern to promote religious values, which seemed more than ever under threat from the materialism of modern culture.[40] One of these was R. A. Butler, and S. J. D. Green shows, in his essay, how his 1944 Education Act was profoundly shaped by his concern at the advance of irreligion and his anxiety to see a Church dimension to the attempt to create a better postwar world. In a salutary reminder of the strongly christian tone of public discourse in the early years of the war, Green argues that a public panic about the lack of religious knowledge in the young helped Butler to achieve two goals of great significance to the Church. Its schools could opt to preserve their powers and status, or to surrender them partially in return for increased financial assistance to improve their quality of teaching. And a christian element would be a compulsory statutory feature of elementary education in all maintained schools for the first time.

The final article in the collection, by Clyde Binfield, demonstrates the continuing importance of religious tone to Liberal political life in twentieth-century England. But it also explores the impact of materialism on that religious tone and therefore on the language and integrity of politics. Dissent has traditionally preached the importance of righteous struggle against sinfulness and the prospects for renaissance through such a struggle, with an eloquence sometimes disproportionate to the cause in hand. But over time it has lost its 'evangelical motor while retaining its evangelical rhetoric', with problematical consequences for political argument and principle. Binfield uses John le Carré's novel, *A Perfect Spy*, to bring out the full, corrupting potential of such a declension, ending in the betrayal of the nation itself. The point is not, of course, that the real-life experience of the Liberal party in the twentieth century can be summarized in a remotely similar way. Indeed it is a necessary aspect of the dissenting identity that it should express itself in a great variety of forms, some of which continue to be strongly religious in motivation. None the less, the essay illuminates several aspects of twentieth-century dissenting political culture, and its subtly distorted relationship with its revered past.

The decline of religion in the public life of twentieth-century England is undeniable. Its influence in parliament and press is much smaller, and the Church's voice in national affairs is noticeably quieter. For all that, it is worth pointing out that the low profile of ecclesiastical institutions in national affairs today does not necessarily imply general indifference to religion.[41] To a significant extent that low profile is the consequence of

[39] K. D. Wald, *Crosses on the Ballot. Patterns of British Voter Alignment since 1885* (Princeton, N.J., 1983), pp. 108–201; D. W. Bebbington, 'Nonconformity and Electoral Sociology, 1867–1918', *Historical Journal*, XXVII (1984), 654–6.

[40] See e.g. P. Williamson, 'The Doctrinal Politics of Stanley Baldwin', and J. P. Parry, 'From the Thirty-Nine Articles to the Thirty-Nine Steps: Reflections on the Thought of John Buchan', both in *Public and Private Doctrine. Essays in British History Presented to Maurice Cowling*, ed. M. Bentley (Cambridge, 1993).

[41] Useful analyses of the state of religion in contemporary Britain include: G. Davie, *Religion in Britain since 1945. Believing Without Belonging* (Oxford, 1994), and *Religion, State, and Society in Modern Britain*, ed. P. Badham (Lewiston, N. Y., 1989).

the long-standing tendencies to pluralism and comprehension in the country's religious life traced in this introduction. For three centuries, parliament's powers over the Church have by and large been exercised in the direction of toleration and latitude, while influential churchmen of all parties have instinctively tended to see anglicanism as a national and inclusive concept rather than a narrow ideal. Since the seventeenth century, the Church has also had to compete with a vigorous dissenting mentality that by definition has been even more unwilling to agree on strict codes of doctrine and conduct. The result has been a colourful variety of religious perspectives, and an innate suspicion, in parliament and in influential anglican circles, of authoritarian attempts to make those perspectives more uniform. The Church of England has developed into a self-consciously broad church. This tendency is manifest in its frequently ridiculed inability to exercise the kind of discipline over its members that many orthodox religious minds consider proper. But the weakness of ecclesiastical authority, and the absence of uniformity, have not prevented religion from playing a large part in political life in the past, and an indefinable but substantial one in the private sphere even in our own time. A parliamentary Church, with external competition on both its 'wings', may not be a noble creature, but it has performed a central role in defending the freedom, and the peculiarities, of the English.

Parliament, Convocation and the Granting of Clerical Supply in Early Modern England

PATRICK CARTER

Writing in 1622 the radical puritan William Ames ridiculed the reforming record of English convocations: 'much evil hath come from among them, and more would but that many times their commission serveth not but onely to give Subsidies, and then to tell the clock'. Eighty years later William Wake, the future primate and authority on convocation, declared that the chief function of these clerical assemblies was 'the business of granting subsidies'.[1] Yet modern historians have largely overlooked this fact. Deterred in part by the scarcity of surviving records, they have confined their consideration of convocation to a few favoured topics: its involvement in the Elizabethan religious settlement, its controversial approval of canons in 1640, and its importance as a forum for clerical political opposition during the 1690s and 1700s. By contrast, convocation's regular role in granting supply to the crown remains largely ignored. At no point is this more striking than in 1640, when convocation's approval of the Laudian canons has been fully integrated into the broader historiography, unlike its equally contentious grant of supply without parliamentary confirmation. In light of this neglect, the accusation advanced by the incendiary Francis Atterbury in his 1697 *Letter to a Convocation-man* rings true today: 'We live in an age when convocations, and the learning that relates to them, are out of fashion, and even Understanding men are content to know as little of an English synod, as of a Jewish Sanhedrin.'[2]

Assembled in their two provincial convocations of Canterbury and York, the clergy of England had offered supply to the crown from as early as the thirteenth century, independent of parliament. This liberty was occasionally challenged, as in 1295 when Edward I, in his fiscal dispute with Archbishop Winchlesey, sought to incorporate the clergy into parliamentary grants by requiring them to send proctors to parliament, but all such attempts to end separate clerical taxation were successfully thwarted. Furthermore, by the later middle ages it was accepted that convocation could accompany its grants with petitions to the crown requesting the redress of clerical grievances; on several occasions supply was withheld until the crown gave evidence of good faith. While provincial convocations (unlike other synods) usually

---

[1] William Ames, *A Reply to Dr Mortons Generall Defence of three nocent Ceremonies* (1622), sig. B1r-v; William Wake, *The State of the Church and Clergy of England in their Councils, Synods, Convocations, Conventions and other Publick Assemblies* (1703), p. 51.

[2] Francis Atterbury, *Letter to a Convocation-man concerning the Rights, Powers, and Privileges of that Body* (1697), p. 28.

met in conjunction with parliaments, they remained sovereign legislative bodies – potent symbols of the privileges of the *Ecclesia Anglicana*.[3]

Under the early Tudors convocations continued to make regular grants, like the *magnum subsidium* of 1489. The sums involved were considerable: the final pre-Reformation clerical subsidy, secured by Cardinal Wolsey in 1523, was calculated to raise £120,000 over five years. The summoning of the Reformation Parliament in 1529, however, signalled the start of a sustained assault upon ecclesiastical privileges, legal and fiscal alike. When in 1531 the English clergy were charged with *praemunire* simply for having exercised their spiritual jurisdictions, the provincial convocations purchased a royal pardon by recognizing a limited royal ecclesiastical supremacy, and by paying a fine of £118,000 (a clerical subsidy in all but name). The next year the legislative independence of convocation was swept away. By their submission to the crown (confirmed by statute in 1534) the clergy acknowledged that all canons enacted by convocation required royal approval. While in theory grants of supply could still be made by convocation alone as the principle of consent remained unaltered, in practice the canons enforcing payment now needed royal confirmation, secured by means of a parliamentary statute incorporating the text of the grant. Finally, in November 1534 even the principle of consent was cast aside, when two new taxes (first fruits and tenths) were imposed upon the English clergy by parliament, without reference to convocation. Nevertheless, despite these attacks convocation still retained the power to initiate grants of supply subject only to confirmation by parliament: a fiscal liberty which survived until the 1660s.

From 1540 (the first post-submission subsidy) the regular process of granting clerical subsidies comprised four steps: drafting and approval by the bishops in the upper House, assent by the lower House, presentation to the sovereign, and finally confirmation by parliament. The order of these actions was significant, for, while following the act of 1534 the legal authority for levying subsidies rested with the crown expressed through parliament, the clergy through convocation retained the power of consent. Writing in 1582 Bishop Aylmer summarized this process as supply 'by a parliament with the consent of a convocation'.[4] Before considering the political implications of ecclesiastical supply, particularly in the early seventeenth century, it is necessary to examine each of these steps in turn.

From at least the fifteenth century, provincial convocations comprised two Houses, with the upper composed of bishops (and abbots until the dissolutions), and the lower of deans, archdeacons and two proctors chosen by the clergy of each diocese. At the start of each convocation the lower House elected a prolocutor to preside over their meetings. This arrangement mirrored that of lay parliaments, although it should be noted that joint sessions of both houses of convocation were much more common. Clerical grants always originated with the bishops, before being presented to the lower House for approval (a reversal of the procedure of lay grants in parliament). Thus in 1566 the bishops discussed the subsidy amongst themselves before summoning the prolocutor of the lower House. The bishops were also anxious that the crown be satisfied. In March

---

[3] Dorothy B. Weske, *Convocation of the Clergy* (1937); Jeffrey H. Denton, *Robert Winchelsey and the Crown, 1294–1313. A Study in the Defense of Ecclesiastical Liberty* (Cambridge, 1980).
[4] B.L., Egerton MS 1693, f. 101r.

1593 Archbishop Whitgift wrote to Lord Buckhurst at court, seeking the queen's view of the subsidy proposal agreed with his colleagues, before presenting it to the lower House.[5] The bishops were keen to avoid criticism, both from the queen and from their fellow clergy. As the lower clergy had regularly voiced their opposition to taxation in the later middle ages, the leaders of the Church were loath to take any risks. Often, as in October 1566, the bishops invited representatives of the lower House to join them in drafting the subsidy book. On occasion these discussions could take some time (it was here that any disagreements and conflicts were resolved); for example in February 1589 the subsidy consultations occupied five separate meetings over a fortnight, concluding with a final conference at Lambeth.[6] In this case the problems probably arose as this was the first multiple subsidy grant, a situation which would become a commonplace under the pressures of war finance in the 1590s. Once the terms of a grant had been agreed, the subsidy book was delivered to the prolocutor of the lower House, where it was read aloud and approved.

The next stage in the process of granting a clerical subsidy was the royal presentation, symbolic of both the clergy's continuing control over supply and their direct relationship with the supreme governor, bypassing parliament. While the bill confirming each grant would receive assent at the close of the parliamentary session in the normal fashion, the subsidy was also presented to the sovereign in person, before the bill was introduced in parliament. Several examples of such ceremonies are known from the reign of Elizabeth. On 7 December 1566 a delegation of bishops led by Archbishop Parker went to court to deliver the Canterbury grant, accompanied by several representatives of the lower clergy. The latter were refused entry to the queen's chamber owing to Elizabeth's indisposition, but the supreme governor was well enough to read through the text of the grant and express her gratitude. A similar episcopal presentation is recorded in 1581.[7] The best documented of these ceremonies occurred in February 1585, when a heated debate arose on the relative value of clerical and lay contributions to crown coffers. In accepting the Canterbury grant, the queen thanked the clergy for their generosity, 'and the rather for that that came voluntarily and frankly wheras the Laity must be intreated and moved therunto'. Angered by this pointed comparison, Lord Treasurer Burghley (also present) was dismissive of the clerical subsidy: 'Madame, these men come with mites, but we will come with pounds.' This reply drew a sharp rejoinder from Elizabeth: 'I esteeme more of their mites, than of your pounds, for that they come of themselves not moved, but you tarry till you be urged thereunto.'[8] This incident hints at the potential of convocation's fiscal autonomy to lead to conflict with parliament, for it offered the crown a convenient instrument to prod parliament towards similar generosity.

Finally, having been approved by the Canterbury convocation and presented to the monarch, the notarized grant passed to parliament and was incorporated into a draft

---

[5] David Wilkins, *Concilia Magnae Britanniae et Hiberniae* (4 vols., 1737), IV, 251; Lambeth Palace Library, MS 2004, f. 3r.

[6] Wilkins, *Concilia*, IV, 251, 355.

[7] John Strype, *Annals of the Reformation* (4 vols., Oxford, 1824), I, pt ii, 239; Wilkins, *Concilia*, IV, 293.

[8] P.R.O., SP 12/176/69. On the context of this exchange, see Patrick Collinson, *The Elizabethan Puritan Movement* (Oxford, 1990), p. 284.

confirming statute, together with the necessary clauses enforcing payment and permitting sequestration of defaulters' benefices. This clerical subsidy bill was introduced into the house of lords by the archbishop of Canterbury, receiving three readings before being sent to the Commons for approval. Although only a legal formality, this legislative process demonstrated the supremacy of statute over the Church. Yet by the later sixteenth century the bill regularly received only a single reading in the Commons; in the Lords the main body of the bill was generally omitted after the first reading.[9] While the Submission of the Clergy made such a process necessary, the perfunctory treatment of clerical subsidies by parliament highlighted the effective fiscal autonomy enjoyed by convocation.

Clerical subsidy grants attracted little attention from parliament in comparison with their lay counterparts, but they did share one important element: their preambles, which fully exploited the possibilities for propaganda which they presented. Richard Hoyle has aptly described the preamble to an Elizabethan lay subsidy bill as a 'eulogy of the nation's good fortune to possess a monarch of such supreme qualities'.[10] The framers of clerical grants produced comparable panegyrics, which naturally emphasized the monarch's ceaseless labours in advancing true religion and frustrating 'the malice of the adversaries of Godes Truth' (1587). In drafting these preambles, the bishops and their advisors regularly recycled earlier texts, simply inserting topical references as in 1571 to 'repressing the detestable Rebellion', or in 1589 to the 'rare and wonderful preparacion of the Spanishe forces readie to have invaded this Realme'. Indeed, with only minor adjustments the same text served for nine Elizabethan grants. This continuity was broken, however, in 1597 when the clerical grant scarcely referred at all to religion, offering instead an extended thanksgiving for the secular benefits of the queen's rule, and stressing the high costs of maintaining peace. The text seems intended to emulate lay grants, but without further insight into its authorship, it is difficult to determine why this was so.[11] Even more extraordinary, however, was the preamble of 1606, an extended hymn in praise of the rule of kings, 'nourcing [nursing] Fathers to the Church of Christ'. Here was a text clearly calculated to appeal to James's regal pride and exalted views of kingship, extolling his 'inflamed and resolute Zeale and Love to the Gospell of Christ, earnest and exquisite Desire and Care for the order and unitie of his Church . . . extraordinarie and right princelie favours afforded to his Ministers and Servants the Pastors and Leaders of his Flocke . . .'[12] The gratitude of Bancroft and his colleagues toward the royal champion of episcopacy is unequivocal, and expressed in language certain to flatter the king. By the next grant in 1610, however, the preambles had returned to their traditional pattern, and the three identical texts of 1624, 1625 and

---

[9] B.L., Cotton MS Titus F II, f. 80v; *C.J.*, I, 91, 131; *L.J.*, II, 252; Geoffrey R. Elton, *The Parliament of England, 1559–1581* (Cambridge, 1986), p. 154; David Dean, *Law-Making and Society in Late Elizabethan England. The Parliament of England, 1584–1601* (Cambridge, 1996), p. 52. In December 1601 one M.P. complained that the clerical subsidy bill had been sent written in a roll like other acts, rather than on a long membrane of parchment under the royal sign manual and seal, as was customary. Simond D'Ewes, *The Journals of all the Parliaments during the Reign of Queen Elizabeth* (1682), p. 688.

[10] Richard W. Hoyle, 'Crown, Parliament and Taxation in Sixteenth-Century England', *English Historical Review*, CIX (1994), 1193.

[11] *Statutes of the Realm* (10 vols., 1810–28), IV, pt ii, 931; Dean, *Law-Making and Society*, p. 54.

[12] *Statutes of the Realm*, IV, pt. ii, 1102.

1628 simply stress the 'extraordinarie Peace and Tranquillitie' enjoyed by the realm – an increasingly implausible (or even impolitic) assertion, given the military activity of the later 1620s.[13] Yet it seems probable that, rather than criticism of those pressing for war, this continuity of pacific preambles simply reflected a lack of attention or interest in drafting the later grants.

Parliament and convocation each played a role in the regular process of granting clerical supply. Yet in exceptional circumstances convocation could still act alone, for the Submission had simply required royal approval of its acts, which in theory at least did not necessarily involve parliament. In 1545 the English clergy presented the crown with a benevolence to help support the invasion of France, without parliamentary sanction. A similar situation arose after 1585 with the advent of war against Spain. In early 1587 the clergy responded to royal necessity by offering a benevolence to supplement their subsidy, in gratitude for 'the free exercise of our mynistery and function, the true preachinge of God, and the syncere admynistringe of His holly Sacraments (to us farre more deare than our lyves and lyvinges)'. This grant lacked parliamentary confirmation; instead convocation relied upon a royal license authorizing it to draw up the requisite orders and canons for collection. Half the value of a standard subsidy, the 1587 benevolence raised almost £15,000 over the succeeding years.[14] Its significance exceeded its financial value, however, for it sowed the seed of a conflict between parliament and convocation which would mature in 1640.

Consideration of convocation's role in granting supply focuses upon Canterbury, for the York convocation was clearly subordinate to its southern cousin. Indeed York's grants were covered by the parliamentary confirmation of clerical subsidies, in advance of the northern clergy's approval. The unicameral northern convocation (for the four bishops were generally absent attending the house of lords at Westminster) received a copy of the recently approved Canterbury subsidy grant and prepared an identical grant of its own. Thus on 7 March 1587 the texts of both the Canterbury subsidy and benevolence grants were received at York, where the dean and chapter had the texts engrossed and approved two days later by 'so many of the convocation together in our chapter house as conveniently we coulde have'.[15] The grants were then returned to the capital for the archbishop's seal, after which he presented them to the queen. The degree to which Lambeth directed this process is demonstrated by the survival at York of copies of early Stuart Canterbury grants, complete with basic diplomatic instructions (like substituting 'Ebor' for 'Cantuar') and guidance for the York notary preparing the final document. Such close control confirms Fuller's frank assessment of the northern convocation's status as 'but the hand of the dial, moving and pointing as directed by the clock of the province of Canterbury'.[16]

Until the political crisis of May 1640, the granting of clerical subsidies rarely prompted conflict between parliament and convocation; as already noted bills

[13] *Ibid.*, p. 1263.
[14] P.R.O., AO 3/344; E 336/21; *The Records of the Northern Convocation*, ed. G. W. Kitchin (Durham, Surtees Soc., CXIII, 1907), pp. 262–3, 274–5.
[15] Borthwick Institute [hereafter B.I.], Conv. 1586/7; *Northern Convocation*, ed. Kitchin, pp. 259–63.
[16] B.I., Conv. 1604/2; Conv. 1605/2; Conv. 1623/3; Thomas Fuller, *The Church History of Britain* (6 vols., Oxford, 1845), VI, p. 175.

confirming clerical grants normally received only perfunctory attention at Westminster. In the charged political climate of the mid 1620s, however, this peaceful relationship began to show signs of strain. In April 1624 parliament and convocation together made immediate action against Jesuits and seminary priests a precondition for granting the funds required to prosecute the looming war with Spain. After some delicate negotiations the king reluctantly agreed, and a proclamation expelling catholic clergy from the realm was issued on 6 May. Yet on 30 April, even before the proclamation had appeared from the printers, convocation hastened to recognize the king's action by granting four subsidies, with the first due only a month later. It has been suggested that this prompt grant may represent the action of a zealous lower House, in the face of episcopal reluctance.[17] Perhaps, but what is clear is that such hasty generosity angered some M.P.s, who felt their clerical allies had betrayed them and handed the king a stick with which to beat parliament. The M.P. Sir Francis Nethersole reported that James (echoing Elizabeth's 1585 speech) 'hath been heard to commend this forwardnes and frankenes of them with an oblique reflexyon upon the backwardnes and cautyousnes of our house'. More significantly, some believed that by preempting the lay subsidy convocation had violated custom and undermined efforts to bind the granting of supply to the redress of grievances. On 13 May, the day before parliament approved its own grant of only three subsidies, John Chamberlain wrote that the recent behaviour of convocation 'beeing contrarie to the usuall forme, which was to go together and in the same manner, breeds distaste'. Sir Dudley Carleton was advised that the clergy's actions left the house of commons 'scandalised'.[18] The tensions evident in 1624 reflected the threat some in parliament perceived in the independent powers of convocation to initiate grants of supply, and in the potential of clerical autonomy to undermine parliamentary opposition to crown policies. Such concerns would prove prescient.

In 1640 the granting of supply by convocation independently of parliament precipitated a constitutional crisis and further harmed the reputation of the clergy. When parliament assembled in April for the first time in over a decade, there were already concerns with the fiscal support offered to Charles by the bishops and clergy, especially during the recent 'Bishops' wars'. In this hostile climate the Canterbury convocation assembled as usual, and at a joint session on 17 April Archbishop Laud urged the clergy to devote their energies to two pressing items of business: the granting of generous subsidies and the compilation of fresh canons. Both were to have momentous consequences. At their next meeting five days later Laud announced to the clergy that, in view of the crown's pressing necessity, the bishops had determined to offer six subsidies; he invited the lower House to signify its assent 'as a manifestation of their singular duty and observance to his Most Gracious Majesty'. After a short but seemly interval, the lower House complied.[19] Thereupon a committee, including Peter Heylyn of

[17] P.R.O., SP 14/163, f. 75r; *Statutes of the Realm*, IV, pt ii, 1263–4; *Stuart Royal Proclamations vol I: James I*, ed. James F. Larkin and Paul L. Hughes (Oxford, 1973), pp. 591–3. On the supply debate in the 1624 parliament, see Thomas Cogswell, *The Blessed Revolution. English Politics and the Coming of War, 1621–1624* (Cambridge, 1989), ch. 7. For the zeal of the lower House during the 1620s, see P.R.O., SP 16/450/73, quoted in Esther S. Cope, 'The Short Parliament of 1640 and Convocation', *Journal of Ecclesiastical History*, XXV (1974), 169.

[18] P.R.O., SP 14/164, ff. 71r, 77v–78r, 117v.

[19] Wilkins, *Concilia*, IV, 539; John Nalson, *An Impartial Collection of the Great Affairs of State* (2 vols., 1682), I, 361–2.

Westminster and Bishop Hall of Exeter, began drawing up the subsidy book, it was empowered to meet unofficially as often as necessary, for there was already anxiety to approve the grant as quickly as possible.[20] At the same time convocation's actions attracted some notice from M.P.s debating the king's request for urgent supply. In vain one member urged his colleagues to consider the clergy's ready response to the king's financial needs.[21]

Convocation's concern for prompt action was justified when parliament was prematurely dissolved on 5 May, before the clerical subsidy grant could be confirmed by statute. In more settled times this should have been followed almost immediately by the dissolution of convocation – an outcome which would have meant forfeiting the proffered clerical subsidy. Ignorant of the fact that convocation could only be dissolved by royal writ (this was of course the first convocation over which Laud had presided as primate), the archbishop ordered its dissolution upon his own authority. A message from convocation reminding him of the need for a royal writ reached him while attending a council meeting. As the king was present, Laud took the opportunity to raise the matter with him. To the archbishop's surprise, Charles refused the writ, and it was decided to allow convocation to continue meeting, to ensure that the desired supply and canons were not lost.[22] A royal commission was issued to this effect, and on 13 May Laud invited the assembled clergy to press on with the subsidy (now termed a benevolence) and the book of canons. Three days later the lower House approved the 'free benevolence or contribution' and at the same time petitioned the bishops to raise several grievances (including impropriations) with the attorney-general. The terms of the benevolence were identical to those of the lost subsidy: four shillings in the pound *per annum* for six years. Even the preamble reproduced verbatim the 1628 grant.[23] No attempt was made to disguise the grant, which remained a clerical subsidy but under a different name.

As M.P.s dispersed, the members of convocation continued to sit at Westminster, guarded by several companies of the Middlesex trained bands to prevent public disturbance. Yet the decision to remain in session also drew criticism from within convocation itself, from clergy who questioned the legality of meeting after the dissolution of parliament. Even Bishop Hall (one of those closely involved in preparing the grant) expressed doubts about the situation. In the lower House Peter Heylyn dismissed such scruples by differentiating between the writs summoning parliaments and convocations and demonstrating the separate characters of the two bodies (an issue which would agitate later scholars).[24] In response to the concerns of some

---

[20] Nalson, *Collection*, I, 362–3. Ominously, on the same day that convocation approved the subsidies (22 April), there was discussion in parliament of the necessity for consent to any canons promulgated by the clergy. *Proceedings of the Short Parliament of 1640*, ed. Esther S. Cope and Willson H. Coates (Camden Soc., 4th ser., XIX, 1977), p. 201.

[21] *The Short Parliament (1640) Diary of Sir Thomas Aston*, ed. Judith D. Maltby (Camden Soc., 4th ser., XXXV, 1988), p. 121.

[22] William Laud, *Works* (7 vols., Oxford, 1847–60), III, 285. Julian Davies argues that the king had determined upon continuing convocation even before parliament was dissolved, in part to challenge the latter's superiority. Julian Davies, *The Caroline Captivity of the Church* (Oxford, 1992), p. 254.

[23] Nalson, *Collection*, I, 364–6, 533–7 (text of grant).

[24] Davies, *Caroline Captivity*, p. 255; *The Works of the Right Reverend Joseph Hall*, ed. P. Wynter (10 vols., 1863), VIII, 280; John Bernard, *Theologo-Historicus, or the True Life of . . . Peter Heylyn* (1683), pp. 180–1.

members, a legal opinion was sought from the king's justices, who ruled that convocation could sit until dissolved by royal writ or commission under the great seal. This judgment both enhanced the autonomy of convocation and diminished the supremacy of parliament over clerical acts and canons. Charles confirmed the judges' ruling in a letter to Laud read out in convocation on 21 May, which commanded the assembled clergy 'to finish and perfect the said concession, and also to make and ordain such decrees, canons or constitutions for the collecting, levying, paying and accounting [of the same]'. This they promptly did.[25] However, some members, like the dean of Exeter, remained opposed, and there was apparent confusion over precisely what was being done. One member later claimed (perhaps disingenuously) that he had never heard the subsidy book read out or approved in the lower House that day.[26] It is clear, however, that many members appreciated the significance of what they were doing, and were concerned about the consequences. Their fears were well-founded. For the moment, however, there remained one final act: the presentation to the king. On the morning of 24 May Bishop Hall, three of his colleagues and several representatives of the lower House presented the benevolence to a grateful Charles, whose thanks were conveyed to convocation three days later by Archbishop Laud. At last, having also approved the new canons, the Canterbury convocation was dissolved by royal writ on 29 May, over three weeks after the termination of parliament. It now remained only for the clergy of the northern province to follow the lead of the southern synod; meeting on 8 June the York convocation approved an identical contribution.[27]

Convocation's actions were not quickly forgotten, either by the king or by his opponents. In furnishing Charles with some of the revenue which he urgently required, the bishops and clergy offered tangible support for his cause and demonstrated gratitude for his defence of their interests. At the same time their willingness to grant supply enraged many, providing evidence of the threat which convocation's continued fiscal autonomy could pose to the constitution. It represented a challenge to parliament's own liberties and powers, as well as to a century of custom. The concerns expressed by some M.P.s in 1624 had now proved accurate. Thus, when the military and financial crisis compelled Charles to summon another parliament later in 1640, the benevolence did not escape censure. On 9 December a Commons' committee was appointed to examine the actions of convocation after 6 May; a week later the Commons passed two unanimous resolutions. The first denounced the 1640 canons; the second declared the benevolence illegal and discharged clergy from their obligation to pay.[28] In raising the matter in the Commons, Francis Rouse declared the benevolence 'wicked', while the Southwark M.P. Edward Bagshaw, an authority on ecclesiastical law, drew attention to the illegality of affixing penalties for non-payment to a grant lacking parliamentary sanction. He ridiculed the clerical grant: 'It is not a subsidy, for then it should have been by the convocation during parliament . . . but it is called a benevolence or

---

[25] Wilkins, *Concilia*, IV, 540–1; Nalson, *Collection*, I, 369.
[26] Davies, *Caroline Captivity*, p. 256.
[27] Nalson, *Collection*, I, 370, 373; B.I., Conv. Book 2; Wilkins, *Concilia*, IV, 533.
[28] Nalson, *Collection*, I, 661, 679; *C.J.*, II, 52; *The Journals of Sir Simonds D'Ewes*, ed. Wallace Notestein (New Haven, 1923), p. 157.

free gift, and yet if any refuse to pay it, he should be deprived, which is a very bull; for if men be compelled to pay it, how can it be said to be a free gift?'[29] When the issue was debated in the house of lords in early 1641 Bishop Hall (closely involved in the preparation of the grant) offered a defence of the clergy's actions founded upon the precedent of the 1587 benevolence and upon the crown's pressing necessity. Recalling his earlier doubts, he declined to argue that convocation's actions had been legal, protesting only that peers would 'but see the difference of times'.[30] Reflecting later upon the clergy's approval of the canons and benevolence, the royalist Clarendon noted how, in a tense political atmosphere, convocation had acted unwisely and 'did many things which in the best times might have been questioned, and therefore were sure to be condemned in the worst', thereby adding 'fuel . . . to the fire that ensued'. Clarendon believed that convocation's behaviour had transformed the hostility directed against some into a 'prejudice upon the whole body of the clergy'.[31] By their willingness to grant supply to the crown in May 1640, the clergy stoked the conflagration which would shortly consume them.

As archbishop of Canterbury, Laud played a major part in the benevolence grant of 1640, and incurred much of the wrath it aroused. Yet for his part the primate placed the responsibility for continuing convocation and securing the benevolence squarely upon the king's shoulders. Laud later related how Charles, anxious not to lose the supply offered by convocation, refused the archbishop the customary writ of dissolution when parliament ended. Moreover Laud claimed that he counselled the king against continuing convocation, but his advice was disregarded in favour of that give by Lord Keeper Finch. Quick to take offence, the archbishop was wounded that Charles chose to consult someone else on an ecclesiastical matter before raising it with his primate, 'that after so many years' faithful service, in a business concerning the Church so nearly, his Majesty would speak with the Lord Keeper, both without me, and before he would move it to me: and somewhat I said thereupon which pleased not'. Julian Davies cites this episode in support of his thesis that Charles directed ecclesiastical policy himself.[32] Yet there is evidence to doubt Laud's ascription of all responsibility to the king. It relates to the role of the Westminster proctor Peter Heylyn. In a biography of his father-in-law, John Bernard describes how Heylyn himself discovered the Elizabethan benevolence precedent, which he immediately showed to the archbishop at Lambeth. Realizing its value, a joyful Laud then carried the news to the king.[33] The archbishop no doubt had cause to minimize his part in the events of May 1640, for the granting of a clerical subsidy without parliamentary approval formed the basis of one of the charges of subverting the laws of the realm levelled against him at his trial. In his defence the primate pleaded the precedent of 1587 (as Bishop Hall had earlier done in the house of lords); he also protested that the

---

[29] *Journals of D'Ewes*, ed. Notestein, p. 125; Edward Bagshaw, *Two Arguments in Parliament* (1641), p. 21

[30] *Works of . . . Joseph Hall*, VIII, 280.

[31] *The History of the Rebellion and Civil Wars in England begun in the year 1641, by Edward, earl of Clarendon*, ed. W. Dunn Macray (6 vols., Oxford, 1888), I, 194.

[32] Laud, *Works*, III, 285.

[33] Bernard, *Theologo-Historicus*, pp. 180–1.

grant was entirely voluntary, and thus did not violate the law by imposing penalties for non-payment without parliamentary sanction.[34]

Following its suspension during the interregnum, convocation played an important part in the re-establishment of the Church, and the Stuart restoration brought the clergy a brief Indian summer of fiscal autonomy. The clerical subsidy granted in July 1663 proved to be the last, however, for in November 1664 a verbal agreement between Archbishop Sheldon and the lord treasurer, Clarendon, established that they would henceforth be included in lay grants.[35] In return for surrendering a right exercised for centuries, the English clergy received the vote in parliamentary elections. Apart from a meeting at Lambeth involving several bishops and privy councillors, there is little evidence of the genesis of the Sheldon-Clarendon pact, although a contemporary petition from convocation to parliament for 'some more equal manner of rating subsidies upon the clergy' may have been part of Sheldon's manoeuvres.[36] The absence of any written agreement compounds the mystery. The fact that several subsequent lay subsidy statutes contained clauses declaring that the inclusion of clergy did not prejudice future rights may suggest that the 1664 arrangement was regarded as temporary. White Kennett later argued that, while the exercise of self-taxation through convocation had been suspended in 1664, the right itself had not been surrendered.[37] Of course in practice this proved a distinction without a difference, for the right was never reasserted. Finally, it is noteworthy (if not surprising) that, while an archiepiscopal circular elicited the views of the bishops on the proposed change, there is no evidence that convocation itself was ever consulted in what Edmund Gibson later described as 'the greatest alteration in our constitution ever made without an express law'.[38]

So why did Sheldon sanction the surrender of convocation's fiscal powers? The most plausible explanation is that he aimed to minimize potential hostility towards the established Church, particularly within parliament. The controversy over supply in 1640 had gravely wounded the Church and helped bring an earlier primate to the block. As well as limiting lay-clerical conflict, the archbishop may have aimed at strengthening the new alliance between gentry and clergy which buttressed the Restoration settlement.[39] For this the loss of fiscal autonomy was perhaps a price worth paying. Ronald Hutton has gone further, regarding 1664 as signalling a shift from an earlier clerical alliance with the crown against parliament to one with parliament against the king.[40] The attitude of Charles II and his brother toward the Church in succeeding decades suggests this may have been prudent. The agreement concluded between archbishop and lord treasurer had a further political consequence, since it enabled some clergy to pursue a more active

[34] H.M.C., *House of Lords MSS*, n.s., XI, 368–9, 372.

[35] Wilkins, *Concilia*, IV, 578; *Statutes of the Realm*, V, 481–8.

[36] Wilkins, *Concilia*, IV, 580.

[37] As in 16 and 17 Cha. II, c.1 s.36, 'Provided always that noe thing herein contained shall be drawn into example to the prejudice of the Auntient Rights belonging unto the Lords Spirituall or Temporall or Clergy of this Realme . . .' (*Statutes of the Realm*, V, 552); White Kennett, *Ecclesiastical Synods and Parliamentary Convocations* (1701), p. 317.

[38] Norman Sykes, *From Sheldon to Secker* (Cambridge, 1959), p. 41.

[39] Norman Ravitch, *Sword and Mitre. Government and Episcopate in France and England in the Age of Aristocracy* (The Hague, 1966), p. 208; Victor Sutch, *Gilbert Sheldon. Architect of Anglican Survival, 1640–1675* (The Hague, 1973), pp. 139–41.

[40] Ronald Hutton, *The Restoration* (Oxford, 1985), pp. 213–14.

role in partisan politics, contributing significantly to the ferment of the later seventeenth century. Sheldon's action may have been motivated by economic concerns as well, reducing the fiscal burden borne by clergy through inclusion in parliamentary supply. The archbishop and his colleagues feared that tax assessments unchanged since 1535 would soon be revised upwards.[41] In replying to Sheldon's circular, the bishop of Lichfield also made the point that, in granting their taxes, clergy found themselves in an invidious position: whatever they might offer could be criticized by some laymen as insufficient.[42] As a result, they were trapped into voting substantial sums in order to counter any potential lay criticism, a policy disastrous for ecclesiastical finances. Far better, the bishop argued, to be included in the same tax regime as the lay population, ensuring an appearance of equity. For there was a long tradition of clerical complaint about the unfair burden of taxation upon the Church, a situation which the 1664 agreement might help resolve (although of course it did not address the payment of first fruits and tenths). Bishop Burnet was clear: for the clergy inclusion in lay taxation 'proved indeed a lighter burden, but was not so honourable as when it was given by themselves'.[43]

The 1664 agreement proved fatal for the future of convocation; deprived of a role in the granting of supply its meetings became merely a formality. For 25 years convocation was prevented from transacting any business, until in 1689 the crown sought the clergy's assistance in implementing the Revolutionary settlement. Tensions between the bishops and the lower House over royal instructions and the disputed election of a prolocutor, however, led to the prompt prorogation of the assembly. Clerical discontent with toleration towards dissenters and the weakening of the authority of church courts encouraged some in the 1690s to campaign for the return of convocation as a clerical voice to defend the interests of the established Church. The 1697 publication of Francis Atterbury's *Letter to a Convocation-man* ignited a fierce controversy. The place of this convocation controversy within late Stuart ecclesiastical politics and the Herculean scholarly and polemical labours of the tory Atterbury and his opponents (led by William Wake and White Kennett) have been extensively examined elsewhere.[44] While not proposing to revisit these debates, it is worthwhile to examine the place occupied by the granting of supply in the opposing views of convocation's powers and privileges.

Seeking a forum in which to challenge the power of the whig bishops, Atterbury argued that convocations, like parliaments, possessed constitutional powers to meet, present grievances and transact appropriate business regardless of the crown's desire for subsidies. Atterbury repeatedly stressed the close parallels between parliaments and convocations: particularly the privileges of the house of commons and the lower House of convocation. The task of refuting Atterbury fell to William Wake, who argued in *The Authority of Christian Princes* that since the middle ages assent to grants

[41] Sykes, *From Sheldon to Secker*, p. 42; Lambeth Palace Lib. MS 2564, pp. 463–4.

[42] H. N. Mukerjee, 'Parliamentary Taxation of the Clergy', *Notes and Queries*, 13th ser., CLXVI (1934), 41.

[43] *Burnet's History of My Own Time pt I: The Reign of Charles II*, ed. Osmund Airy (2 vols., Oxford, 1897), I, 352–3.

[44] G. V. Bennett, *The Tory Crisis in Church and State 1688–1730. The Career of Francis Atterbury, Bishop of Rochester* (Oxford, 1975), esp. pp. 48–56; and Norman Sykes, *William Wake, Archbishop of Canterbury, 1657–1737* (2 vols., Cambridge, 1957), I.

of supply had been the chief function of convocations. They transacted as little other business 'with their often-meeting then, as they do with their seldom-meeting now'. Wake also remarked on the irony that such zealous defenders of the established church should press for frequent meetings of an assembly which had always been to their financial disadvantage.[45] In his several rejoinders to Wake, Atterbury reiterated the similarities between convocation and parliament and suggested that the absence of other business besides supply in much of the surviving records reflected the bias of the documents, whose purpose was to record fiscal precedents rather than serve as a full register of business transacted. By surrendering their right to grant supply in 1664, the clergy had 'slept over their privileges', a negligence which Atterbury was determined to prevent in future.[46]

Renewing efforts to demolish his opponent by distinguishing between parliaments and convocations, Wake argued in his 1703 *State of the Church and Clergy of England* that even the granting of subsidies by convocation was an ecclesiastical and not a parliamentary matter. As evidence for his contention Wake pointed to the practice since 1540 of requiring parliamentary confirmation of the clerical grant by means of statute. Here the bishops acted in both their ecclesiastical and parliamentary capacities: in the former by assenting to the grant in convocation, in the latter by voting for the clerical subsidy bill in the Lords.[47] Wake was ably assisted by the medievalist White Kennett, who composed a learned and (mercifully) briefer critique of Atterbury's arguments. He maintained that the provincial convocations which met in conjunction with parliaments were 'for civil, not ecclesiastical purposes'. Kennett pointed out that all other activities of convocations (including Atterbury's oft cited right to petition for redress of grievances) were contingent upon its principal function of granting of supply. It followed therefore that a future working convocation would be obliged to offer subsidies if it intended to transact any other business. The consequences of this, both financial and political, could be severe. If parliament refused willingly to exempt clergy once more from its own grants, double taxation could result and the fiscal burden upon the Church would be unbearable. More realistically, such a change would weaken the alliance between clergy and laity promoted in 1664, with unpredictable consequences. How might the Church then fare, under a future king hostile to the established Church? Kennett concluded by urging the proponents of an active convocation to reconsider: 'We are at present Safe and Happy, if we know how to consult our own Safety, or how to prize our own Happiness.'[48] In the event Kennett's concerns proved too pessimistic, for, although the campaign for the summoning of convocation enjoyed temporary success in the early eighteenth century, the clergy never again sought (nor were offered) any power to tax themselves.

Relying upon their exhaustive research in both civil and ecclesiastical records, Wake and Kennett demolished Atterbury's polemical claims of close parallels between parlia-

---

[45] Atterbury, *Letter to a Convocation-man*, p. 44; William Wake, *The Authority of Christian Princes over their Ecclesiastical Synods Asserted* (1697), pp. 107, 227–8, 281–2.

[46] Francis Atterbury, *The Rights, Powers, and Priviledges of an English Convocation, Stated and Vindicated* (1700), pp. 269–71; Atterbury, *The Power of the Lower House of Convocation to Adjourn Itself* (1701), p. 21.

[47] Wake, *State of the Church*, pp. 51–2.

[48] Kennett, *Ecclesiastical Synods*, pp. 56–7, 94, 317–18; G. V. Bennett, *White Kennett 1660–1728, Bishop of Peterborough* (1957), pp. 36–43.

ment and convocation. In so doing, however, they may have encouraged later historians to marginalize the place of convocation in the constitutional history of the early modern period, a history long dominated by questions of parliament's powers and privileges. Religious historians have considered the role of convocation in formulating doctrine and drafting canons, while passing silently over the clergy's continuing function of granting supply to the crown. No longer should this be acceptable, for this fiscal function lay at the heart of convocation's existence – and its demise.

Parliament, the Royal Supremacy and the Church

CONRAD RUSSELL

More by accident than by design, this essay makes a logical sequel to Patrick Carter's. As his dealt with the financial autonomy of the clergy, this deals with the legislative and jurisdictional autonomy of the clergy. As that dealt with the power to vote clerical subsidies, so this deals with the power to make canons. Since the body of 32 people appointed by the Act for the Submission of the Clergy reported to Mary in 1553, and had their report resolutely pigeonholed by Elizabeth, the legal status of canon law in the Church of England was still unresolved when Bishop Williams, in 1641, tried to get Cranmer's *Reformatio Legum Ecclesiasticarum* implemented. He failed. 1641 was no time for constructive measures.

From 1534 to 1640, the clergy's claim to an independent jurisdiction, as well as their independent legislative power, were matters of recurring dispute. Though the politics of these two issues were separable, the issues of law and political theory in terms of which the arguments were conducted were very much the same. It is those arguments which form the substance of this essay.

In 1604, Lord Chancellor Ellesmere asked the assembled judges in Star Chamber whether the deprivation of ministers for refusing to conform themselves to the ceremonies appointed by the last canons was lawful. He was told it was lawful

> because the King hath the supreme ecclesiastical power which he hath delegated to the commissioners, whereby they had the power of deprivation by the canon law of the realm. And the statute of 1 Elizabeth c.1, which appoints commissioners to be made by the Queen, doth not confer any new power, but explain and declare the ancient power. And therefore they held it clear that the King without Parliament might make orders and constitutions for the government of the clergy, and might deprive them if they obeyed not. And so the canons might deprive them. But they could not make any constitutions without the king.[1]

This clearly orchestrated performance sets out what might be described as the 'episcopal' view of the royal supremacy. For the avoidance of clarity, it should be remembered that those who set out this view were the common law judges.

That view never held a monopoly. Also in 1604, the *Apology of the Commons* declared that

> your Majestie should be misinformed if any man should deliver that the Kings of England have any absolute power in themselves either to alter religion (which God

---

[1] Sir George Croke, *Reports*, II (1791), 37.

defend should be in the power of any mortal man whatsoever) or to make any lawes concerning the same, otherwise then, as in temporall causes, by consent of Parliament.[2]

For the further avoidance of clarity, we should remember what, by now, we hope every schoolboy knows, that the Commons did not write the *Apology of the Commons*. Yet somebody did write it, and in relation to this paragraph, it is a plausible hypothesis that that someone was Nicholas Fuller, who was a member of the relevant committee, and whose views it closely resembles.

However much we muddy the waters about parties, people and groupings, the underlying intellectual issue is clear enough. Had the idea of the omnicompetence of statute obliterated the belief in the legislative independence of the clergy? In the words of Sir Francis Knollys, writing to Burghley in 1593, 'these civilians and other confederates . . . would fain have a kind of monarchy in the . . . clergy government, as is in the temporalty; the which government they would have to be exempted from the temporal government'.[3] In other words, to pilfer Jenny Wormald's title, were Church and state two bodies or one? That issue remained live from the Reformation to the civil war.

It derived its vitality from crucial ambiguities in the original Henrician legislation. The governing document of the royal supremacy was the Act of Supremacy of 1534. That document was a declaratory act: it did not make the king supreme head of the church, but declared that he was so already. With the natural instinct of any parliamentarian seeking a majority, the act failed to answer the crucial question by what law, and by what authority, he was supreme head of the Church. All it said about his powers as supreme head was that he had

> full power and authority from time to time to visit, repress, redress, reform, order, correct, restrain and amend all such errors, heresies, abuses, offences, contempts, and enormities, whatsoever they may be, which by any manner spiritual authority or jurisdiction ought or may *lawfully* be reformed, repressed, ordered, redressed, corrected, restrained or amended.[4]

The relentless hammer-blow repetition of Henrician draftsmanship drew the eye away from the gaping hole surrounding the meaning of the word 'lawfully'. The act gives no inkling of whether the limits of spiritual jurisdiction are laid down by canon, common or statute law, or by what permutation of the three of them. It says, in effect, that it is lawful for the king to do what he may lawfully do. It was a good part of the propaganda smokescreen which pretended that the king was doing nothing new, but it created a lawyers' paradise.

This hole was filled in in two other Henrician acts, and, disastrously, they did it in different ways. The 'two bodies' theory beloved of ecclesiastical lawyers was set out in the Act in Restraint of Appeals. It is easy to see why the act which gave Cranmer power to confer the divorce should have been drafted to stress the independence of

[2] H.M.C., *Salisbury MSS*, XXIII, 148–9. For the membership of the committee which drew up the Apology, see *C.J.*, I, 222, 230.
[3] Sir John Neale, *Elizabeth I and Her Parliaments* (2 vols., 1957), II, 271–2.
[4] 26 Hen. VIII, c.1: G.R. Elton, *The Tudor Constitution* (Cambridge, 1960), p. 356.

spiritual jurisdiction, yet again the act was drafted without enough thought for what it might say to lawyers in later generations. It set out a belief in a body politic 'divided in terms and by names of spiritualty and temporalty',

> the body spiritual whereof having power when any question of the law divine happened to come in question or of spiritual learning, then it was declared, interpreted and shewed by that part of the body politic called the spiritualty, now being usually called the English church, which always hath been reputed and also found of that sort that both for knowledge and integrity and sufficiency of number, it hath been always thought and is also at this hour sufficient and meet of itself, without the intermeddling of any exterior person or persons, to declare and determine all such doubts, and to administer all such duties, as to their rooms spiritual doth appertain.[5]

This was the ideal text to wave at common lawyers bearing prohibitions.

Unfortunately, this was not all. If the Act in Restraint of Appeals was Bancroft's act, the Act for the Submission of the Clergy was Coke's act. After requiring all future canons to have the royal assent, it required that

> no canons, constitution or ordinance shall be made or put in execution within this realm by authority of the Convocation of the clergy which shall be contrariant or repugnant to the King's prerogative royal, or the customs, laws or statutes of this realm; anything contained in this Act to the contrary hereof notwithstanding.[6]

This was the crucial document for those who wished to regard spiritual jurisdiction as the junior authority, to be delimited by the superior force of parliamentary statute, and controlled by the damoclean threat of *praemunire*. It was a view which encouraged people to see all spiritual jurisdiction as a delegated power.

The question of authority in doctrine was left strictly alone. The main occasion when doctrine was laid down in an act of parliament was the Act of Six Articles. Yet that act scrupulously refrains from enacting doctrine by authority of parliament. The six articles of doctrine come *before* the enacting clause, and therefore are not governed by it. The doctrine is not enacted by parliament: it 'was and is finally resolved, accorded and agreed in manner and form following'.[7] The enacting clause covers only the penalties for dissent from these doctrines. They are not made doctrine by act of parliament: they are confirmed because they are already doctrine. The question who had power to make doctrine was never satisfactorily settled. The Elizabethan Act of Uniformity tied it to the scriptures and the first four general councils, but did not say who was to decide what they said. In 1606, when Sandys introduced a bill which would have provided that a 'substantial point' of religion could only be settled by parliament with the advice and consent of the clergy in convocation, one of the biggest objections made in the House was that they should not suggest that it was possible that any 'substantial point' of religion might ever be altered.[8] Almost the only suggestion that parliament had authority in doctrine came from Pym in 1629.

---

5   24 Hen. VIII, c.12: *ibid.*, p. 344.
6   25 Hen. VIII, c.19: *ibid.*, p. 340.
7   31 Hen. VIII, c.14: *ibid.*, pp. 390–1.
8   *The Parliamentary Diary of Robert Bowyer*, ed. D. H. Willson (Minneapolis, 1931), p. 52.

His source, ironically, was the Act of Attainder of Thomas Cromwell, on the ground that only parliament could have the authority to pronounce that the men Cromwell favoured were heretics. For good measure, he added the often forgotten point that there was no national convocation, but two independent convocations of Canterbury and York.[9] In practice, authority in doctrine remained with convocation, provided that they did not use it in a way a parliament found offensive.

On the whole, the questions the Henrician legislation left open do not seem to have become daily matter of dispute until the second half of Elizabeth's reign. It is at least possible to speculate on why this should be so. Questions of rival jurisdiction are always capable of being exciting to those whose authority and income is at stake, but they rarely excite members of the public until there is a reasonable possibility that the two jurisdictions might give different judgments. If one jurisdiction may imprison or deprive a man, while the other will let him go scot-free, then the conflict of jurisdictions may become very interesting indeed. It is with the first generation of established protestants secure in command, the generation of Beale, Morrice, Fuller, Wentworth and Coke, that a clear divergence between the dominant faction among the laity and the ecclesiastical authorities starts informing conflicts over jurisdiction.

Two acts of Elizabeth's reign accentuated this trend. One was the Act of Supremacy, authorizing Elizabeth to appoint a high commission by letters patent. The high commission claimed the power to imprison. If this power had been conferred by the statute, then lawyers would have been constrained to accept the authority of the statute. It was not: it was conferred by letters patent issued pursuant to the act. The power was conferred by what, in modern times, is known as delegated legislation. Salisbury, writing to James, saw no reason for distress in this fact. He said

> the authority by which the Commissioners proceed in anything is by your letters patent under the Great Seal, which are grounded upon an Act of Parliament. You can then easily conclude that if they do more than you have authorized them, their acts are void.

It is very clear in this picture that it is James, not parliament, who is envisaged as doing the authorizing. Nicholas Fuller, of course, was not satisfied. He seized on the central problem of delegated legislation: it transferred the authority to make law. In this construction, he said 'whatever should be conteyned in the Letters Patents should be as a law'.[10] Any common lawyer was trained not to recognize letters patent as having the authority to make law, so those who wished to uphold the high commission were driven back on the two kingdoms theory of the Act in Restraint of Appeals. Here was fertile ground for building rival theories.

The other statute which gave rise to debate was the act of 1571 confirming the 39 articles, Peter Wentworth's solitary parliamentary victory. That act confirmed only those articles which concerned doctrine, not those which concerned discipline. This immediately set up a situation in which many clergy could be deprived according to ecclesiastical law, but not according to secular law. It then became very interesting indeed which law governed the case.

---

[9] Conrad Russell, *Parliaments and English Politics 1621–1629* (Oxford, 1979), pp. 410–1.

[10] H.M.C., *Salisbury MSS*, XIX, 344–5; Nicholas Fuller, *The Argument of Master Nicholas Fuller in the Case of Thomas Lad and Richard Maunsell* (1607), p. 29.

The third event which accentuated debate on these issues was the canons of 1604. These canons laid down a long series of offences for which clergy might be deprived, many of which were offences only by virtue of the authority of the canons, and not of any statute or common law. It thus became extremely interesting to clergy threatened with deprivation, as well as to their parishioners and their patrons, whether this authority was legally sufficient. It was those canons which started many of the stories which led to the headline conflicts between James and Coke. James and Bancroft rode out the storm, but James did not confirm the canons of 1606. The next attempt to make binding canons was in the ill-starred convocation of 1640. That led to a storm which swept the power to make canons away altogether.

The tendency of common law judges to review the competence of the church was much accentuated by the canons of 1604, but it ran back to the act of 1571, which confirmed those among the 39 articles which concerned matters of faith or sacraments. They took it as their business to decide, case by case, what these matters were. Attorney General Hobart, in the case of prohibitions under James, tried to argue that this took the common law judges outside their sphere of competence. He said: 'the judges of common lawe or jurie doe take upon them to determine what concernes faith or sacraments, what not, wherein they ought to judge according to the judgements of the Church of England'. This claim that matters ought to be decided by those competent to understand them was always at the heart of the case for clerical independence, as it is now at the heart of the case for academic freedom. Sir John Bennett, in a treatise of the interpretation of statutes, rehearsed the two bodies doctrine of the Act in Restraint of Appeals, and added that judges could not expound statutes if they did not know the matter.[11]

The other strong point of the ecclesiastical case, even more in politics than in law, was the ability to rely on the name and authority of the king, and therefore to tar their rivals with the brush of disloyalty. One of the opening memoranda submitted to James on his accession told him that royal authority in ecclesiastical cases 'appertaines to the kinge as supreme magistrate in a Christian commonwealth'. It did not come by law, still less by a declaratory Act of Supremacy. It came, in this version, direct from God. That power, he was told, allowed him to summon 'general assemblies of the clergy', and 'to confirme ecclesiasticall canons, and give them the force of lawes'. Another memorandum delivered to James early in his reign said such points were decided by the bishops and clergy 'out of the scriptures, councells and Fathers', 'none other sitting with them but themselves', and became law if the king on 'mature deliberation' approved them.[12] James needed no second urging to an assumption of responsibility so delightful to a king of Scots. In his *Meditation Upon . . . St. Matthew*, he said 'it is the kings office toe oversee and compel the church to doe her office, to purge all abuses in her, and by his sword to procure her due reverence and obedience of all his temporal subjects.'[13] The view was the more persuasive to James because it came to him with the authority of Sir Edward Coke. In Cawdry's Case of 1591, Coke closely followed the two bodies theory of the

[11] Bodl., MS Barlow 9, ff. 51, 54.

[12] P.R.O., S.P. 14/6/46, 14/8/20. The second of these bears a note, not in the author's hand, saying 'Dudley Carleton'. This note might indicate ownership, rather than authorship, of the MS.

[13] King James I, *A Meditation Upon the 27, 28, 29 Verses of the 27 Chapter of St. Matthew* (1620), pp. 36–7. Unlike most of King James's political works, this actually is a work of James I and not of James VI, though it is easy to imagine that James VI envied him the ability to write it.

Act in Restraint of Appeals, much of which found its way *verbatim* into his report. He added:

> and as in temporal causes the King by the mouth of his judges in his courts of justice doth judge and determine the same by the temporal laws of England, so in causes ecclesiastical and spiritual . . . (*the conusance whereof belong not to the common laws of England*) the same are to be determined and decided by ecclesiastical judges, according to the King's ecclesiastical laws of this realm.[14]

Those words must have haunted Coke a few years later.

In the case of the high commission, early in the next reign, Coke took a very different line. He said the high commission could not arrest on suspicion, for 'the King by his commission cannot alter the ecclesiastical law, nor the proceedings of it'. So far, this is simply the point about delegated legislation. However, he also cited with approval the case of Simpson in 1602. Simpson had shot dead a pursuivant sent to arrest him by the high commission. Anderson, of all unlikely judges, had held that since the arrest was tortious, the killing was in self-defence and no murder. That is the supremacy of the common law being claimed in the most extreme terms. In the case of convocations, Coke had shifted his allegiance from the Act in Restraint of Appeals to the Act for the Submission of the Clergy. He spelt out the four conditions required by that act for canons to be lawful, that they should not be against the prerogative of the King, nor against common law, nor against statute, nor against any custom of the realm. Here we have the Coke of judicial review, firmly dedicated to the supervisory superiority of the common law over all other sources of authority. For good measure, he threw in the rejection of canon law over bastardy in the Statute of Merton: '*nolumus leges Angliae mutare*'. He also added a stress on representation and consent which was to become more and more characteristic of the lay case against the power to make canons. He said convocation might make canons by which the spiritualty might be bound 'for that they all, or by representation, or in person, are present, but not the temporalty'.[15] This doctrine reduced the clergy to the private status of a college governing body.

It is this universalism of the common law which became a popular doctrine among members of parliament. Nicholas Fuller's 1610 bill against the *ex officio* oath begins by reciting the due process clause of Magna Carta, asserts that only common law procedure with presentment and accuser constitutes due process, and makes future use of the *ex officio* oath into a *praemunire*. It is a very clear assumption that the common law is the governing law, and that the king's authority can only mean his authority by the common law. It altogether denies the idea of an autonomous realm of spiritual jurisdiction. In his speech in the case of Mansell and Lad in 1607, Fuller spelt out the thinking behind this position rather more clearly. He said:

> the lawes of England are the high inheritance of the realme, by which both the King and the subject are directed; and that such grants, charters and commissions as tend to charge the body, lands or goods of the subjects, otherwise then according to the due

---

[14] Elton, *Tudor Constitution*, pp. 226–7; Sir Edward Coke, *Fifth Report* [hereafter *Co. Rep.*] (1826), pp. xxvii–xxviii. My italics.
[15] *12 Co. Rep.*, pp. 50, 72–3.

course of the lawes of the realme, are not lawfull, or of force, unless the same charters and commissions, doe receive life and strength, from some Act of Parliament.

As he spelt out later in the speech, 'without lawes there would be neither king nor inheritance in England'. It was indeed the law which made the king. For Fuller, who made a curious mixture of More and Cromwell by treating the Mosaic law as a fundamental law while believing in parliamentary sovereignty, the common law was the *fons et origo* of the royal supremacy.[16]

From the late Elizabethan period down to the death of Bancroft, a long succession of bills embodying such principles sailed through the Commons, usually with very little recorded discussion. All of them asserted the supremacy of the common law and statute over ecclesiastical jurisdiction, and all of them attacked the legislative independence of the clergy in one form or another. A regular team of godly members pushed these bills through, seconding each other's motions and staffing each other's committees. Over and over again, the names of Hastings, Fuller, Sir Anthony Cope, Thomas Wentworth, Sir John Heigham, Sir Nathaniel Bacon and the rest crop up side by side with each other. It is dangerously easy to assume because the bills were not more disputed, that these men spoke for the Commons, or still worse, for the parliament.

One clue to suggest that this might not be so is that none of these bills reached the statute book in the sessions of 1604, 1606, 1607 or 1610. Over and over again, they 'fell asleep' or worse in the house of lords. We get a rare glimpse of what strong feelings such bills could arouse in the Lords from Archbishop Bancroft's speech against the Bill of Non-Residence and Pluralities in 1610, which concluded: 'For this Bill, I could be content to agree this bill should be committed, but to the pit of Hell; and I crave pardon if my speech do not comfort to every man's disposition.'[17] He was immediately supported by the bishops of London, Oxford, Durham and Lincoln. The bill clearly enjoyed some support among the peers, but Salisbury, in spite of signs of sneaking sympathy for the bill, could not support a bill which caused such offence to his colleagues, and it was laid aside. Assaults on their order united the bishops in a way issues of theology did not, and bills with so strong a hostile feeling against the church were always likely to promote the reciprocal hostility to which Bancroft so freely gave expression. The support given in the 1620s by such bishops as Williams and Harsnet to measures the crown did not want came from a world in which such issues of ecclesiastical law had given way to issues of theology, foreign affairs and court faction, which did not threaten the interests of bishops as an order.

The next clue comes from an unwise speech by Sir Thomas Holcroft, on 15 December 1606. He protested that Sir Thomas Vavasour, knight marshal of the household, had been heard saying: 'he cared not what they did in the Lower House: he knew there would be a stop above'.[18] Vavasour's words are so painfully true that they must give us pause. What he thought, others with the same evidence before them may have thought also. We have perhaps given too much importance to the passage of bills through the

---

[16] H.M.C., *House of Lords MSS*, new ser., XI, 125–6, and Fuller's bill on subscription, *ibid.*, p. 127. Fuller, *Lad and Maunsell*, pp. 3, 14.

[17] Elizabeth Read Foster, *Proceedings in Parliament 1610* (2 vols., New Haven, 1966), I, 219–27, 229–36.

[18] *C.J.*, I, 1010.

house of commons. The passage of bills through the seventeenth-century house of commons was like their passage through the twentieth-century house of lords: it gave no entry to the legislative pipeline in the other House. It was therefore of no political significance unless forces of sufficient power were able to take charge of the bill and help it through the other House. Where this was not so, Vavasour was quite right: there is no sense in shooting down what is about to crash anyway.

In these circumstances, it is only worth dignifying a bill by an attempt to kill it if success is reasonably certain. Otherwise, there is a risk of a damaging political reverse for no political gain. Does this explain why bills passed through the Commons so easily?

There are only two divisions in the years 1604 to 1614 which help to gauge the strength of religious groups in the House. These are the two divisions on whether to sit on Ascension day, in 1604 and 1614. In 1604, there was a narrow majority of 137 to 128 in favour of the godly preference for sitting. In 1614 there was a clear majority against sitting, given by the *Commons' Journal* as 248 to 141, and by Holles as 248 to 191.[19] These figures, tentative though any conclusion from them must be, do not suggest that Fuller, Hastings and their associates enjoyed an overwhelming natural majority.

It is perhaps suspicious that the diaries and the *Journals* do not record more debate on these bills. A bill which provokes little debate is likely to be one which is not much opposed because no one thinks anything will come of it. We must make do with occasional scraps, either on bills, or on the ecclesiastical grievances.

The 1606 Bill against the Residence of Married Men in Colleges, which was designed to prevent marriage by Oxford and Cambridge heads of houses, was not a conventional godly bill, but it is interesting none the less. The move away from celibacy by law might have been expected to attract some godly support. Instead, it drew vigorous praise for virginity from Hoskins, which provoked Bowyer to accuse him of being popish. William Hakewill, who was certainly no puritan, said 'who knoweth not how the manners of young men are corrupted and drawn from their studyes by the ordinary sight and conversation with women'. On a third reading, the bill was carried, but only by 169 to 104.[20]

Silenced ministers are a more typical godly issue. They were introduced as a grievance by Sir Edward Montague and Sir Francis Hastings in 1604, and played their part in leading up to the debacle of the Apology.

The story of religious jurisdiction in 1604 survives only in tantalizing scraps, creating lines between which it is very tempting to read. The serious story begins on 18 April, when Hastings reported that the House wanted a conference with the Lords touching matters of religion and ecclesiastical government. The king, he said, had suggested that they confer with the bishops in their capacity as lords of parliament. The fact that the Lords replied that they 'do like of it'[21] suggests that Hastings had correctly reported the king's wishes. On 5 May, articles for this conference were agreed. They were prefaced by a resolution that no subscription could be required but by parliament, and followed by a resolution to draw a bill for ecclesiastical courts. The first article

---

[19] *Ibid.*, p. 972. Maija Jansson, *Proceedings in Parliament 1614* (American Philosophical Society, CLXXII, Philadelphia, 1988), p. 405. H.M.C., *Portland MSS*, IX, 136.

[20] *Bowyer*, ed. Willson, pp. 58–9; *C.J.*, I, 276.

[21] *C.J.*, I, 949; *L.J.*, II, 282.

demanded that the thirty-nine articles be 'explained' by parliament – a demand which came perilously close to a demand for parliamentary authority in doctrine. The second demanded that none should be made ministers unless they were graduates with a certificate of fitness to preach from their colleges or from six preachers of the county. The third was that there should be no more dispensations for pluralism, and the fourth for increase in livings worth less than £20. The fifth asked the Lords to join in a petition that no subscription should be required but by the 1571 act, and the sixth demanded that there should be no more deprivations for not using the surplice or the cross in baptism.[22]

Hastings' report of the conference with the Lords appears to have been delivered in two parts. In the first appears the ominous question 'what the king may do out of his regal power, without law'. In the second part of Hastings' report appears the even more ominous entry: 'a motion that some of the Convocation House might attend, to deliver such reasons – not assented unto'. Anyone who has followed the story so far must be tempted to see in these entries an opening up of the fundamental question where authority in the Church resided.[23]

Richard Bancroft knew, perhaps better than anyone else involved, the anti-Melvillian fears which such questions could raise in James VI. For so skilled a court politician, this was an opportunity not to be missed. Hastings delivered the second half of his report on 24 May, six days before James's speech of 30 May, at which the Commons 'conceived some grief'. Since that speech, which is the moment at which the session broke down, is wholly lost, it is not possible to prove that the issue of authority in the Church, as well as those of the union and purveyance and wardship, contributed to the speech. However, if we accept the entirely plausible hypothesis that the Apology is a reply to James's speech of 30 May, it does cover these issues at some length.

What can only be hypothesis on 30 May appears clearly in the record on 4 June. On that day the religious conference with the Lords, which had been postponed on 31 May, was resumed. Sir Edward Montague recorded:

> This afternoon we met with the Lords about matter of religion, who refused to join with us in a petition. And the bishop of London [Bancroft] read a writing from the Convocation, inhibiting the bishops to confer with us, for that the laity had not to meddle in these matters now the King had granted to them letters patents, protesting that if they did proceed, they would appeal to the king.[24]

It appears Bancroft had persuaded the king that anything other than the episcopal version of the royal supremacy carried a threat to his authority. It is a consequence Hastings should have foreseen.

Hastings reported this conference to the Commons on 8 June. He said an 'instrument' had been read by a bishop, coming from the convocation house. In this 'a

---

[22] *C.J.*, I, 199–200 and 965. For the Godly Ministry Bill, incorporating a revised version of Article 2, see H.M.C., *House of Lords MSS*, new ser., XI, 80–1. It fell asleep after one reading in the Lords. For a modified version of this bill introduced in 1606, see *ibid.*, pp. 98–100. It too fell asleep after one reading in the Lords.

[23] *C.J.*, I, 975, 979.

[24] H.M.C., *Buccleuch MSS*, III, 89. For evidence for regarding the Apology as a reply to James's speech of 30 May, see *C.J.*, I, 230–1.

mislike uttered, that the House of Commons should deal in any matter of religion'. This, of course, was too much for the Commons. Sir Vincent Skinner pointed out that the Church was mentioned in the writ, as it still is. Nathaniel Bacon proposed to proceed by petition, 'for all matters introduced into the church, savouring of popery'. Hext, the nearest the seventeenth century knew to 'disgusted of Tunbridge Wells', moved 'that the bishops' canons be looked into, by authority whereof the subject is sued, and much grieved'. Yelverton and Fuller took the debate back onto Eltonian grounds of sovereignty. Yelverton said that 'an Act of Parliament will bind the matter of ceremony, more than a Convocation pamphlet', adding for good measure that 'papists get too much encouragement out of the Convocation House'. Fuller reacted to a proposal for a petition for the silenced ministers by proposing to make laws to bind as well as to beg for mercy. For good measure, they condemned Dr Howson for speeches of 'scandal and scorn' of the house of commons.[25] All the big theoretical issues were opened up in these few exchanges. Both sides were showing an adamant determination to have the whole loaf, and not just a half. These exchanges foreshadowed the legislative programme of the godly group in the Commons for the next ten years, and they ushered in what was probably the worst ten years in Church-state relations, though not in religion as a whole, between the Reformation and the civil war. Bancroft and Fuller may have been distinguished intellects, but as politicians they deserved each other.

In 1606, the issue of silenced ministers was raised both as a bill preferred by Hastings, and as a grievance preferred by Fuller. It was the grievance and not the bill which attracted the recorded debate. Heigham, Morrice, Sir Anthony Cope, Trevor and Wingfield set up the usual chorus, but Sir Richard Spencer declared himself 'against the self-weening opinion of some ministers', and said that 'ceremonies agreed on by a general convocation, not to be subject to any private man'. Spencer was a maverick, and proves nothing. It is the response to him which is interesting. Sir William Strode, probably much against his own inclination, proposed a conference with the bishops, while Sir George More, the embodiment of conventional wisdom, moved to investigate whether they were justly deprived. Spencer had been taken seriously. When the issue was introduced by Digges in 1610, and his name suggested that the ear of the archbishop might not be out of reach, Spencer tried again. This time he drew the support of Dudley Carleton, who said they should not count as a grievance what was done *more majorum*, and they should be relieved and not restored. He was also supported by Christopher Brooke, John Donne's best man, who said they were not deprived under the canons, but by the statutes of 1 and 13 Elizabeth.[26] To speculate that these men were the tip of an iceberg is legitimate, but it is in the nature of icebergs that one cannot even guess their size. The issue of the learned ministry drew a proposal from Sir Richard Lovelace that they should confer with the Lords first, while the Sabbath Bill became lost in the piscatorial politics of Great Yarmouth.[27] Clearly, not all undercurrents were godly.

The death of Richard Bancroft led to a drop in temperature, but in these issues, if not in issues of theology, Abbot held to the same position as his predecessor. He may have

---

[25] *C.J.*, I, 235, 989.
[26] *Ibid.*, pp. 274, 285, 290, 420–1.
[27] *Bowyer*, ed. Willson, pp. 34–5; *C.J.*, I, 267.

been less provocative in the use of his powers, and more ready to confer about their use, as he did in the middle 1620s. Yet his theoretical claims remained the same, as did those of members of the Commons like Thomas Wentworth or Pym. A period of comparative calm began to break down in 1629, and when the storm broke again in 1640, both sides were rehearsing a well-known script.

Overall, the conclusion must be that 30 years of parliamentary and legal agitation achieved remarkably little. The legal route for a while looked the more promising, but the dismissal of Chief Justice Coke in 1616 put a stop to that. The parliamentary route may have restrained bishops and high commission from doing what they might otherwise have done, but the haul of failed bills achieved very little except the irritation of the king. Carleton's attack on silenced ministers in 1610 is perhaps a telltale sign that defences of them were regarded as 'unhelpful'.

The one really important contribution these arguments made was to the task of public education. When the chance came again, with the drive to condemn the canons of 1640, it came to a House admirably educated in basic arguments. It was also one more inclined than its predecessors to argue the case from representation and consent which Coke had argued in the case of convocation. The attack on the canons of 1640 was a high-level intellectual debate. Yet intellect does not win political victories. Power does. What had changed in 1640 is that the Lords were in no position to resist. The bishops had lost the support of a much-increased number of peers. Laud knew his impeachment was following hard behind the condemnation of the canons, and many bishops, and some lay lords too, may have feared that too vigorous a defence of the canons would leave them to be impeached too. It was much more important that the Scots, camped around Newcastle, were as determined to see the canons go as any English member. Since it was their power which had blunted the king's weapon of dissolution, it was again they, and not the power of public opinion, which made Pym and Glyn successful where Hastings and Fuller had failed. The attempt to control ecclesiastical jurisdiction by merely parliamentary power reminds me of the cartoon on the publication of C. P. Snow's *Corridors of Power*. An indignant cleaner, shaking a hoover plug, is saying: 'I must remember to tell C. P. Snow there's no power in this corridor.'

Oliver Cromwell, the First Protectorate Parliament and Religious Reform*

DAVID L. SMITH

The first Protectorate parliament is one of the more obscure of seventeenth-century English parliaments. Apart from Peter Gaunt's important research, the parliament has been relatively neglected and it remains less familiar than the apparently more colourful Rump, or Barebone's, or second Protectorate parliaments.[1] Yet, despite the brevity of its existence, the first Protectorate parliament nevertheless repays careful study. Its proceedings reveal much about the contrasting religious priorities of Cromwell and many members of parliament, and that divergence in turn throws a great deal of light on why Cromwell was never able to establish a stable working relationship with any of the interregnum parliaments. In this paper, I shall argue that the key to the collapse of the first Protectorate parliament lay in Cromwell's attempt to use a body designed as 'the representative of the whole realm' to advance what remained a minority agenda, 'liberty of conscience'. He believed that parliament had a crucial role to play in reconciling the interests of the godly with those of the whole nation. Yet in the end, the first Protectorate parliament was a profound disappointment to him, for his wish to liberate the godly proved incompatible with the determination of many members to prevent heresies and blasphemies. At the heart of this parliament's failure, there thus lay fundamentally contrasted visions of the kind of religious reform that parliament should promote.

* I am very grateful to John Morrill and Graham Seel for reading and commenting on a draft of this article, and to Elliot Vernon and Patrick Little for drawing my attention to several sources and for helpful advice on specific points.

[1] Whereas the Rump and Barebone's parliaments have both been the subject of outstanding monographs published during the last 25 years (Blair Worden, *The Rump Parliament, 1648–53* [Cambridge, 1974], and Austin Woolrych, *Commonwealth to Protectorate* [Oxford, 1982]), the first two Protectorate parliaments have been much less studied. Of the two, the second is the more fully researched: see, especially, Ivan Roots, 'Lawmaking in the Second Protectorate Parliament', in *British Government and Administration. Essays presented to S. B. Chrimes*, ed. H. Hearder and H. R. Loyn (Cardiff, 1974), pp. 132–43; and Carol S. Egloff, 'The Search for a Settlement: Exclusion from the Second Protectorate Parliament. Part I: The Process and its Architects', *Parliamentary History*, XVII (1998), 178–97. On the first Protectorate parliament there is little apart from two excellent articles by Peter Gaunt: Peter Gaunt, 'Law-Making in the First Protectorate Parliament', in *Politics and People in Revolutionary England. Essays in Honour of Ivan Roots*, ed. Colin Jones, Malyn Newitt and Stephen Roberts (Oxford, 1986), pp. 163–86; and 'Cromwell's Purge? Exclusions and the First Protectorate Parliament', *Parliamentary History*, VI (1987), 1–22. See also Peter Gaunt, 'The Councils of the Protectorate, from December 1653 to September 1658', University of Exeter Ph.D., 1983, ch. 5; and Sarah E. Jones, 'The Composition and Activity of the Protectorate Parliaments', University of Exeter Ph.D., 1988.

Much of the received picture of the first Protectorate parliament still derives in some measure from Cromwell's celebrated denunciation of the parliament when he dissolved it, at the earliest possible constitutional opportunity, on 22 January 1655:

> I do not know whether you have been alive or dead. I have not heard from you all this time; I have not . . . Instead of peace and settlement, instead of mercy and truth being brought together, righteousness and peace kissing each other . . . weeds and nettles, briers and thorns, have thriven under your shadow![2]

To Cromwell, the parliament had simply missed the point of its calling by concentrating on revising the Instrument of Government rather than liberating the godly. This view was echoed in Thomas Carlyle's withering condemnation of this 'most poor hidebound pedant Parliament; which reckoned itself careful of the liberties of England; and was careful only of the sheepskin formulas of these'.[3] S. R. Gardiner argued that the parliament witnessed a power struggle between the civilian politicians and the army leaders, resulting almost inevitably in an impasse.[4] Hugh Trevor-Roper suggested instead that the main problem lay in Cromwell's failure to manage this and other parliaments at all effectively.[5] Most recently, Carol Egloff has written that 'the disastrous session, which produced no legislation but instead witnessed a concerted attempt to dismantle the Instrument and replace it with a parliamentary constitution, made it abundantly clear to the military Cromwellians that the members of future parliaments must be more carefully controlled'.[6] Although there is much in these interpretations that is persuasive, an exploration of the theme of religious reform in this parliament suggests that it is necessary not so much to refute them as to extend and nuance them.

First of all, it is worth stressing, as Peter Gaunt has done, that the parliament's business record demonstrates that its members were very active during the 20-week session.[7] In all, over 40 bills were considered,[8] several of which addressed issues of religious reform, including a bill 'for setling Tenths, and all Impropriacons, belonging to the State, for the maintenance of ministers', a bill 'against the Quakers, Heresies, and Blasphemyes', and another 'for the restoreinge [of] Cathedralls'.[9] The principal source of disagreement between Cromwell and a majority of members seems not to have been over whether religious reform was necessary, but over what sort of religious reform was desirable. Religion was undoubtedly a priority, and the French ambassador recorded that during Cromwell's opening speech on 4 September 1654, 'as often as he spoke . . . of liberty and religion, . . . the members did seem to rejoice with acclamations of joy'.[10] But the

---

[2] *The Letters and Speeches of Oliver Cromwell, with Elucidations by Thomas Carlyle*, ed. S. C. Lomas (3 vols., 1904), II, 407, 409.

[3] *Ibid.*, p. 431.

[4] S. R. Gardiner, *History of the Commonwealth and Protectorate, 1649–1656* (4 vols., 1903; repr. 1989), III, 178–255.

[5] Hugh Trevor-Roper, 'Oliver Cromwell and his Parliaments', in *Religion, the Reformation and Social Change* (3rd edn., 1984), pp. 345–91.

[6] Egloff, 'Search for a Settlement', p. 183.

[7] Gaunt, 'Law-Making in the First Protectorate Parliament', esp. pp. 169–76.

[8] *Ibid.*, p. 174; Jones, 'Composition and Activity of the Protectorate Parliaments', p. 128.

[9] See the draft list of bills intended for the first Protectorate parliament in B.L., Stowe MS 322 (Revenue papers), f. 74r-v.

[10] *A Collection of the State Papers of John Thurloe*, ed. Thomas Birch (7 vols., 1742), II, 588: Bordeaux to the Count de Brienne, 14 Sept. 1654 [n.s.].

more specific the debates became, the more divergences opened up over what kind of church parliament should promote and construct.

It is virtually impossible to reconstruct the religious attitudes of most members of the Protectorate parliaments. Sarah Jones has argued that only a minority were 'active' or 'expressed opinions' that reveal their religious sympathies, and that the religious affiliations of nearly 70 per cent of members of the first Protectorate parliament remain unknown. Jones argues that of the remainder, presbyterians constituted 18 per cent, independents four per cent, 'radicals' (quakers, baptists etc.) three per cent, and anglicans two per cent.[11] However, these figures are necessarily approximate and it is often difficult to make distinctions with any degree of precision: in particular, presbyterians and independents were even more problematic terms by 1654 than in the later 1640s. It is nevertheless worth noting that various contemporary observers reported the prominence of what they termed presbyterians: Sir Edward Nicholas wrote that 'there are many that now perswade the King to some extraordinary complyaunce with the Presbiterian party, for that soe many of that faccon are chosen to sit in the approching mock Parliament',[12] while the Venetian secretary in England, Lorenzo Paulucci, observed that 'the members returned for the new Parliament are not quite to the Protector's satisfaction. He wanted a majority of his own creatures, whereas a great part of those already chosen prove to be Presbyterians, the enemies of the dominant military party on which the government depends.'[13]

The influence of such people among the parliament's most active members can be discerned in the religious reforms that were adopted for inclusion in the draft 'constitutional bill' to which the parliament devoted so much of its time.[14] Initially, the parliament had envisaged creating an assembly of divines which would advise members on religious reform.[15] However, on 5 October, a grand committee for religion was appointed to meet on two afternoons a week, to discuss 'matters of religion' with the advice of between 12 and 20 ministers.[16] The religious measures that the House subsequently adopted fell into two main categories: the provision and maintenance of the ministry, and the prevention of what were deemed religious errors, heresies and blasphemies. On both issues, the principal concern was to create structures that would regulate the nation's religious life. As the French ambassador observed in late October: 'The Parliament is still taken up about religion: I am afraid they are not good enough to

---

[11] Jones, 'Composition and Activity of the Protectorate Parliaments', p. 74.

[12] P.R.O., SP 18/74/115: [Sir Edward Nicholas] to Mr Jane, 22 Aug./1 Sept. 1654.

[13] C[alendar] [of] S[tate] P[apers] V[enetian], XXIX (1653–4), 235–6: Lorenzo Paulucci to Giovanni Sagredo, 17 July 1654. This situation was not significantly altered by the fact that before the parliament assembled the council 'purged' less than a dozen members, only two of whom apparently had presbyterian sympathies. Nor was it decisively changed when over 100 members withdrew on 12 September rather than sign a recognition promising to accept 'the [Instrument of] Government, as it is settled in a single person and a Parliament'. See Gaunt, 'Cromwell's Purge?'; and Gardiner, *History of the Commonwealth and Protectorate*, III, 173–8, 193–7.

[14] The text of this 'constitutional bill' is printed in *Constitutional Documents of the Puritan Revolution, 1625–1660*, ed. S. R. Gardiner (3rd edn., Oxford, 1906), pp. 427–47.

[15] C.J., VII, 367. See also *Diary of Thomas Burton, Esq.*, ed. J. T. Rutt (4 vols., 1828), I, xxvii (this and subsequent references are to the journal of Guibon Goddard, printed as an introduction to Burton's diary).

[16] C.J., VII, 373; *Diary of Thomas Burton*, ed. Rutt, I, xlvi.

be fathers of the Church, to form a true canonical one. In all likelihood, they will set the Presbytery uppermost, and give toleration to the others.'[17]

Within a month of its assembling, the parliament turned to the issue of the ministry. Before it had met, Cromwell had issued two protectoral ordinances specifically designed to improve the quality of the ministry: that of March 1654 established a national body of 'triers' to vet all new clergy, while the following August county commissioners known as 'ejectors' were set up to expel 'scandalous, ignorant and insufficient ministers and schoolmasters'.[18] The parliament referred both these ordinances to a large committee of 94 members.[19] This committee initially suggested suspending the ordinance for the 'ejectors' while they drafted a new bill, but that proposal was narrowly defeated.[20] I have not found any hints in the surviving sources as to the contents of this new bill. We do know, however, that it was read twice during the course of November and after the second reading was referred back to the committee, 'upon some exceptions', never to resurface during the parliament's lifetime.[21] Pending further progress on that bill, the parliament resolved on 7 December that,

> until some better provision be made by the Parliament, for the encouragement and maintenance of able, godly, and painful ministers, and public preachers of the Gospel, for instructing the people, and for discovery and confutation of errors, heresy and whatsoever is contrary to sound doctrine, the present public maintenance shall not be taken away, nor impeached.[22]

This was accompanied by a resolution that 'the true reformed Protestant Christian religion as it is contained in the Holy Scriptures of the Old and New Testament, and no other, shall be asserted and maintained as the public profession of these nations'.[23] The next day (8 December), after 'a long debate',[24] the parliament resolved that any subsequent bills that required,

> from such ministers and preachers of the Gospel as shall receive public maintenance for instructing the people, a submission and conformity to the public profession aforesaid, or enjoining attendance unto the preaching of the word and other religious duties on the Lord's day . . . shall pass into and become laws within twenty days after the presentation to the Lord Protector, although he shall not give his consent thereunto.[25]

This represented a firm rebuff to Cromwell and a clear indication of the importance that the majority of members attached to public conformity by a national ministry.

---

[17] *Thurloe State Papers*, ed. Birch, II, 697: Bordeaux to the Count de Chavost, 6 Nov. 1654 [n.s.].

[18] *Acts and Ordinances of the Interregnum, 1642–1660*, ed. C. H. Firth and R. S. Rait (3 vols., 1911), II, 855–8, 968–90.

[19] *C.J.*, VII, 370, 371. See also *Diary of Thomas Burton*, ed. Rutt, I, xli.

[20] *C.J.*, VII, 377, 381, 382. See also *Diary of Thomas Burton*, ed. Rutt, I, lxii.

[21] *C.J.*, VII, 377, 381, 382, 384, 385–7. See also *Diary of Thomas Burton*, ed. Rutt, I, lxii, lxxv, lxxix, lxxxix.

[22] *C.J.*, VII, 397. See also *Diary of Thomas Burton*, ed. Rutt, I, cxii. This clause was adopted as chapter 44 of the draft 'constitutional bill'. *Constitutional Documents*, ed. Gardiner, p. 443.

[23] *C.J.*, VII, 397. See also *Diary of Thomas Burton*, ed. Rutt, I, cxii. This clause was adopted as chapter 41 of the 'constitutional bill'. *Constitutional Documents*, ed. Gardiner, p. 442.

[24] Bulstrode Whitelocke, *Memorials of the English Affairs* (4 vols., Oxford, 1838), IV, 159.

[25] *C.J.*, VII, 398. See also *Diary of Thomas Burton*, ed. Rutt, I, cxii–cxiii. This clause was adopted as chapter 42 of the 'constitutional bill'. *Constitutional Documents*, ed. Gardiner, pp. 442–3.

These steps to maintain the ministry and the 'public profession' of religion were complemented by measures to suppress 'damnable heresies' and blasphemies. Throughout the deliberations on this subject, liberty of conscience remained a much lower priority, to be denied whenever it conflicted with the prevention of errors, heresies and blasphemies, or the maintenance of public order. Thus, on 15 December, after two days of 'long debates',[26] the House resolved that,

> without the consent of the Lord Protector and Parliament, no law or statute be made for the restraining of such tender consciences as shall differ in doctrine, worship or discipline, from the public profession aforesaid and shall not abuse this liberty to the civil injury of others, or the disturbance of the public peace.

To this, however, was added the crucial proviso that,

> such bills as shall be agreed upon by the Parliament, for the restraining of atheism, blasphemy, damnable heresies, to be particularly enumerated by this Parliament, popery, prelacy, licentiousness, or profaneness; or such as shall preach, print, or avowedly maintain any thing contrary to the fundamental principles of doctrine held forth in the public profession . . . shall pass into, and become laws, within twenty days after their presentation to the Lord Protector, although he shall not give his consent thereunto.[27]

This remarkable final clause constituted further direct defiance of Cromwell and his promotion of liberty of conscience.

The most specific illustration of the difference between Cromwell and the parliament over liberty of conscience was the case of the socinian John Biddle. In his two books, *A Two-Fold Catechism* and *The Apostolical and True Opinion, concerning the Holy Trinity, revived and asserted*, Biddle had denied the Trinity and the divinity of Christ, and London presbyterians were quick to identify him as a target.[28] He was interrogated by a parliamentary committee, and the House subsequently endorsed the committee's verdict that the *Two-Fold Catechism* expressed 'many blasphemous and heretical opinions', and that *The Apostolical and True Opinion* was 'full of horrid, blasphemous, and execrable opinions, denying the Deity of Christ and of the Holy Ghost'.[29] Biddle was imprisoned and his books burnt; and his case soon prompted a broader attack on the quakers, against whom a bill was prepared.[30] Although Cromwell did not prevent Biddle's punishment,

[26] Whitelocke, *Memorials*, IV, 161; *Diary of Thomas Burton*, ed. Rutt, I, cxviii–cxix.

[27] *C.J.*, VII, 401. See also *Diary of Thomas Burton*, ed. Rutt, I, cxviii–cxix. This clause was adopted as chapter 43 of the 'constitutional bill'. *Constitutional Documents*, ed. Gardiner, p. 443. Earlier, the parliament had resolved by 85 votes to 84 (11 Dec.) to provide 'a particular enumeration of heresies' after the words 'damnable heresies' (*C.J.*, VII, 399), and then (13 Dec.) to include the specific words 'blasphemy', 'popery', 'prelacy', 'licentiousness' and 'profaneness' (*C.J.*, VII, 400). These resolutions were subsequently confirmed on 3, 12 and 15 January (*C.J.*, VII, 412, 414, 416).

[28] Blair Worden, 'Toleration and the Cromwellian Protectorate', in *Persecution and Toleration*, ed. W.J. Sheils (Studies in Church History, XXI, 1984), pp. 199–233, esp. pp. 218–21.

[29] *Diary of Thomas Burton*, ed. Rutt, I, cxxix–cxxx. Parliament's handling of Biddle's case can be reconstructed from *ibid.*, pp. cxiv–cxvii, cxxiii, cxxviii–cxxx; and *C.J.*, VII, 400, 404, 416.

[30] *C.J.*, VII, 410; *Diary of Thomas Burton*, ed. Rutt, I, cxxvii. The attack on quakers was also prompted by the bizarre protest outside the palace of Westminster of Theauraujohn Tany, for whom see especially Ariel Hessayon, ' "Gold Tried in the Fire": The Prophet Theauraujohn Tany and the Puritan Revolution', University of Cambridge Ph.D., 1996.

it was characteristic that he ensured that Biddle was imprisoned on the Scilly Isles, beyond parliament's reach, and also granted him a weekly allowance of ten shillings.[31]

To the lord protector, who in his opening speech had called 'liberty of conscience and liberty of the subjects' 'two as glorious things to be contended for, as any God hath given us',[32] the attitudes of some of the parliament's most able and active members were profoundly disappointing. In that speech he went on to lament that there was

> too much of an imposing spirit in matter of conscience; a spirit unchristian enough in any times, most unfit for these; denying liberty of conscience to those who have earned it with their blood; who have gained civil liberty, and religious also, for those who would thus impose upon them

(at which point Carlyle interpolated in his edition: 'stifled murmurs from the Presbyterian sect').[33] In his great speech of 12 September, Cromwell declared that 'liberty of conscience in religion' was 'a fundamental' and 'a natural right'.[34] But such 'a thing ought to be very reciprocal', and in his final speech Cromwell denounced the parliament's failure to give 'a just liberty to godly men of different judgments', and to settle 'peace and quietness amongst all professing godliness', adding: 'is there not upon the spirits of men a strange itch? Nothing will satisfy them unless they can put their finger upon their brethren's consciences, to pinch them there.'[35] On this point Cromwell was fundamentally at odds with the prevailing mood of the parliament. Moreover, the specific limitations that the 'constitutional bill' placed on his capacity to promote liberty of conscience must have heightened his resentment of the parliament's systematic curtailing of other protectoral powers established in the Instrument of Government.

Cromwell's anger at the parliament's failure to ensure liberty of conscience was widely shared among the soldiery. Towards the end of 1654, the army presented a petition to Cromwell that included the demands that 'liberty of conscience be allowed, but not to papistry in publicke worshipp', and that 'a law be made for the righting [of] persons wronged for liberty of conscience'.[36] The Venetian ambassador noted wrily that when, 'in spite of the article in the paper presented by some of the Army against interference in religion', the parliament 'decided that the religion generally professed here must be the Protestant', this outcome 'possibly dissatisfied the military'.[37] In fact, a number of the most prominent members, including such figures as John FitzJames, John Bulkeley, Sir Richard Onslow, John Birch, John Ashe and Robert Shapcote, had a long history of antipathy towards the independent cause espoused by the army. With the exception of FitzJames, who had not sat in the Long Parliament, all these members

---

[31] Worden, 'Toleration and the Cromwellian Protectorate', pp. 221–2; J. C. Davis, 'Cromwell's Religion', in *Oliver Cromwell and the English Revolution*, ed. John Morrill (Harlow, 1990), pp. 196–7.

[32] *Letters and Speeches of Cromwell*, ed. Lomas, II, 345.

[33] *Ibid.*, p. 346.

[34] *Ibid.*, p. 382.

[35] *Ibid.*, pp. 416–17.

[36] *The Clarke Papers. Selections from the Papers of William Clarke*, ed. C. H. Firth (4 vols., Camden Soc., new ser., XLIX, LIV, LXI, LXII, 1891–1901), III 13. Cf. *A Perfect Account of the Daily Intelligence from the Armies in England, Scotland and Ireland, and the Navy at Sea* (1–8 Nov. 1654), sig. 9Q (B.L., Thomason Tracts, E 816/9).

had been imprisoned or secluded at Pride's purge.[38] The tensions that erupted during the first Protectorate parliament between on the one hand Cromwell and the army, and on the other a number of active members of presbyterian sympathies, thus represented in part the continuation of a long-term fissure within the parliamentarian cause that could be traced back to the later 1640s.

Those within parliament who opposed the unqualified grant of liberty of conscience had close links with like-minded laity and divines in the wider world. Blair Worden has shown how they forged in particular 'an effective alliance with the Presbyterian machine of the City of London'.[39] That machine had two principal motors: the Stationers' Company and the London Provincial Assembly. One leading member of the latter, the presbyterian minister Jeremiah Whitaker, wrote to Cromwell in the summer of 1654 begging him to 'consider seriously how religion is not onely weakened by divisione, but almost wasted by the daily growth of Atheisme and the Prophane: the reignes of Government time let lose, and now lost, in the Church totally'. Horrified to see 'sabboths generally prophaned, ordinances despised, the consciences of men growing wanton abusing liberty to all licentuousnes', Whitaker hoped that the lord protector would 'appoint such Justices whose principles and practices lead them to restrain vice, who do account the Sabboth their delight, that so [lesser?] officers may bee by them encouraged [to] repress prophanes'.[40] No evidence survives of any reply from Cromwell to Whitaker, but the letter is indicative of presbyterian hopes within the city of London. These were again plainly apparent in a petition that the common council submitted to Cromwell towards the end of 1654 'to encourage the Parliament about settling Church government'. To this, Cromwell responded plaintively: 'where shall wee have men of a universall spirit? Every one desires to have liberty, but none will give it.'[41]

It is occasionally possible to reconstruct links between certain members of the first Protectorate parliament and ministers or laymen of similar views outside parliament. The letter-book of one member unsympathetic to liberty of conscience, John FitzJames, reveals that he maintained an extensive correspondence with those of a like persuasion including not only other members, such as Robert Shapcote and Robert Beake, but also ministers like Stanley Gower and William Mew as well as gentry such as Andrew Bromhall and Robert Lewen.[42] FitzJames's own scepticism about liberty of conscience

[38] For Bulkeley, see David Underdown, *Pride's Purge. Politics in the Puritan Revolution* (1971), p. 369. For Onslow, see Mary Frear Keeler, *The Long Parliament, 1640–1641. A Biographical Study of its Members* (Memoirs of the American Philosophical Society, XXXVI, Philadelphia, 1954), p. 290; Underdown, *Pride's Purge*, p. 381; and the D[ictionary] [of] N[ational] B[iography]. For Birch, see Underdown, *Pride's Purge*, p. 368; and the D.N.B. For Ashe, see Keeler, *Long Parliament*, p. 91; and Underdown, *Pride's Purge*, p. 367. For Shapcote, see Underdown, *Pride's Purge*, p. 385.

[39] Worden, 'Toleration and the Cromwellian Protectorate', p. 218.

[40] B.L., Add. MS 4159, f. 113r: Jeremiah Whitaker to Oliver Cromwell, [? summer 1654]. I am most grateful to Elliot Vernon for giving me a transcript of this letter, for advice on its date and significance, and for a helpful discussion about Whitaker.

[41] *The Clarke Papers*, ed. Firth, II, xxxv–xxxvi.

[42] Northumberland MS 551, ff. 3v–13v (duke of Northumberland, Alnwick Castle, Northumberland), letter-book of John FitzJames, V, 9 Sept. 1654–2 Sept. 1656. I am most grateful to Patrick Little for drawing this source to my attention, and to his grace the duke of Northumberland for granting me permission to consult the microfilm of it in the British Library (B.L., Microfilm M 331).

was well captured when he wrote to Shapcote: 'whether a religion that pleases *all* interests can please *one* God, there's the question.'[43] As in earlier seventeenth-century parliaments, an elaborate network existed that transmitted news of parliamentary proceedings back to the provinces, and in turn enabled those at Westminster to draw advice and encouragement from friends and relatives outside the capital.[44]

It is also worth remembering that, under the terms of the Instrument of Government, the first Protectorate parliament included representatives from Scotland and Ireland.[45] The Instrument stipulated that there should be 30 Scottish members and 30 Irish, although the actual numbers returned were probably 22 and somewhere between 15 and 25 respectively.[46] The influence of these members within the parliament generally, and on religious issues specifically, is extremely difficult to determine. However, it is likely that at least some of these members were of presbyterian sympathies and that their presence therefore tended to strengthen hostility towards liberty of conscience. The member for County Cork, Lord Broghill, provides a good case-study of this. Broghill was well connected in both Ireland and Scotland: the owner of extensive lands in Ireland, he was appointed lord president of the Scottish council in 1655, and in the second Protectorate parliament he sat for both County Cork and Edinburgh.[47] In the first Protectorate parliament he was appointed to the committee to review the ordinance 'for ejecting scandalous, ignorant and insufficient ministers and schoolmasters', and acted as a teller for the noes who opposed its suspension.[48] On 12 December 1654, he was appointed to a committee 'to consider of the particular enumeration of damnable heresies'.[49] Later, on 3 January 1655, he acted as a teller for the yeas in favour of retaining the words 'to be particularly enumerated by the Parliament' after 'damnable heresies' in the House's resolution of 15 December.[50] Broghill's friends included the presbyterian minister Richard Baxter, and Broghill nominated Baxter to the group of divines chosen to confer with parliament's sub-committee on religion.[51] Baxter subsequently wrote of his hostility to 'an universall toleration for all that shall seeke the subversion of the faith of Christ'. Although keen to 'distinguish betweene tolerable and intollerable errours, and restraine only the latter', he was vehemently opposed to 'licentious toleration of Church destroyers'.[52] Broghill's role on committees and as a teller during the first

[43] Alnwick Castle, Northumberland MS 551, f. 8v: John FitzJames to Robert Shapcote, 8/18 Nov. 1654. Original emphasis.

[44] Cf. Richard Cust, 'News and Politics in Early Seventeenth-Century England', *Past and Present*, No. 112 (1986), 60–90.

[45] *Constitutional Documents*, ed. Gardiner, p. 407 (Instrument of Government, IX).

[46] For the Scottish elections, and the 22 members returned (of whom nine were English), see F. D. Dow, *Cromwellian Scotland, 1651–1660* (Edinburgh, 1979), pp. 148–54. For information about the Irish members, and this estimate of their numbers, I am indebted to Patrick Little.

[47] I am very grateful to Patrick Little for this information, and for a helpful discussion about Broghill. For useful outlines of Broghill's career, see the article on him in the *D.N.B.*, and also Dow, *Cromwellian Scotland*, pp. 162–210.

[48] *C.J.*, VII, 370, 382. The noes carried the day by 77 votes to 67.

[49] *Ibid.*, p. 399.

[50] *Ibid.*, p. 412. The yeas carried the day by 81 votes to 75. The resolution is quoted above, p.42.

[51] *Calendar of the Correspondence of Richard Baxter*, ed. N. H. Keeble and Geoffrey F. Nuttall (2 vols., Oxford, 1991), I, 160, 162, 189. I am very grateful to Patrick Little for these references.

[52] *Ibid.*, pp. 222–6: Baxter to Edward Harley, 15 Sept. 1656 (quotations at pp. 223, 226). I owe this reference to Patrick Little.

Protectorate parliament suggests that his own stance on religious issues was consistent with Baxter's position.

The lack of sympathy within parliament towards liberty of conscience was crucial in explaining why Cromwell did not find the assembly, in Bulstrode Whitelocke's phrase, 'pliable to his purposes'.[53] The chances of achieving such pliability were not enhanced by the fact that those councillors of state who sat in the parliament do not appear to have formed a coherent group: there is little sign that they attempted to co-ordinate their activities or to set a lead in the House. The government did not introduce any clear legislative programme, and parliamentary business proceeded on an *ad hoc* basis.[54] In part this reflected Cromwell's conviction that he should not interfere directly in the parliament's deliberations.[55] However, the problem went much deeper than that, and it ultimately revealed a basic tension within Cromwell's own concept of the role of parliament which prevented him from achieving a stable working relationship with any of the interregnum parliaments. Throughout his career, he believed that parliament had a constitutional role of central importance: as he put it on 12 September, 'the government by a single person and a Parliament is a fundamental. It is the *esse*, it is constitutive.'[56] Yet how did this relate to that other 'fundamental', liberty of conscience? Cromwell wished to use parliament to unify the interests of the nation with those of the people of God. He was attracted to the Instrument of Government because he felt that within it 'a just liberty to the people of God, and the just rights of the people in these nations [were] provided for'.[57] He believed that if parliament, the 'representative of the whole realm', promoted liberty of conscience, then the interests of the nation and of the godly would eventually be reconciled. This was what a 'pliable' parliament would have done. Unfortunately, this parliament, from which only a few of the most obviously hostile individuals had been purged before the session opened,[58] contained a core of members who were vehemently opposed to any agenda that might lift the lid off a seething mass of sectarian errors and blasphemies.

The story of the first Protectorate parliament was thus part of a wider pattern that characterized Cromwell's relations with successive parliaments throughout the interregnum. His fundamental conviction that parliament had a crucial role to play in reconciling the interests of the godly with those of the nation as a whole helps to explain why he remained committed to working with parliaments. There was not a single calendar year throughout the Commonwealth and Protectorate when a parliament did not meet at some stage. Yet always they disappointed him, for the 'representative of the whole realm' never produced an assembly in which a majority of members shared his and the army's commitment to liberty of conscience. Much of the problem lay in the way that Cromwell viewed the relationship between parliament, the nation and the people of God. Committed to the belief that England was an elect nation, he

---

[53] *The Diary of Bulstrode Whitelocke, 1605–1675*, ed. Ruth Spalding (British Academy, Records of Social and Economic History, new ser., XIII, Oxford, 1990), p. 400: 3 Feb. 1655. The same phrase also appears in Whitelocke, *Memorials*, IV, 182: 1 Feb. 1655.

[54] Gaunt, 'Councils of the Protectorate', pp. 129–42.

[55] See, e.g., *Letters and Speeches of Cromwell*, ed. Lomas, II, 359, 407.

[56] *Ibid.*, p. 381.

[57] *Ibid.*, p. 419.

[58] Gaunt, 'Cromwell's Purge?'.

wanted the godly people to become ever more numerous until they ultimately comprised the whole nation. In that way, the visible and invisible churches would eventually become coterminous. He hoped that parliament, by promulgating liberty of conscience and fostering peaceful co-existence amongst 'God's children', would play a central part in this process. Yet, as Cromwell complained to his confidant Lieutenant-Colonel Wilks in January 1655, 'whosoever labours to walk with an even foot between the several interests of the people of God for healing and accommodating their differences is sure to have reproaches and anger from some of all sorts.'[59] The first Protectorate parliament, like those before and after, continued to reflect the widespread civilian unease about liberating the sects. The parliament had been elected on a revised franchise, with a major redistribution of seats towards the counties and a £200 property qualification.[60] As a result, it manifested many of the attitudes that were apparently mainstream within the political and social *élite*, and was deeply reluctant to espouse what remained a minority agenda.

Cromwell's commitment to liberty of conscience thus generated profound tensions between the 'single person and a parliament' which dogged the entire history of the interregnum. By struggling to create an identity between the interests of the nation and those of the godly, he doomed himself to a relationship with parliaments characterized by constant frustration and mutual bafflement. His dealings with parliament in 1654–5 set the pattern for the rest of the Protectorate. Just as he saw the Instrument of Government as a way of reconciling 'a just liberty to the people of God' with 'the just rights of the people in these nations',[61] so, in April 1657, he praised the framers of the Humble Petition and Advice on the grounds that,

> I think you have provided for the liberty of the people of God, and for the liberty of the nation. And I say he sings sweetly that sings a song of reconciliation betwixt these two interests! And it is a pitiful fancy, and wild and ignorant to think they are inconsistent. Certainly they may consist![62]

Yet, like the other interregnum parliaments, the deliberations of the first Protectorate parliament repeatedly demonstrated their essential inconsistency.

When members assembled at Westminster in the autumn of 1654, neither they, nor the lord protector, nor the army leaders doubted that parliament had a crucial role to play in settling the church and the religious life of the nation. In that sense, the relationship between parliament and the church was taken as a given. But what sort of settlement was to be constructed? How rigid should the national structures be, and what measure of liberty of conscience was acceptable? Perhaps more than any other single issue, the differences of opinion between Cromwell and a significant core of members were responsible for destabilizing the parliament and frustrating the lord protector's high hopes of it. In many ways it was a tension within Cromwell's own vision, between

---

[59] *Letters and Speeches of Cromwell*, ed. Lomas, III, 460: Cromwell to Lieutenant-Colonel Wilks [? 14–18 Jan. 1655].

[60] Vernon F. Snow, 'Parliamentary Reapportionment Proposals in the Puritan Revolution', *E.H.R.*, LXXIV (1959), 409–42. The revised distribution of seats is set out in the Instrument of Government, printed in *Constitutional Documents*, ed. Gardiner, pp. 407–9.

[61] *Letters and Speeches of Cromwell*, ed. Lomas, II, 419.

[62] *Ibid.*, III, 101.

his commitment to parliament and his pursuit of liberty of conscience, that doomed both to failure. He was trying to embrace as 'fundamentals' two objectives that were ultimately incompatible. It is uncertain how far he ever perceived this. But we can occasionally hear him, so to speak whistling in the dark, hoping against hope that the two might be reconciled, as for example when he told representatives of the second Protectorate parliament on 3 April 1657:

> If anyone whatsoever think the interest of Christians and the interest of the nation inconsistent, or two different things, I wish my soul may never enter into their secrets . . . And upon these two interests, if God shall account me worthy, I shall live and die. And . . . if I were to give an account before a greater tribunal than any earthly one; and if I were asked why I have engaged all along in the late war, I could give no answer but it would be a wicked one if it did not comprehend these two ends.[63]

Ironically, it was precisely the attempt to tie those two ends together that had earlier brought the first Protectorate parliament to deadlock; and behind Cromwell's brave words in April 1657, there must surely have lurked, at least in part, the memory of that previous parliamentary disaster.

---

[63] *Ibid.*, p. 31.

Parliament and Popery in England, 1700–1780

COLIN HAYDON

In 1706, Squire Blundell of Little Crosby, Lancashire, anxiously waited to see whether parliament would tighten one of the provisions of the 1700 Act against Popery.[1] He probably expected the Lords and Commons to do so, as two of the pillars of the protestant constitution. Under the second Test Act (1678), catholics had been debarred from sitting in both Houses;[2] and under William III's Act for the Security of the Crown (1696), catholics were forbidden to vote (although they sometimes did so).[3] In terms of political theory, papists seemed to deny the sovereignty of the king-in-parliament. As John Locke put it in his first *Letter on Toleration* (1689), their church 'is so constituted that all who enter it *ipso facto* pass into the allegiance and service of another prince'.[4] From 1693, parliament annually imposed a double land tax on the papists, whilst preachers frequently reminded the Lords and M.P.s of the iniquities of popery. In 1715, Thomas Linford, preaching before the Commons, inveighed against the '*Popish Pretender*, back'd with a Foreign Power', and, in 1747, Bishop Lavington told the Lords that popery was the '*scandal and scourge of the Christian world*'.[5]

None the less, to Blundell's relief, the expected alteration to the law was not made;[6] and, in practice, there was considerable flexibility in parliament's behaviour towards the papists between 1700 and 1780 – a flexibility which is not altogether surprising. As the century progressed, support for religious toleration became increasingly widespread. It was also repeatedly argued that the protestant state, unlike catholic sovereigns, did not penalize minorities on account of their religion, but because of their politics.[7] Moreover, hostile legislation could alienate catholic allies. It was feared that the proper enforcement of William III's Act against Popery might do so.[8] And in 1706, following the Lords' receipt of a petition denouncing overt popish proselytizing in Lancashire, the

[1] 11 & 12 Will. III, c. 4.

[2] 30 Car. II, Stat. II, c. 1.

[3] 7 & 8 Will. III, c. 27; Edward Hughes, *North County Life in the Eighteenth Century. The North-East, 1700–1750* (1952), p. 260, n. 3; *The Jerningham Letters (1780–1843)*, ed. Egerton Castle (2 vols., 1896), I, 217–18.

[4] John Locke, *Epistola de Tolerantia/A Letter on Toleration*, ed. Raymond Klibansky and J. W. Gough (Oxford, 1968), p. 133.

[5] Thomas Linford, *God, A Tower of Salvation to the King* (1715), p. 21; George Lavington, *A Sermon Preached before the House of Lords . . . May 29, 1747* (1747), p. 23.

[6] *The Great Diurnal of Nicholas Blundell of Little Crosby, Lancashire*, transcribed and annotated by Frank Tyrer, ed. J. J. Bagley (3 vols., Record Soc. of Lancashire and Cheshire, CX, CXII, CXIV, 1968–72), I, 105.

[7] E.g., H.M.C., *Polwarth MSS*, III, 202–3: Lord Carteret to Lords Polwarth and Whitworth, 19 Nov. 1722.

Commons debated closing certain of the act's loopholes respecting the inheritance of property by papists – the cause of Blundell's alarm.[9] They decided to refrain (by 119 to 43 votes), however, partly because such a measure would antagonize catholic allies, thereby lessening 'the force of the queen's intercession in favour of the Protestants, who lived in the dominions of those princes'.[10] There were, of course, zealots who wanted the anti-catholic statutes fully implemented or strengthened. The S.P.C.K.'s archive contains proposals for such courses of action dating from the early eighteenth century.[11] Later, in 1768, following an alarm about the 'growth of popery', Thomas Hollis, Johnson's 'strenuous Whig', published in *The London Chronicle* his 'Plan for preventing the growth of Popery in England', propounding a new set of anti-catholic laws.[12] But advocates of such schemes were likely to be disappointed: parliament proceeded at its own pace respecting the penal code.

This essay seeks to examine this give-and-take attitude in more detail.

1

By the start of the eighteenth century, there was a massive array of anti-papist laws, dating from the reigns of Elizabeth I, James I, Charles II and William III, dealing with recusancy, oaths, priests, papists' property, education overseas, arms, horses, movement and so forth. Richard Burn, in *The Justice of the Peace and Parish Officer*, categorized them under no fewer than 36 heads.[13] Had the statutes been rigorously enforced, catholicism could scarcely have survived in England. Priests could not have operated. Catholic landed estates – where a missioner acted as an aristocratic family's chaplain and as a pastor to the local catholic community – would have withered away. In fact, a total enforcement of the laws was impraticable. In 1723, following the Atterbury plot, the government ordered a massive tendering of the anti-catholic oaths: recusants were liable to a penal levy. This imposed a huge burden on J.P.s – in rural Devonshire, some 27,000 people signed or marked the rolls in a period of six months – and it graphically shows the impossibility of fully implementing all the statutes.[14] But that was never realistically envisaged. As Burn observed:

> 'Tis true, these laws in the present age have been permitted to sleep in a great measure . . .: but they are suffered nevertheless to continue in force; perhaps that it may appear to the enemies of our constitution, that if they are spared, it is not for want of power, but of inclination to punish.[15]

[9] William Cobbett, *The Parliamentary History of England, from the Earliest Period to the Year 1803* (36 vols., 1806–20), VI, 514–15.

[10] *C.J.*, XV, 185; Cobbett, *Parl. Hist.*, VI, 515.

[11] Cambridge University Library, Archive of the S.P.C.K., CP I, Papers and Memorials, ff. 3–8, 9–10, 12–19, 20–2; Private Letters, 1718–20, ff. 45–6: H. Newman to C. Talbot, 31 Dec. 1718.

[12] *Memoirs of Thomas Hollis*, [ed. Francis Blackburne] (2 vols., 1780), I, 359–61, II, 706–8; *London Chronicle*, 22–4 Sept. 1768.

[13] Richard Burn, *The Justice of the Peace and Parish Officer* (12th edn., 4 vols., 1772), IV, 1–25.

[14] Colin Haydon, *Anti-Catholicism in Eighteenth-Century England, c.1714–80. A Political and Social Study* (Manchester, 1993), pp. 120–1; Paul Langford, *Public Life and the Propertied Englishman, 1689–1798* (Oxford, 1991), pp. 104–5.

[15] Burn, *Justice of the Peace*, IV, 3.

Blackstone agreed: 'these laws are seldom exerted to their utmost rigor', he noted in his *Commentaries on the Laws of England*.[16] Lord Mansfield deplored anti-papist prejudice; and, when priests were prosecuted in George III's reign, by demanding absolute proof of ordination, he effectively made conviction impossible. His views on the penal code, unsurprisingly therefore, went beyond Burn's and Blackstone's. The statutes, he said, 'were not meant to be enforced except at proper seasons, when there is a necessity for it; or, more properly speaking, they were not meant to be enforced at all, but were merely made *in terrorem*'.[17]

Of course, even at the end of the period under consideration, catholics continued to suffer disabilities – the exclusion from public life, the prohibition of practising at the bar and the double land tax. Technically, too, their worship remained illegal. None the less, as Burn's, Blackstone's and Mansfield's words indicate, the retention of the penal statutes – statutes which appeared increasingly obsolete as the years passed – was *principally* ideological: it was a continuing affirmation of the state's protestantism. As such, it was, for some, as potent a symbol as is the right to march on protestant anniversaries for Ulster's Orangemen in our own time. Adjustments to the penal code could, therefore, prove highly controversial and engender a dismay that was quite disproportionate to their practical consequences. As we shall see, the provisions of the first Catholic Relief Act (1778) were very circumscribed. But John Wesley strongly opposed the measure: not because he favoured persecution (he was well aware of catholic missioners' activities), but largely because he saw it as a symbolic acceptance or encouragement of popish proselytizing by the protestant legislature.

> 'But the late Act, you say, does not either *Tolerate* or *Encourage* Roman Catholics.' I appeal to Matter of Fact. Do not the Romanists themselves understand it as a Toleration? You know they do. And does it not already (let alone what it *may* do by and by) *Encourage* them to Preach openly, to build Chappels (at BATH and elsewhere,) to raise Seminerais [*sic*], and to make numerous Converts day by day to their intolerant, Persecuting Principles?[18]

The disjuncture between protestant theory respecting papists and practical realities seems, at first sight, to be again apparent in Locke's concern that each Roman catholic community constituted a foreign enclave within the kingdom, an *imperium in imperio*.[19] None the less, this contention acquires some credibility when one reads notes by exasperated officials or the clergy, unable to have the law enforced when confronted by powerful popish families. In 1717, one government commissioner, operating in the north of England, recorded the treatment of an agent sent to implement the law in two catholic strongholds: the 'Scarsebricks Tennants near Ormskirk putt a General laugh upon the Man yt went to Sum'on them, and at Southworth [one of the seats of the Gerard family] they all shutt their Doors and would not speak to him'.[20] Similarly, in

---

[16] William Blackstone, *Commentaries on the Laws of England* (4 vols., Oxford, 1765–9), IV, 56–7.

[17] John, Lord Campbell, *The Lives of the Chief Justices of England* (3rd edn., 4 vols., 1874), III, 401.

[18] *A Letter from the Rev. Mr. John Wesley, A.M. To the Printer of the Public Advertiser* (n.p., 1780).

[19] Locke, *Epistola de Tolerantia*, p. 133.

[20] Patrick Purcell, 'The Jacobite Rising of 1715 and the English Catholics', *E.H.R.*, XLIV (1929), 429.

the aftermath of the '15, when the government was unusually anxious to stop popish proselytizing, the bishop of Lichfield observed that, at Norbury in Derbyshire, the Fitzherbert family's position was unassailable and nothing could be done about the conversions made by their priest.[21] General concerns of these kinds had, of course, always been present in some measure since the break with Rome. After the revolution of 1688, however (and this was all too reminiscent of Elizabeth I's reign), Locke's thesis was given a further, horribly alarming, dimension by the issue of the contested succession, with the protestant monarchy at threat from a catholic claimant. It was widely assumed by protestants that the English papists were staunch jacobites, who, if the opportunity arose, would endeavour to restore the catholic Stuart dynasty to the throne. During the first half of the eighteenth century, therefore, parliament's view of the catholic minority was deeply influenced by concerns about jacobitism.

Dr Mullett has recently contended that the 'English Catholic community survived the '15 successfully because of low levels of active involvement in it by the majority of recusants outside the ranks of the northern gentry.'[22] There is much to commend this argument, particularly when a long-term perspective is adopted. The number of catholic rebels when compared with the catholic population at large was very limited; but, during the period of crisis, protestants were less likely to be struck by this than by the conspicuous catholic presence in the English jacobite army. Professor Monod has suggested that papists constituted between two-thirds and three-quarters of the troops.[23] Writing to Alexander Pope from Blagdon in Devonshire, Edward Blount dissociated the mass of catholics from the rebels: 'What a dismal scene has there been open'd in the North. What ruin have those unfortunate rash gentlemen drawn upon themselves and their miserable followers, and perchance upon many others too, who upon no account would be their followers?'[24] Parliament's perception was, however, quite different. The chief superior of the English Jesuits was greatly alarmed at 'the present threats and violent proceedings of the Parliament that met after the unfortunate miscarriage of the Preston business'. The rebellion, he maintained, had so incensed the Lords and Commons 'against the whole body of Catholics' that he thought parliament was intent 'on measures of destroying them root and branch'.[25] A range of security measures were implemented against the papists before and during the rebellion by J.P.s anxious to show their support for the central government.[26] At the start of 1716, the Lords was the dismal scene of the catholic earl of Derwentwater's impeachment (along with his co-religionists Nithsdale and Widdrington).[27] The execution of Derwentwater – young, handsome, and regarded almost as a martyr (it was supposed his apostasy would have bought his life) – mortified English catholics: a high mass was held for him at the

---

[21] Richard Clark, 'Anglicanism, Recusancy, and Dissent in Derbyshire, 1603–1730', University of Oxford D.Phil., 1979, p. 279; Christ Church, Oxford, Wake MSS, Epist. XXI, 233, 235: Edward Chandler to William Wake, 21 May, 18 June 1720.

[22] Michael A. Mullett, *Catholics in Britain and Ireland, 1558–1829* (Basingstoke, 1998), p. 87. Cf. B. Gordon Blackwood, 'Lancashire Catholics, Protestants and Jacobites during the 1715 Rebellion', *Recusant History*, XXII (1994), 41–59.

[23] Paul Kléber Monod, *Jacobitism and the English People, 1688–1788* (Cambridge, 1989), p. 322.

[24] *The Correspondence of Alexander Pope*, ed. George Sherburn (5 vols., Oxford, 1956), I, 320.

[25] H.M.C., *Stuart MSS*, III, 349: Father Blake to Thomas Lawson, 24 Dec. 1716.

[26] Haydon, *Anti-Catholicism*, pp. 86–91.

[27] T. B. Howell, *A Complete Collection of State Trials* (33 vols., 1809–26), XV, cols. 761–806.

French envoy's residence and was attended by a number of prominent papists.[28] The rebellion's aftermath also brought two anti-catholic acts. First, there was the act for 'appointing Commissioners to enquire of the Estates of certain Traitors, and of Popish Recusants, and of Estates given to superstitious Uses'.[29] One of its aims was to produce an inventory of the estates of those rebels attainted by midsummer 1718, as these lands were forfeit to the crown. The other was to uncover the property which formed the catholic church's endowments and to confiscate it. The second measure was the 'Act to oblige Papists to register their Names and real Estates', the preamble of which declared that 'all [the papists] or the greatest Part of them, [have] been concerned in stirring up and supporting the late unnatural Rebellion', so that it 'appears by their Behaviour, that they take themselves to be obliged, by the Principles they profess, to be Enemies to his Majesty and to the present happy Establishment'.[30] All those who did not take the oaths of fidelity had to register their property and, in line with Elizabethan and Jacobean legislation, the crown was entitled to two-thirds of it (though the reminder of this was another paper tiger).

The papists were dismayed, but, regarding these measures' implementation, one again observes flexibility and an inability or reluctance to trap the quarry ruthlessly. Although the forfeited estates commissioners often found difficulty in obtaining the evidence they needed for their work, and local society – including 'persons who would be thought friends to the Government'[31] – sometimes closed ranks to shield the papists, the confiscation of rebels' lands, notably in Lancashire and Northumberland, was vigorously pursued. However, the pressure to make catholics register their estates slackened as the whig regime became more self-assured. A new act (1717) extended the time for registration;[32] so did later acts of George II's and George III's reigns. (In provincial archives, one finds registration deeds completed decades after 1715.) It is very revealing that one of these acts was passed in 1746,[33] when, following the rebellion of Charles Edward Stuart, parliament might well have displayed renewed hostility to his co-religionists. Peaceable catholics, it appeared, might be protected. Equally, the legislation to sequestrate the property used to support the popish church, and hence strangle catholicism in England, was not properly implemented. The government did not expect it to be; and, given that these endowments were often protected by legal devices of monstrous complexity, the attempt was, in practice, scarcely viable.

There was, however, one further measure designed to punish catholics for their jacobite connexions. Following the Atterbury plot (in which the papists' involvement had, in fact, been minimal), the government produced a bill for raising a levy of £100,000 on the popish community. The catholics were horrified. Bishop Giffard wrote: 'Now to complete our misery, a Bill is prepared to be brought into Parliament which will reduce all Catholics to the extremity of want.'[34] The levy was to be imposed on all those who would not swear allegiance to George I and refused the

[28] *Great Diurnal of Blundell*, ed. Bagley, II, 159.

[29] 1 Geo. I, Stat. 2, c. 50.

[30] 1 Geo. I, Stat. 2, c. 55.

[31] Purcell, 'Jacobite Rising', p. 426.

[32] 3 Geo. I, c. 18.

[33] 19 Geo. II, c. 16.

[34] Dom Basil Hemphill, *The Early Vicars Apostolic of England, 1685–1750* (1954), p. 92.

sacramental test. The bill produced heated debate in parliament. In particular, the tory lawyer Thomas Lutwyche denounced it as a species of religious persecution,[35] and Sir Edward Knatchbull noted the tartness of the criticism in his parliamentary diary:

> A second reading of the Papists' Bill and a strong debate against the commitment, the arguments against it were persecution impolitic and impracticable, persecution because it taxed people for their religion, impolitic because it would disoblige our popish allies, and impracticable because many of the estates that were registered [i.e. in or after 1715] had been since alienated and come into Protestant hands, and another reason because it was partial and did not take notice nor subject the Scotch Papists to it . . .[36]

Despite such arguments, the bill was passed in both Houses – but only by 69 to 55 in the Lords.[37] Although probably only two-thirds of the projected figure was collected,[38] the levy was in addition to the double land tax, and, from her study of the evidence from Staffordshire, Marie Rowlands concludes that the county's papists 'in the difficult 1720s at least, felt themselves to be under considerable pressure'.[39] It is feasible that such anxiety was much more widespread.

2

In his *State and Behaviour of English Catholics*, published in 1780, Joseph Berington observed that 'very few Catholics . . . were engaged in the rebellion' of 1745.[40] The recognition of this, the demise of jacobitism, and the *de facto* recognition of George III by the papacy after James Edward's death in 1766, put an end to serious political concerns about the papists. Blackstone was soon arguing in his *Commentaries* that 'when all fears of a pretender shall have vanished, and the power and influence of the pope shall become feeble, ridiculous, and despicable . . ., it probably would not then be amiss to review and soften these rigorous edicts'.[41] Whilst popery was still condemned as wicked and abhorrent, the behaviour of papists became an increasingly insignificant matter in the legislature's eyes. It is revealing that, in 1753, when parliament passed Hardwicke's Marriage Act,[42] no thought was apparently given to its implications for catholics. The requirement that all marriages should be performed in an anglican church by an anglican clergyman meant that henceforth catholics, until 1837,[43] were usually married

---

[35] Romney Sedgwick, *The House of Commons, 1715–1754* (2 vols., 1970), II, 231. The Lutwyches were Nonjurors in the 1690s: Monod, *Jacobitism*, p. 142.

[36] *The Parliamentary Diary of Sir Edward Knatchbull, 1722–1730*, ed. A. N. Newman (Camden Soc., 3rd ser., XCIV, 1963), p. 22.

[37] 9 Geo. I, c. 18; Cobbett, *Parl. Hist.*, VIII, 363.

[38] W. R. Ward, *The English Land Tax in the Eighteenth Century* (1953), p. 70.

[39] Marie Rowlands, 'Staffordshire Papists and the Levy of 1723', *Staffordshire Catholic History*, II (1962), 37.

[40] [Joseph Berington], *The State and Behaviour of English Catholics. From the Reformation to the Year 1780* (1780), p. 94.

[41] Blackstone, *Commentaries*, IV, 57.

[42] 26 Geo. II, c. 33.

[43] 7 Will. IV & 1 Vict., c. 22.

both in the parish church and by a catholic priest. This was both offensive and cumbersome and the matter occasioned some disagreement in the hierarchy – notably between Bishops Challoner and Stonor – on the precise status of the marriage ceremony (a debate usefully summarized by John Bossy).[44] Yet, whilst parliament acted without considering the catholics (or dissenters other than quakers) on this occasion, other issues pertaining to the papists forced themselves on its attention; and under George III, it, significantly, sought to mitigate anti-catholic agitation or action. In the mid 1760s, there was considerable alarm, notably in the London press, that popery was increasing vastly in England.[45] And, in order to allay these fears, the bishops organized a census of papists in 1767.[46] The returns demonstrated convincingly that the alarm was unjustified. They produced a figure of 69,376 catholics in England and Wales,[47] whereas one newspaper report of 1765 had stated that there were some 200,000 catholics in and about the capital.[48] And, in 1772, parliament passed a private act with a clear symbolic import. Anne Benison, a catholic heiress, had married a protestant, John Fenwick, and made over her property to him. He wished to transfer it back, but died before doing so, and his brother was determined to use the penal laws to stop Mrs Fenwick recovering her land. The case went before king's bench, the exchequer and chancery, but 12 Geo. III, c. 122 secured her a pleasing financial settlement:[49] as Burke put it in 1780, 'the legislature itself rushed in, and by a special act of Parliament rescued her from the injustice of its own statutes'.[50]

Other aid to catholics in the 1760s and '70s included Mansfield's judgment blocking the prosecution of priests. The concessions to catholics appeared especially significant since parliament, in 1772 and 1773, refused to relieve dissenting ministers and schoolmasters of the need to subscribe to the doctrinal articles of the established church as a condition of registration.[51] Even more symbolic, however, appeared parliament's oversight of the various reforms in Ireland of the later eighteenth century,[52] and, above all, the passing of the Quebec Act of 1774, which gave catholics a place on the legislative council of Canada, perpetuated the French legal system in civil cases and established a system of endowments for the popish clergy.[53] This provoked anger 'without doors', and also among some at Westminster. In the Lords, Chatham denounced the bill as a violation of the protestant constitution. He declared that 'all establishments by law are to be Protestant', and told the bishops that 'as by the Bill the Catholic religion was made the established religion of that vast continent, it was impossible they could be silent on

[44] John Bossy, 'Challoner and the Marriage Act', in *Challoner and his Church. A Catholic Bishop in Georgian England*, ed. Eamon Duffy (1981), pp. 126–36.

[45] Haydon, *Anti-Catholicism*, pp. 189–91.

[46] *Annual Register*, X (1767), 'Chronicle', 109.

[47] John Bossy, *The English Catholic Community, 1570–1850* (1975), p. 184.

[48] Martin H. Fitzpatrick, 'Rational Dissent in Late Eighteenth-Century England, with Particular Reference to the Growth of Toleration', University of Wales (Aberystwyth) Ph.D., 1982, pp. 158–9.

[49] Haydon, *Anti-Catholicism*, p. 174; Langford, *Public Life*, p. 99.

[50] *The Writings and Speeches of Edmund Burke. Volume III: Party, Parliament, and the American War, 1774–1780*, ed. W. M. Elofson with John A. Woods (Oxford, 1996), p. 643.

[51] G. M. Ditchfield, 'The Subscription Issue in British Parliamentary Politics, 1772–79', *Parliamentary History*, VII (1988), 45–80.

[52] R. B. McDowell, *Ireland in the Age of Imperialism and Revolution, 1760–1801* (Oxford, 1979), pp. 209–348.

[53] 14 Geo. III, c. 83.

the occasion'.[54] (In fact, several bishops withdrew because of this speech, but only Shipley of St Asaph voted against the bill, and Archbishop Cornwallis later spoke for it.)[55] In the debate in the Commons on 10 June, Sergeant Glynn stated that the day 'would be handed down to posterity as a day when the members of a British House of Commons preferred Popery and French laws to the established religion and laws of their own country'.[56] None the less, the bill was passed – late in the session when few M.P.s or peers were in London (it went through by 56 votes to 20 in the Commons and 26 votes to 7 in the Lords).[57] When, on 22 June, the king came to Westminster to give it the royal assent, there were disturbances in the streets.[58] Still, in 1775, when Camden in the Lords, and Sir George Savile in the Commons, tried to secure its repeal, they were unsuccessful (though 86 M.P.s supported the attempt).[59] In 1778, Savile again proposed the act's repeal, but this was rejected in the Commons by 96 to 54 votes.[60]

By contrast with the Quebec Act, the first Catholic Relief Act of 1778 was, in terms of its exact stipulations, a very limited measure which, for this reason, unsurprisingly glided through both Houses. It was introduced by Savile, who, though thoroughly hostile to popery and its expansion, wished to 'assert the principles of the Protestant religion, to which all persecution was, or ought to be, wholly adverse'.[61] But soon the legislation produced bewilderment and agitation 'without doors', and ultimately the Gordon riots of 1780.[62] In part, it was the furious reaction to the act which secured its depiction in catholic historiography as a measure of tremendous importance. In *The Life and Times of Bishop Challoner*, an elderly classic, published in 1909, Edwin Burton described it as a, perhaps the, turning-point in English, post-Reformation, catholic history.

> When the year 1778 opened, the social and legal condition of Catholics was neither better nor worse than it had been for three-quarters of a century. Nor did any one anticipate a change. Yet it was the year 1778 which was to bring the first relief from the long persecution, and which, ever since, has rightly been regarded as the beginning of that slow restoration of our rights which was to culminate in Catholic Emancipation.[63]

Such writing is a species of whig history:[64] Burton sketched a line of progress from 1778 to the 1791 Relief Act (giving catholics freedom of worship) and emancipation in 1829,

[54] For Chatham's objections to the bill, see Cobbett, *Parl. Hist.*, XVII, 1402–4.
[55] *The Last Journals of Horace Walpole during the Reign of George III from 1771–1783*, ed. A. Francis Steuart (2 vols., 1910), I, 354–5; Cobbett, *Parl. Hist.*, XVIII, 671.
[56] Cobbett, *Parl. Hist.*, XVII, 1395.
[57] *C.J.*, XXXIV, 813; Cobbett, *Parl. Hist.*, XVII, 1407.
[58] Haydon, *Anti-Catholicism*, p. 196.
[59] Cobbett, *Parl. Hist.*, XVIII, 655–84.
[60] *Ibid.*, XIX, 1127–30; *C.J.*, XXXVI (1776–8), 923.
[61] Nigel Abercrombie, 'The First Relief Act', in *Challoner and his Church*, ed. Duffy, p. 189.
[62] 18 Geo. III, c. 60.
[63] Edwin H. Burton, *The Life and Times of Bishop Challoner (1691–1781)* (2 vols., 1909, repr. Farnborough, 1970), II, 181.
[64] Cf. Macaulay's opinion that the 'Declaration of Right, though it made nothing law which had not been law before, contained the germ of the law which gave religious freedom to the Dissenter, . . . of the law which abolished the sacramental test, [and] of the law which relieved the Roman Catholics from civil disabilities . . .' Lord Macaulay, *The History of England from the Accession of James the Second*, ed. C. H. Firth (6 vols., 1913–15), III, 1311.

and thought this progress would continue, maintaining that eventually (with statutes permitting catholics to hold the great seal or the viceroyalty of Ireland, and to inherit the crown) 'we shall enter upon our full inheritance of freedom'.[65] Such an approach is understandable: as the first major law in favour of the papists since the Elizabethan settlement, the act enjoys a reputation out of all proportion to its provisions. Nor is the approach illegitimate: contemporaries quickly perceived the symbolic significance of the legislation, as Wesley's objections to it illustrate. None the less, one must draw a clear distinction between the act's symbolic importance and the precise changes in law which it effected.

In terms of its provisions, the 1778 act was not a milestone. It did not give catholics freedom of worship, and Mansfield observed at Lord George Gordon's trial, 'it is most injurious to say this bill . . . is a toleration of Popery'.[66] Strictly, papists remained subject to most of the penalties enacted in the reigns of Queen Elizabeth, James I and Charles II, though this was ignored by the authorities. The act's immediate background lay in the government's desire to employ catholic troops in the American war, and in the consequent need to produce a conciliatory token for the catholic body, and in the lobbying of a group of catholic gentlemen.[67] Its broader context was the *de facto* shelving of the penal laws by magistrates in the course of the eighteenth century, and especially after 1746; the willingness to spare peaceable catholics unnecessary inconvenience (as shown by the extensions of time permitted for the registration of property); and a disbelief that antiquated legislation still had the potential to ruin harmless individuals, such as Anne Fenwick. When the bill was debated, there was also the recollection of the prosecution by William Payne, a London constable, of 16 priests and nine catholic schoolmasters between 1767 and 1771,[68] the authorities' dismay when the penal laws were activated by one of 'the lowest and most despicable of mankind',[69] and the resulting embarrassing need to circumvent those laws' stipulations (either by clever arguments in the courts or by the use of a royal pardon).[70] The act therefore put what was normal practice by the later eighteenth century – and practice approved by the *élite* – on a proper legal footing. In return for taking a specially drafted oath of allegiance, catholics might in future be able to purchase land legally. Catholic priests and schoolmasters were no longer to be liable to life imprisonment if apprehended, whilst rewards for informers against priests were ended. Formally removing only specific, moribund, disabilities, this was not necessarily forward-looking but rather a recognition of the *status quo* that had evolved by the 1770s.[71]

The Protestant Association, formed in 1779, however, seized only on the act's symbolic import, seeing the measure as an affront to the constitution. Either its repeal, or

---

[65] Burton, *Challoner*, II, 181. He also perceived the act in providential terms. *Ibid.*, II, 182.

[66] *State Trials*, XXI, col. 645.

[67] Robert Kent Donovan, 'The Military Origins of the Roman Catholic Relief Programme of 1778', *Historical Journal*, XXVIII (1985), 79–102; Abercrombie, 'First Relief Act', pp. 174–93.

[68] This was, Eamon Duffy notes, 'on a scale unknown since the Popish Plot'. Eamon Duffy, 'Richard Challoner, 1691–1781: A Memoir', in *Challoner and his Church*, ed. Duffy, p. 22.

[69] Cobbett, *Parl. Hist.*, XIX, 1145.

[70] Haydon, *Anti-Catholicism*, pp. 172–4.

[71] The wording of the act is curiously backward-looking in so far as Jesuits are mentioned, despite the order's suppression in 1773.

significant qualifications to it, it declared, were needed to ensure 'the Protestant religion would be preserved; the British constitution secured'.[72] It is probable that the Association's supporters did not properly appreciate the act's limitations. In *The Life of Lord George Gordon* (1795), Robert Watson, Gordon's friend and secretary, wrote of the government's decision to 'repeal the statutes enacted against' the catholics and of 'the Bill for repealing the penal statutes in force against them':[73] one suspects that Gordon and his followers saw the measure in this light. A similar act for Scotland, proposed for 1779, would be, it was claimed by some opponents, *'an express violation of the Claim of Right 1689, and of the Union 1707, or rather of an essential condition of the very existence of that treaty'*.[74] Some of the petitions which were sent to parliament contained large numbers of signatures: that from within the compass of the synod of Glasgow and Ayr had 20,000; that from Newcastle upon Tyne and its environs, 7,661; and London's gargantuan petition, 44,000.[75] Some emphasized that the measure, like the Quebec Bill, had been introduced late in the session: the sense of the people had not been tested. This was true; the bishop of Peterborough had noted this when the bill was before the Lords.[76]

Despite the petitions and the Gordon riots which engulfed London from 2 to 8 June 1780 (and which had faint echoes in the English provinces),[77] parliament neither repealed, nor modified, the Relief Act. It could not yield; and at Gordon's trial, Mansfield spoke for it, declaring: 'nothing can be so dishonourable to government, as to be forced to make, or to repeal, by an armed multitude, any law; from that moment there is an end of all legislative authority'.[78] Still, when compared with parliament's capitulation to opinion 'without doors' regarding the Jewish Naturalization Act of 1753,[79] this shows considerable resolution: the preamble to the act which repealed that legislation had justified the volte-face on the grounds that *'occasion has been taken from the said act to raise discontents, and to disquiet the minds of many of his Majesty's subjects'* – a comment which could obviously be applied with a vengeance to the first Catholic Relief Act.[80] This constancy in 1780 was perhaps another example of the hubris which parliament had developed in the 1760s and 1770s and displayed respecting the printing of its proceedings, the other Wilkes affairs and the American colonies; whilst the events of 1778 to 1780 prefigured the gulf between parliament and the nation over the granting of catholic emancipation in 1829. Yet there was some give-and-take too. The bishops ordered another census of papists in order to calm fresh fears about the 'growth of popery'.[81] And following riots in Edinburgh and Glasgow in 1779, any attempt to pass a

[72] *An Appeal from the Protestant Association to the People of Great Britain* (1779), p. 62.
[73] Robert Watson, *The Life of Lord George Gordon* (1795), pp. 9, 10.
[74] *Scotland's Opposition to the Popish Bill* (Edinburgh, 1780), p. 324.
[75] Eugene Charlton Black, *The Association. British Extraparliamentary Political Organization, 1769–1793* (Cambridge, Mass., 1963), p. 139; *C.J.*, XXXVII, 900, 901; P.R.O., T.S. 11/388 1212; W. Vincent Smith, *Catholic Tyneside* (Newcastle upon Tyne, [1930]), p. 54; *State Trials*, XXI, col. 620.
[76] Cobbett, *Parl. Hist.*, XIX, 1144.
[77] Haydon, *Anti-Catholicism*, pp. 204–44.
[78] *State Trials*, XXI, col. 646.
[79] Thomas W. Perry, *Public Opinion, Propaganda, and Politics in Eighteenth-Century England. A Study of the Jew Bill of 1753* (Cambridge, Mass., 1962).
[80] 27 Geo. II, c. 1.
[81] Paul Langford, *A Polite and Commercial Peoples. England, 1727–1783* (Oxford, 1989), p. 551.

similar me.sure for Scotland was dropped.[82] (The first catholic relief measure for the country was passed in 1793, and was cannily entitled '*An act for requiring a certain form of oath of abjuration, and declaration, from his Majesty's subjects, professing the Roman catholick religion, in . . .* Scotland'.)[83] The Commons even supported a small sop to 'protestant' opinion in late June 1780. They passed a bill, introduced by Savile, '*for securing the Protestant Religion*'; its terms prohibited papists from teaching protestant children. But it was lost in the Lords.[84]

3

Two general questions remain to be addressed respecting parliament's stance towards the catholic minority. First, to what extent did the catholics themselves lobby for a mitigation of their ill-treatment? And secondly, how significantly did the anti-papist statutes condition protestant attitudes to the catholics in the country at large?

Regarding the first question, there were occasions when catholics worked strenuously to forestall new legislation against them. Led by the duke of Norfolk, they made 'weighty intercessions with the considerable men of the House of Commons' against the 1706 proposal to tighten the laws concerning popish property.[85] After the '15, they spent considerable sums of money – 'which might have been otherwise and better employed' – in order to obtain more time for the registration of their lands.[86] Following the Atterbury plot, an Oxfordshire clergyman noted how papists hastened 'up to town from all parts of the country hereabouts',[87] presumably to intercede with the powerful. The envoys of catholic states also intervened on behalf of the catholic minority and maintained close ties with its leaders.[88]

There were drawbacks to sustained lobbying, however. Strident complaints could alienate and prove counter-productive. Diplomatic pressure might be firmly rebuffed. This was the case with attempts to prevent the 1723 levy, and the French envoy reported to Dubois that, as France exerted more pressure, government attitudes would harden proportionally.[89] Few politicians wished to appear sympathetic to popery and thereby court opprobrium. In the Oxfordshire election campaign of 1754, Sir James Dashwood was criticized for buying an estate on a papist's behalf,[90] whilst, in the Gordon riots, Lord Mansfield's Bloomsbury house was destroyed and Savile's home attacked.[91] Lobbying behind the scenes was plainly sensible. Within the English catholic community, there was a spectrum of opinion, particularly in jacobite times, as to whether a principled accommodation with the government was possible; and a failure

---

[82] Black, *Association*, pp. 142–4.
[83] 33 Geo. III, c. 44.
[84] Cobbett, *Parl. Hist.*, XXI, 714–26, 754–66.
[85] *C.J.*, XV, 184; Cobbett, *Parl. Hist.*, VI, 515.
[86] H.M.C., *Stuart MSS*, IV, 331: J. Menzies to duke of Mar, 28 May/8 June 1717.
[87] H.M.C., *Portland MSS*, VII, 339: Dr William Stratford to Edward Harley. 8 Nov. 1722.
[88] Jeremy Black, *British Foreign Policy in the Age of Walpole* (Edinburgh, 1985), p. 128.
[89] *Ibid.*
[90] *Jackson's Oxford Journal*, 9 Mar. 1754.
[91] Haydon, *Anti-Catholicism*, pp. 214, 227.

to speak with one voice might prove disastrous. In 1719, Stanhope in fact backed a scheme for a measure of toleration for the papists, but it ultimately foundered, chiefly because of disagreements about it among the catholics themselves.[92] There was always the danger that the clergy and the laity might take divergent views. It was no coincidence that the first Relief Act was secured by the negotiations of laymen alone. The prime mover, Wiliam Sheldon of Gray's Inn, maintained 'the English Roman Catholic Gentleman [*sic*] could judge and act for themselves in every concern of that kind, nor could they suffer the Clergy to interfere'.[93] Sir Robert Throckmorton reportedly growled, 'we don't want bishops' at the gentlemen's meetings.[94] And generally, passive, uncomplaining behaviour was itself a species of lobbying and likely to conciliate the legislature. Prudent behaviour reaped rewards. In 1733, there was the threat of renewed persecution in the north, following some conversions. None the less, it was noted that 'provided ye Cath. gentry dont at least oppose ye government in ye Elections, tis hopt they will continue their wonted Indulgence'.[95]

Turning to the second question, it is difficult to gauge the degree to which the penal code shaped popular attitudes to catholics, because the sources pertaining to the matter are fragmentary, and sometimes cryptic. None the less, there are snippets of evidence which suggest that the law, as an expression of state ideology, was perceived by the 'meaner sort' as legitimizing their anti-catholic behaviour; and that, consequently, it could foster casual brutality. John Morris was the son of catholic parents, but later became a methodist and published an account of his life in the *Arminian Magazine* in 1795. In it, he recalled how, following the '45, a soldier came to Stretford, near Manchester, where the family lived

> and tarried all night at a public-house. A man in the neighbourhood, who was a bitter enemy to my parents, because they were Papists, dropt into the soldier's company, and they drank together till they were intoxicated. The man told the soldier, that if he would go to my father's house, and demand such a sum of money, he might have it, *because we were Papists, and no Law would be granted us.*[96]

This garbled notion was partially confirmed by the sequel. The soldier took some money, but was subsequently apprehended by a constable; yet 'upon acknowledging his fault, and returning the money, he was dismissed'.[97] There was, moreover, a tendentious, but erroneous, basis for the assumption that there was no law for papists: under Jacobean legislation, a popish recusant convict could not plead in court, except in cases concerning his property.[98] Burn observed that 'divers authors . . . have fallen into confusion' by 'the want of attending to . . . [the] distinction' between a '*popish recusant,*

---

[92] Hemphill, *Early Vicars Apostolic*, pp. 110–15; Eamon Duffy, ' "Englishmen in Vaine": Roman Catholic Allegiance to George I', in *Religion and National Identity*, ed. Stuart Mews (Studies in Church History, XVIII, Oxford, 1982), pp. 356–62.

[93] Abercrombie, 'First Relief Act', p. 180.

[94] *Ibid.*, n. 14.

[95] Birmingham Roman Catholic Diocesan Archives, Archive of the archbishop of Birmingham, C. 421.

[96] 'The Life of Mr. John Morris, of Manchester. Written by himself ', *Arminian Magazine*, XVIII (1795), 19. My italics.

[97] *Ibid.*

[98] 3 & 4 Jac. I, c. 5.

... a papist who ... refuseth [to attend anglican services,] ... and a *popish recusant convict*, ... a papish legally convicted thereof '.[99] That there was popular confusion, therefore, regarding the papists' legal standing is scarcely surprising. Comparably, a belief prevailed that the early methodists did not enjoy the law's protection, and this encouraged the mobbing of some preachers. The supposition did not derive simply from ignorance: it was probably suspected that the first preaching-houses and preachers were not licensed as the Toleration Act required, and that field meetings violated the Conventicle Act's provisions.[100]

When anti-catholic riots occurred, there was often a generalized sense that the mob's behaviour was legitimate. A number of such disturbances occurred following the jacobite army's retreat from Derby in 1745, and at Stokesley in Yorkshire, where a catholic chapel was wrecked, one of rioters mounted the market cross and told the rest of 'the great service they had done to their king and country, in destroying the Mass-house that day'.[101] At Hereford in 1756, when a group of women 'duked [a popish farmer] so Longe in the river, ... [that] he was almost drownded', an observer felt 'theire was a just provication for resentement': the man had apparently 'been heard to Say that he rather would Sell to the french for 5. Shill. than to his own Country for 7. shs. 6 pen'.[102] But sometimes the rioters' ill-defined notion of legitimacy was buttressed by their deliberate imitation of the measures which those in authority, under the penal code, might take against the papists. This is highly reminiscent of the action of grain rioters, described by E. P. Thompson, in setting a 'just price' for corn, as J.P.s were meant to do.[103] Thus, in the Gordon riots, mobs attempted to ascertain whether potential victims were indeed Roman catholics. To achieve this, they sometimes entered a house in order to search for popish books,[104] as two J.P.s were empowered to do under one of James I's acts against popish recusants.[105] Crowds might stage 'trials', making householders and witnesses swear on a Bible that the former were not papists; pulling in neighbours and others to testify to the religion of possible catholics; or obtaining relevant written evidence.[106] Early in the riots, the Bavarian and Sardinian embassy chapels were attacked and their contents burnt in the streets.[107] Even this was an echo of the law. As 3 and 4 Jac. I, c. 5 decreed,

> any altar, pix, beads, pictures, or such like popish relicks, or any popish book or books, ... as in the opinion of the ... justices, mayor, bailiff or chief officer, ... shall

[99] Burn, *Justice of the Peace*, IV, 2.

[100] John Walsh, 'Methodism and the Mob in the Eighteenth Century', in *Popular Belief and Practice*, ed. G. J. Cuming and Derek Baker (Studies in Church History, VIII, Cambridge, 1972), p. 217.

[101] *Gentleman's Magazine*, XVI (1746), 40.

[102] National Library of Wales, 478 E, f. 16v: D. W. Linden to J. Williams, 10 Dec. 1756.

[103] E. P. Thompson, 'The Moral Economy of the English Crowd in the Eighteenth Century', *Past and Present*, No. 50 (1971), 76–136.

[104] P.R.O., S.P. Dom. 37/20/289; *The Whole Proceedings on the King's Commission of the Peace, Oyer and Terminer, and Gaol Delivery for the City of London; and also, the Gaol Delivery for the County of Middlesex; Held ... on the 28th of June, 1780, and the following Days*, ed. Joseph Gurney (1780), pp. 405–6, 463, 485, 492, 526, 532.

[105] 3 & 4 Jac. I, c. 5.

[106] P.R.O., S.P. Dom. 37/21/277–8, 279, 280, 310; *Whole Proceedings*, pp. 457, 460, 463; Black, *Association*, pp. 164–5.

[107] George Rudé, *Hanoverian London, 1714–1808* (1971), pp. 221–2.

be thought unmeet for . . . [a] recusant . . . to have or use the same, shall be presently defaced and burnt, if it be meet to be burned.

Some mobs took trouble to ensure that the bonfires would not damage nearby houses: their targets were specific, and their actions, in their own eyes, not excessive.

4

This essay has illustrated parliament's changing perception of the catholic population in the eighteenth century. The shift resulted, above all, from the demise of jacobitism and is nicely encapsulated by two views of the catholic minority, the first from 1716, the second from 1778. In 1716, the Septennial Act was, in part, justified in terms of 'a restless and Popish Faction . . . designing and endeavouring to renew the Rebellion within this Kingdom, and an Invasion from Abroad'.[108] By contrast, when the first Catholic Relief Bill was considered in the Lords, Rockingham saw the catholic minority as 'a very dutiful and loyal part of the King's subjects'.[109] Yet, even though, for parliament, political change was of paramount importance in revising old views of catholics, the shift must also be seen in a wider cultural and intellectual context.[110] And here, in particular, there is the tantalizing issue of oath taking. It was long argued that no protestant government could trust the oaths of papists. They were not obliged, it was maintained, to keep faith with heretics, and their church might absolve them from their commitments. This was a watertight, self-confirming belief system: it was impossible for catholics to counter it effectively. In 1716, indeed, when some sought an oath of submission to the government, the duke of Mar despaired of their finding a suitable formula.[111] Yet in 1778, parliament simply accepted a carefully-worded oath of allegiance, which, by that time, could readily be taken by catholics. (There was an objection to the oath from Lord Hillsborough – but that was to its 'language', and 'some Lord observed to him, it came from Ireland'.)[112] The intellectual change merits proper analysis – part of its background was the changing attitude to state oaths described by Paul Langford[113] – and it mystified some at the time – not least John Wesley, who denounced it in his *Popery Calmly Considered* of 1779.[114] For reasons of space, however, it is not possible to examine it here.

5

In a now elderly essay on the anti-catholic laws' administration, Rupert C. Jarvis observed:

[108] 1 Geo. I, Stat. II, c. 38.
[109] Cobbett, *Parl. Hist.*, XIX, 1144. In the Commons, Charles Turner stated that 'Roman Catholics were good people; kind at home; did charity among their neighbours'. Abercrombie, 'First Relief Act', p. 190.
[110] Haydon, *Anti-Catholicism*, pp. 164–203.
[111] Duffy, ' "Englishmen in Vaine" ', pp. 345–65; H.M.C., *Stuart MSS*, III, 4: duke of Mar to Mary of Modena, 1 Oct. 1716.
[112] Abercrombie, 'First Relief Act', p. 191.
[113] Langford, *Public Life*, pp. 98–118.
[114] John Wesley, *Popery Calmly Considered* (2nd edn., 1779), pp. 22–3.

A study of contemporary manuscript sources, as distinct from a study of the text of the statutes, provides a more agreeable picture than is usually presented of mid-eighteenth-century religious toleration in England. There was, in other words, a greater contrast than has hitherto been fully realized between the law of the land as it was enacted in the capital and the law as it was administered and enforced in the country.[115]

Subsequent research has endorsed Jarvis' contention;[116] but one should not underestimate the degree to which parliament was itself responsive to changing political circumstances and shifts of educated opinion during the eighteenth century. Its outlook was pragmatic and flexible, not hidebound, and its adjustments to the penal code not only dictated but also broadly kept in step with magistrates' altering practice in the provinces. One can probably observe this at the start of the century. Bishop Burnet maintained that the Act against Popery of 1700 originated in factious squabbling at Westminster and between the court and its opponents.[117] But remarks by Samuel Pepys suggest a desire to ensure that the statutes were not simply perceived as so outdated as to be wholly unenforceable:

> [A] thing, indeed, there is, that looks somewhat a mitigation of our present laws, by repealing so much thereof as subjected to death every Romish Priest found among us, by condemning them now to perpetual imprisonment only; but this . . . [the Roman catholics] take to be much worse than what they were before exposed to, because so seldom found, by the tenderness of our Juries, exacted from them.[118]

The trimming of the penal code to conform to new thinking and the practice of J.P.s, juries, or judges had obvious parallels in, first, the educated's rejection of witchcraft trials and then, the Witchcraft Act's repeal; and in the *de facto* acceptance of office-holding by dissenters, ratified by indemnity acts almost annually from 1727. Macaulay maintained that the Toleration Act 'removed a vast mass of evil without shocking a vast mass of prejudice'.[119] Given the jacobite threat before 1746 and age-old English anti-catholicism, it behoved parliament to proceed with firmness respecting the papist minority during the first half of the eighteenth century and prudently when displaying greater generosity during the second. Usually its decisions were well judged; but the 1778 Relief Act shocked a vast mass of anti-popish prejudice and the Gordon riots emphatically underlined the need for caution when adjusting those laws that proclaimed the state's protestant identity.

---

[115] Rupert C. Jarvis, *Collected Papers on the Jacobite Risings* (2 vols., Manchester, 1971–2), II, 303.

[116] See, e.g., Haydon, *Anti-Catholicism*, pp. 86–91, 131–3.

[117] *Bishop Burnet's History of his Own Time*, ed. M. J. Routh (6 vols., Oxford, 1823), IV, 408–11; cf. *Writings and Speeches of Burke. Vol. III*, pp. 641–2.

[118] *Diary and Correspondence of Samuel Pepys, Esq., F.R.S.*, ed. Richard, Lord Braybrooke, and Mynors Bright (6 vols., 1876–9), VI, 217: Samuel Pepys to John Jackson, 12 Apr. 1700.

[119] Macaulay, *History of England*, III, 1390. He, of course, tended to judge the subject of religious intolerance anachronistically, and was unable to appreciate the sincerely-held theological objections of the intolerant.

Ecclesiastical Legislation During the Ministry of the Younger Pitt, 1783–1801*

G.M. DITCHFIELD

That the ideological legacy bequeathed by Pitt's first administration to nineteenth-century toryism was a highly ambiguous one has long been apparent to scholars. Such was Pitt's reputation that different elements sought to recreate him in their own image. In particular, it was important for those whose first priority was the defence of the anglican constitution to be able to appeal to the authority of Pitt in support of their ideals. The depiction of Pitt as devout christian, receiving the sacrament on his death-bed, helped to sustain that process. It was perhaps assisted by the way in which Pitt benefited from evangelical support, especially in the years immediately after 1784, when his public commitment to retrenchment and economical reform, not to mention his apparent lack of most of the Fox-like vices, allowed him to be presented as a champion of 'virtue'.[1]

As James Sack has shown, this image of Pitt as pious christian was the fraudulent creation of his friends, notably Bishop Pretyman, and was designed to demonstrate his essential consistency with a certain type of early nineteenth-century toryism which could then use his name as sanctification for the constitutional arrangements which endured until 1828–9.[2] Hence Pretyman, crediting Pitt with what he called 'zeal in defence of the national faith', appeared to attribute to him a measure of theological as well as constitutional conviction.[3] But the forging of the staunchly anglican image of Pitt was not only the work of his friends; it resulted even more emphatically from the polemic of some of his most severe critics. Joseph Priestley may be said to have began the process in 1787, after Pitt had declined to support the repeal of the Test and Corporation Acts: 'Educated as you have been by clergymen, who are interested in the support of the present establishment, and whose minds may therefore be supposed to be biassed in favour of it, it is not much to be wondered at, that you should have adopted their idea of its inseparable connection with the political

* I wish to thank Professor Michael McCahill and Dr Stephen Taylor for valuable comments on an earlier draft of this paper. I am grateful to the British Academy for a grant which provided financial support for the necessary research.
[1] See Boyd Hilton, *The Age of Atonement. The Influence of Evangelicalism on Social and Economic Thought, 1785–1865* (Oxford: paperback edn., 1991), p. 204.

[2] J. J. Sack, 'The Memory of Burke and the Memory of Pitt: English Conservatism Confronts its Past, 1806–1829', *Historical Journal*, XXX (1987), 623–40; idem, *From Jacobite to Conservative. Reaction and Orthodoxy in Britain, c. 1760–1832* (Cambridge, 1993), pp. 83–90.

[3] George Pretyman Tomline, *Memoirs of the Life of the Right Honorable William Pitt* (2 vols., London, 1821), II, 615.

constitution of this country', adding, with reference to Pretyman, 'If, Sir, you must be guided by a bishop, it is to be lamented that you did not make a better choice.'[4] Five years later, the unitarian Samuel Heywood, reflecting a widespread sense that Pitt was guilty of some kind of betrayal of dissenting expectations, complained 'It was not natural to expect that a son of the great Earl of Chatham should be the "issue of his loins" only, and "not the child of his principles" '; to him, Pitt was now in close association with high churchmen.[5]

This perception of Pitt's ministry as a diehard anglican one filtered into the work of several modern historians. In a study of eighteenth-century movements for legal toleration, published in 1962, R. B. Barlow devoted a chapter to the failure to obtain repeal of the Test and Corporation Acts and entitled it 'The principles of Pitt triumphant'.[6] Quoting with approval the remark of the unitarian lawyer Michael Dodson, that 'the principles of William Pitt could triumph only for one last season because they belonged wholly to the past', Barlow saw Pitt as the spokesman of a dying age, desperately clinging to outdated privileges.[7] Such a view, moreover, was highly acceptable to those contemporaries and historians who saw Pitt's ministry as 'repressive' in a secular sense. Thomas Beddoes, writing in 1796, was not the last to caricature the administration as one which cloaked its crimes under a religious halo: Pitt, in this version, was 'surrounded by a little group of pietists . . . the most bloody of tyrants had the cant and leer of a modern saint'.[8] Historians of secular radicalism have endorsed this verdict, seeing the ministry as obstructing the inevitable and desirable march of progress with such draconian retaliation as the Alien Act, Seditious Meetings Act and Combination Laws.[9] What might be termed the 'anglicanization' of Pitt's memory was just as inaccurate as its 'christianization', if less consciously fraudulent. Each helped to form an impression of a ministry defending the institutions of an 'unreformed' state not only against the assaults of atheistical jacobinism, but also against even the most moderate religious reform.

A depiction of unbridled reaction, especially for the 1790s, has not survived the scrutiny of recent historiography, notably the magisterial biography by John Ehrman.[10] It is the purpose of this essay to ask whether the pattern of ecclesiastical legislation provides evidence as to the allegedly anglican ethos of the ministry. It will suggest that the supposed anglican champion and ecclesiastical tyrant, far from pursuing a consistent anglican agenda, presided over some of the most fundamental legislative changes in religion since 1688 and in so doing undermined that very 'confessional state' on behalf of which he was accused of conducting an unremitting defence. It will further claim that in the ecclesiastical sense the ministry's policies were far from repressive. In particular,

---

[4] Joseph Priestley, *A Letter to the Right Honourable William Pitt* (2nd edn., 1787), pp. 2, 14.

[5] Samuel Heywood, *High Church Politics. Being a Seasonable Appeal to the Friends of the British Constitution, against the Practices and Principles of High Churchmen* (1792), pp. 13, 21.

[6] R. B. Barlow, *Citizenship and Conscience. A Study in the Theory and Practice of Religious Toleration in England during the Eighteenth Century* (Philadelphia, 1962), ch. 7.

[7] *Ibid.*, p. 298 and ch. 7, *passim*.

[8] Thomas Beddoes, *An Essay on the Public Merits of Mr Pitt* (1796), p. 51.

[9] See, for instance, Albert Goodwin, *The Friends of Liberty. The English Democratic Movement in the Age of the French Revolution* (1979), p. 83.

[10] John Ehrman, *The Younger Pitt. The Years of Acclaim* (1969); *The Younger Pitt. The Reluctant Transition* (1983); *The Younger Pitt. The Consuming Struggle* (1996).

the ministry had, by the time of its dissolution, transformed the question of catholic emancipation from a near-impossibility, of fringe interest, to the verge of practical reality. Although explanations for Pitt's resignation in March 1801 which rely exclusively on the first minister's differences with George III over emancipation have rightly been discounted,[11] the end of the ministry was nevertheless inextricably bound up with a crucial ecclesiastical issue.[12]

Superficially, there appears to be a disparity between the level of ecclesiastical debate and the prominence of religious issues in politics on the one hand, and the apparent paucity of ecclesiastical legislation on the other. Legislation that was specifically ecclesiastical, or religious in a broader sense, made up a very small proportion of the whole. During 18 parliamentary sessions, from May 1784 to December 1800, there was passed a total of 3,954 acts, some two-thirds of them public, or public and personal acts; of these, 230, or 5.8 per cent, may be strictly defined as ecclesiastical.[13] The compilation and analysis of failed legislative initiatives edited by Julian Hoppit found 1,297 such failures over the same 18 sessions, with only 40, or three per cent, falling within the editor's widely-drawn category of 'religious'.[14] These figures should not cause surprise. Nor are they solely explained by the obvious point that administrations were not necessarily expected to legislate in general matters or that much ecclesiastical administration did not require legislation at all. There were fears that legislation of an excessively erastian kind would threaten ecclesiastical property or clerical authority.[15] William Wilberforce felt deterred from introducing a 'general law' to promote the construction of new churches, 'with a right of patronage', through lack of parliamentary support.[16] Yet by the end of the ministry, the national Church had been significantly re-shaped by parliament's passage of the fifth article of the Act of Union, which united the churches of England and Ireland into 'one Protestant Episcopal Church, to be called *The United Church of England and Ireland*'.[17]

The term 'ecclesiastical legislation' is open to wide definitions. Much of the public and private legislation of this period carried ecclesiastical implications. The effect of warfare on taxation, manpower, overseas trade and the cost of provisions and labour could not but affect an institution which was a major landowner and unavoidably involved in the national economy. But for the purposes of this paper, ecclesiastical legislation may be said to have belonged to one of three broad categories. The first category, which is discussed in section one of this paper, governed the status, endowments, jurisdiction and worship of the Church of England as an institution. This would include, for instance, the relevant clauses of the statutes which provided for the interests of the

[11] See C. J. Fedorak, 'Catholic Emancipation and the Resignation of William Pitt in 1801', *Albion*, XXIV (1992), 49–64; and Ehrman, *The Younger Pitt. The Consuming Struggle*, ch. 15.

[12] Ehrman, *The Younger Pitt. The Consuming Struggle*, ch. 15, *passim*.

[13] There were 2,544 public, including (from 1798) public and personal, acts, and 1,410 private acts between May 1784 and November 1800.

[14] *Failed Legislation, 1660–1800. Extracted from the Commons and Lords Journals*, ed. Julian Hoppit (1997), pp. 6–8.

[15] See, for example, Morgan Cove, *An Inquiry into the Necessity, Justice & Policy of a Commutation of Tithes* (Hereford, 1800), pp. 7, 36; John Sturges, *Thoughts on the Residence of the Clergy and on the Provisions of the Statute of the Twenty-First Year of Henry VIII c.13* (2nd edn., 1802), p. 38.

[16] R. I. and S. Wilberforce, *The Life of William Wilberforce* (5 vols., 1838), II, 362.

[17] 39 & 40 Geo. III, c. 67.

church in the redemption of the land tax in 1798 and immediately thereafter.[18] The second category, which forms the basis of section two of this paper, covered the church's relations with non-anglican denominations, and concerned itself, in practice, with the freedom of worship and civil participation of protestant dissenters and catholics.

The third category comprises the attempted regulation by parliament of public and private morality. In this area there was little actual legislation during Pitt's ministry. Where legislation was carried, it tended to be of a relatively minor or technical nature, such as the acts allowing bills of exchange which fell due on Good Friday to be payable the day before (1799), restricting the work of bakers on Sundays (1794) and the reinforcement of the bigamy law (1795).[19] More wide-ranging efforts to secure 'moral' legislation failed, such as the Bill for the Better Observation of the Lord's Day (1795) and the attempt to curb Sunday newspapers (1799).[20] The best example of such a failure is the Adultery Bill of 1800 which, with much else, would have outlawed the marriage of 'guilty' parties in adultery cases. Its third reading was carried by the narrow majority of eight votes in the house of lords on 23 May 1800, with much episcopal and some ministerial support, although with strong opposition from the court, led by the royal dukes, before going down to defeat in the Commons.[21] A key reason for such failures was the reluctance of the ministry itself to give official sanction, let alone to promote, measures of this kind. Indeed, ministerial acquiescence allowed the passage of J. P. Bastard's act to regulate the church courts in 1787 (27 Geo. III, c. 44), which forbade the bringing of prosecutions for immorality after the lapse of six months. It was opposed by John Moore, archbishop of Canterbury, was criticized by two of the ministry's own law officers and excoriated by the high Church Oxonian Sir William Dolben.[22] Partly because it won the predictable support of anti-clerical whigs in the Commons and partly because Bastard had wanted to abolish altogether the right of the Church courts to hear such prosecutions, it was a measure which helps to explain episcopal suspicion of lay initiatives in the area of morality.[23] As John Butler, bishop of Oxford, complained in 1787, 'The morals of the People may be encouraged by Laws, but they must originate from the Clergy. . . . Laws have a natural tendency to become dormant, and so have magistrates.'[24] Much more might be expected from royal proclamation, as in 1787, and by voluntary organizations with semi-official patronage. The overall effect of legislation in the sphere of morality was to reduce the scope of the church courts and thus to effect a slight reduction in the extent to which morality was regulated according to specifically anglican teaching.

---

[18] In particular 39 Geo. III, c. 22.

[19] Respectively 39 & 40 Geo. III, c. 42; 34 Geo. III, c. 61, and 35 Geo. III, c. 67.

[20] The bill to render more effective the act of 29 Car. II for better observation of the Lord's Day was killed off by long postponement in the Commons: *C.J.* L, 419 (13 Apr. 1795). The second reading of the bill to curb Sunday newspapers was postponed on 11 June 1799. *C.J.* LIV, 616.

[21] Twenty of the 26 bishops voted for the third reading of the Adultery Bill in person or by proxy, as did Grenville, Camden, Spencer and Portland. There is a division list in several London newspapers, including the *General Evening Post*, 27–29 May 1800.

[22] Debrett, *Parliamentary Register*, XXII, 127–32 (20 Apr. 1787).

[23] 27 Geo. III, c. 44.

[24] Surrey History Centre, 173/2/2, Butler Correspondence with Lord Onslow, No. 44: Butler to Onslow, 12 Sept. 1787.

The legislation of 1784 to 1800 must, of course, be considered in historical context. That context took four particularly important forms. Firstly, the demise of jacobitism as registered by the death of the Young Pretender in 1788 not only contributed to a slight but significant easing of *élite* anti-catholicism but also opened the possibility of legislative relief for the worship of the Scottish Episcopalian Church, although such a measure was not carried quickly or without bitter controversy.[25] Secondly, this was a period of threats of warfare, over the Dutch in 1787, over Nootka Sound in 1790 and Ochakov in 1791, followed in 1793 by the most expensive war in the country's history. The unprecedented demands upon manpower and on the nation's financial resources undoubtedly helps to explain the acts of 1798 and 1799 extending earlier legislation to permit foreign protestants to hold military commissions,[26] and it is difficult to believe that the act of 1794, allowing French subjects to enlist in the British army without penalty for profess- ing the catholic religion or failing to declare their adherence to it,[27] would have been proposed in peacetime conditions. The voluntary contributions and the redemption of the land tax substantially affected the Church; its leaders were to the fore in the former and there were specifically ecclesiastical clauses in the latter.[28] Thirdly, the context was one of domestic radicalism and fears of revolution, fuelled by the food crises of 1795 and 1800 and anxieties over the growth of popular, and allegedly dangerous, non-anglican sects. Finally, the threat of disorder, and subsequently the actuality of rebellion, in Ireland brought Irish as well as English ecclesiastical questions to the centre of politics.

1

Some of the most significant legislation which affected the structure of the Church of England concerned the anglican communion internationally, and especially in the colonial area. A residue of the American war was a group of exiled American loyalists, many of them episcopalian clergy, who formed an embittered high church pressure group in Britain as well as in Canada. They received a substantial measure of sympathy in episcopal circles. Partly because of ecclesiastical lobbying on their behalf, the ministry recognized a limited obligation to them. Hence parliament passed five acts between 1785 and 1789 appointing commissioners to assess the claims of dispossessed loyalists,[29] followed by two general compensation acts in 1788 and 1790 and a specific act to confer an annuity upon the loyalist Penn family.[30] Pitt proposed the sum of £150,000 compensation in 1785 and this was followed by subsequent distributions.[31]

[25] F. C. Mather, *High Church Prophet. Bishop Samuel Horsley (1733–1806) and the Caroline Tradition in the Later Georgian Church* (Oxford, 1992), ch. 6.

[26] 38 Geo. III, c. 13; and 39 Geo. III, c. 104.

[27] 34 Geo. III, c. 43.

[28] See 38 Geo. III, c. 60, making the land tax permanent, subject to redemption; 39 & 40 Geo. III, c. 30, for extending the period of preference for redemption.

[29] Respectively 25 Geo. III, c. 75; 26 Geo. III, c. 68; 27 Geo. III, c. 29; 28 Geo. III, c. 44; and 29 Geo. III, c. 62.

[30] Respectively 28 Geo. III, c. 40; 30 Geo. III, c. 34; and 30 Geo. III, c. 46.

[31] Mary Beth Norton, *The British-Americans. The Loyalist Exiles in England, 1774–1789* (Boston, 1972), pp. 209ff, 309 n. 55. Some loyalists were, none the less, excluded altogether from the compensation acts.

The colonial high church lobby was deeply distressed by the fear that the election of a bishop in the newly-independent states was a dangerously 'presbyterian' gesture. The obstacle of the oath of allegiance prevented the consecration by the English hierarchy of Samuel Seabury as the first bishop of the Protestant Episcopal Church of America. The ministry moved towards satisfying the colonial high churchmen, albeit belatedly, by the act of 1784 (24 Geo. III, c. 35), allowing episcopal consecration of citizens belonging to 'countries out of His Majesty's Dominions' as deacons and priests without the oath of allegiance, and the act of 1786 (26 Geo. III, c. 84), empowering the archbishops of Canterbury and York to consecrate bishops in similar circumstances. Legislation was not required for the bishopric of Nova Scotia, set up by letters patent in 1787. While the purely spiritual nature of the powers of the bishop of Nova Scotia might, as Peter Doll suggests, have gratified the anti-erastianism of the high church lobby, the decisive factor was Pitt's anxiety for good relations with the United States. The former colleague of Shelburne had no intention of alienating the former colonies, with which he sought closer commercial relations, by a display of anglican civil expansionism. It was the sense that this was so, as well as the recollection of Pitt's association with the author of *Observations on the Nature of Civil Liberty*, that provoked Seabury's despairing cry 'I am confident that Dr Price has had more weight with him, than the whole bench of Bishops.'[32]

One would acknowledge that the ministry appreciated the value of anglicanism as a means of inducing civil loyalty among the francophone majority in Quebec and that this consideration influenced the preparation of the Canada Act of 1791.[33] William Cleaver indeed lobbied Grenville with elaborate schemes for exhibitions at the English universities to provide for Nova Scotia and Quebec a supply of clergy untainted by American principles.[34] In the higher reaches of the ministry Grenville, indeed, was the closest to a devout anglican, with evangelical sympathies, although he did not become a member of the S.P.C.K. until 1801.[35] But although the act was designed to implant anglicanism, alongside a hereditary aristocracy, in Canada it fell short of what such churchmen as Cleaver had wanted. While endowing the Church of England in Canada with a landed provision to sustain its clergy, it did not establish the Church there – the question of 'establishment' was to be left to the individual legislatures.[36] A college was, admittedly, founded in Nova Scotia (although it did not receive a charter until 1802), but the proposed exhibitions at the English universities never materialized. The notion that the policy of Pitt's ministry towards the Church in North America reflected a missionary, expansionist zeal needs to be tempered by an important qualification. The

[32] Quoted in Peter Doll, 'Imperial Anglicanism in North America 1745–1795', University of Oxford D. Phil., 1989, p. 260. I am most grateful to Dr Doll for providing me with a copy of his dissertation.

[33] Grenville to Archbishop Moore, 31 Jan. 1791, quoted in Peter Jupp, *Lord Grenville, 1759–1834* (Oxford, 1985), p. 95.

[34] B.L., Add. MS 59001, ff. 38–44: William Cleaver to Grenville, 30 May 1790; *The Later Correspondence of George III*, ed. A. Aspinall (5 vols., Cambridge, 1966–70), I, 472–4: Grenville to Cleaver, 11 Apr. 1790.

[35] A list of members of the S.P.C.K., together with their years of joining, is printed with *A Sermon preached in the Cathedral Church of St Paul, London, on Thursday, June 16, 1808 . . . By the Very Reverend John Chappel Woodhouse, D.D.* (London, 1808).

[36] Doll, 'Imperial Anglicanism', p. 291.

testimony of the colonial clergy, soured as it was by the experience of defeat and dispossession and convinced that rebellion in America could have been averted had a colonial episcopate been established earlier in the century, hardly represented anglican opinion as a whole.

In theory a clear structure existed whereby the episcopate could prepare such legislation as it believed to be in the interests of the Church, or propose such legislation to the ministry. There were small committees of bishops for this purpose, as well as less frequent general meetings of such members of the bench who could be persuaded to attend.[37] Yet, apart from the resolution of a majority of bishops to oppose the repeal of the Test and Corporation Acts in 1787, there was never a united episcopal leadership, let alone one in close alliance with Pitt's administration, and particular initiatives were usually the province of individual bishops. There were, to be sure, clerical pressures to which government responded. Pitt, for instance, consulted Pretyman, himself a statistician, over the implications for ecclesiastical estates of the redemption of the land tax, and received a welter of unsolicited advice from Samuel Horsley.[38] This was far from the only instance. As George Rose wrote to Pretyman, in connexion with the Registry Act of 1794, 'We repeal the Tax on Births & Burials at the instance of the Clergy through your Lordship. I trust therefore you will not saddle us with it again in any other Shape.'[39] Similarly, clerical influence secured the exemption of the licences granted to stipendiary curates from stamp duty in 1788 (28 Geo. III, c. 28) and the restoration of that exemption ten years later.[40] But the Stipendiary Curates Act of 1796 (36 Geo. III c. 83), raising the theoretical maximum of curates' stipends to £75, incurred the episcopal unease encountered by subsequent measures of that kind, with a fear of an erastian threat to Church property and an erosion of the appropriate sense of ecclesiastical hierarchy.

There was undoubtedly a sharp sense of injustice on the part of elements within the parochial clergy over the laws governing residence and the threats of prosecutions for their infraction. Several writers urged a relaxation of what they regarded as the excessive rigidity of the Henrician statute of residence. As John Sturges, chancellor of Winchester, put it, 'However great the advantages of Residence may be, it is what ought not and cannot be enforced indiscriminately.'[41] There were, accordingly, moves for a residence bill, following the initiatives of Sir William Scott, together with proposals for the imposition of a tax upon non-residence with the proceeds to be applied to the augmentation of small livings.[42] It was not a matter which the administration could ignore. On the one hand it needed to uphold the status of the established clergy; on the other hand, there remained an old-whig suspicion of

---

[37] Lambeth Palace Library, Porteus notebooks, MSS 2098, f. 7; 2101, f. 32; Suffolk R.O., HA119/T108 45. I am grateful to Dr Michael McCahill for advice on this point.

[38] Suffolk R.O., T108/42: Pitt to Pretyman, 20 Feb. 1799; Mather, *High Church Prophet*, pp. 145–9.

[39] Suffolk R.O., T108/44/1: Rose to Pretyman, 3 Nov. 1796. The act in question was 34 Geo. III, c. 11 ('An Act for repealing the Duties on the registry of Burials, Births, Marriages and Christenings').

[40] The act of 1797 (37 Geo. III, c. 90) had re-imposed the stamp duty on the licences of stipendiary curates; the act of 1798 (38 Geo. III, c. 56) restored the exemption.

[41] John Sturges, *Thoughts on the Residence of the Clergy and on the Provisions of the Statute of the Twenty First Year of Henry VIII c. 13* (2nd edn., 1802), p. 11.

[42] B.L., Add. MS 59307, ff. 1–28, 63–82, 84–95; P.R.O., 30/8/310, ff. 135–62.

the spiritual power of the bishops. While agreeing with Pretyman on the need for 'reasonable and temperate measures tending to give to the ecclesiastical jurisdiction of the bishop over his clergy such a degree of weight and efficacy as to provide an effectual control and superintendence where our church Establishment supposes it to exist,' Grenville warned him of a distaste for 'that sort of spiritual authority which, extending itself far into the temporal concerns of the laity, has formerly been justly odious in this kingdom'.[43] Richard Hurd recognized the existence of the same suspicion when he admitted that 'all motions in Parliament for strengthening the hands of the Bishops, and increasing their discretionary powers, will, I doubt, be received coldly.'[44] Sturges resignedly accepted that 'with so suspicious an eye has this Nation looked at all Ecclesiastical Power from the intemperate use made of it in the time of Popery' that parliament would look askance at a measure which gave a considerable degree of discretionary power to the bench.[45]

These proposals crystallized into what Pitt himself termed 'our Ecclesiastical Plan' of early 1800.[46] Its central features were an augmentation of livings to a minimum of £70 *per annum* for curates, to be charged, where necessary, on the consolidated fund, the repeal of the statute providing for lay prosecution for non-residence, and a system of episcopal jurisdiction and superintendence of residence.[47] It encountered serious objections from the judge of the consistory court and vicar-general of the province of Canterbury, Sir William Scott. He complained that the provisions for clerical incomes would, by establishing a new body of trustees, create 'a new estate in the Church independent of the bishops', that the power 'of clipping large livings and uniting small ones' would attack property rights and lead to a 'presbyterian equality', while at the same time undermining episcopal jurisdiction in cases of non-residence.[48] Pitt was able to assure Pretyman in March 1800 that Scott's objections were 'entirely removed', but the difficulties raised by Archbishop Moore could not be remedied so easily.[49] While approving the plan for the augmentation of small livings, Moore believed 'the line of residence too strictly drawn', and was 'full of apprehensions as to the system of inspection and report'.[50] The lateness of the session curtailed further progress and no measure to reform the residence laws had passed when the ministry fell.[51] The episode is none the less revealing about the ministry's attitude towards an urgent material issue affecting the Church. It certainly appreciated the importance of an assiduous established clergy as a vehicle for social harmony.[52] At the same time, the ministry was in principle prepared to override custom in the pursuit of that objective and was only restrained from seriously challenging that custom in legislative enactment by an almost unanimous episcopal opposition.

---

[43] H.M.C., *Fortescue MSS*, VI, 7–8.
[44] Francis Kilvert, *Memoirs of the Life and Writings of the Right Rev. Richard Hurd* (1860), p. 323.
[45] Sturges, *Thoughts on Residence*, pp. 41–2.
[46] Suffolk R.O., T108/42: Pitt to Pretyman, 28 Mar. 1800.
[47] H.M.C., *Fortescue MSS*, VI, 160, 192, 197, 265.
[48] *Ibid.*, pp. 86–9: Scott to Grenville, 27 Dec. 1799 (mis-dated 1797).
[49] Suffolk R.O., T108/42: Pitt to Pretyman, 28 Mar. 1800; H.M.C., *Fortescue MSS*, VI, 152–3.
[50] H.M.C., *Fortescue MSS*, VI, 197.
[51] Scott's clergy residence act was finally passed in 1803.
[52] See, e.g., H.M.C., *Fortescue MSS*, VI, 11.

A similar attitude underlay the ministry's response to the question of the legally obligatory payment of tithe in kind. Pitt himself had far more sympathy with the agricultural improving interest than with clerical opposition to commutation.[53] Much has been written of the way in which the clergy profited from the commutation of tithes under enclosure legislation, and, indeed, of the 479 enclosure acts passed in the 1790s, 352 involved commutation of tithe, usually by allocation of land.[54] A sense of perspective, however, is provided by the fact that during the entire age of parliamentary enclosure no more than 20 per cent of parishes were enclosed with commutation and some 15 per cent were enclosed without it.[55] Far from a ubiquitous sense of clerical prosperity, there was considerable unease about the loss of a perquisite which involved a property right as well as a source of income.[56] Pitt, by contrast, believed that commutation would remove what he called a 'great obstacle to the improvement and prosperity of any country',[57] and was far from committed to the maintenance of the existing tithe system. Here he was indeed the pupil of Paley, supposedly his favourite author. In the *Principles of Moral and Political Philosophy* (1785), Paley had denounced tithe as 'noxious', and asserted that 'No measure of such extensive concern appears to me so practicable, nor any single alteration so beneficial, as the conversion of tithes into corn-rents.'[58] Pretyman also favoured corn rents and it was on this basis that in 1791 Pitt proposed a general commutation to Moore, presenting it shrewdly in terms of the advantage of the Church and as a means of diffusing a potential source of agitation.[59] But here he encountered not only the hostility of the increasingly recalcitrant Thurlow in cabinet, but also the opposition of a group of intellectually formidable, as well as politically influential, clerical economists.

In fact there was vehement clerical opposition to any kind of pressure on tithe-holders to accept commutation, either in terms of land or corn rent. In committee on the Weldon Enclosure Bill in 1792 it was left to the unlikely alliance of the high Church Samuel Horsley and the unitarian eleventh duke of Norfolk to protest against the commutation provisions in the bill. Horsley declared, 'Where the consent of the clergyman has not been given, Parliament ought not to give its sanction to the proposed commutation without the most satisfactory proof of the adequacy of the allotment.'[60] Only with the granting of additional compensation was the Weldon Enclosure Act (32 Geo. III, c. 65) carried. Morgan Cove condemned corn rents as an equivalent, citing the difficulty of assessing a corn rent which adequately reflected the variations in the value of tithes in different parishes, the 'great fluctuation' in the price of corn, and the

[53] Pitt to Rutland, 7 Nov. 1786, in Earl Stanhope, *Life of the Right Honourable William Pitt* (4 vols., 2nd edn., 1862), I, 318–9.

[54] Eric J. Evans, *The Contentious Tithe. The Tithe Problem and English Agriculture, 1750–1850* (1976), pp. 95, 112 n. 20.

[55] Peter Virgin, *The Church in an Age of Negligence. Ecclesiastical Structure and Problems of Church Reform 1700–1840* (Cambridge, 1988), p. 59.

[56] Virgin, *Church in an Age of Negligence*, pp. 55, 57.

[57] Stanhope, *Pitt*, p. 318.

[58] *The Works of William Paley, D.D.* (5 vols., 1819), II, 105–6.

[59] Stanhope, *Pitt*, II, 131–2; *Maidstone Journal*, 3 May 1791.

[60] *The Speeches in Parliament of Samuel Horsley, LL.D., F.R.S., F.A.S. Late Lord Bishop of St Asaph* (Dundee, 1813), pp. 89–90; Mather, *High Church Prophet*, pp. 143–4.

reduction in that price promised by agricultural improvers in the event of a general commutation.[61] When a group of hop farmers in Farnham, Surrey, petitioned parliament to prevent the lessee of the rectory from raising the tithe composition on hops, the consequent bill met high church obstruction – Sir William Dolben was a teller against it – and made little progress.[62]

Effective clerical resistance thwarted not only the commutation proposal of 1791 but also its successor in 1798, which followed immediately upon the redemption of the land tax. Pitt's second plan would have vested the income from the sale of tithe in government stock, to fund clerical incomes.[63] One motive for the proposal, in the words of John Mitford, M.P., who advised Pitt, was anxiety over, 'the effect of litigation alienating the Minds of the People from the Clergy'.[64] But again the plan was blocked by episcopal opposition.[65] Even the whiggish Bishop Watson, who generally favoured the scheme, objected that he (and parliament) would never agree unless the full value of the tithe were paid for its surrender.[66] But Pitt's genuine commitment to tithe reform was not affected by the French revolution, as his papers abundantly reveal, and plans for radical changes to the tithe system both in England and Ireland were in contemplation at the time of the Act of Union.[67] The ministry's approach is better reflected in the aspirations of the Board of Agriculture than in the critique offered against it by clerical economists such as Morgan Cove.[68]

Clerical resistance to commutation is explained firstly by the way in which the question was perceived in a sectarian light. A topical fear of disendowment at the hands of rampant dissent informed at least some of the opposition to the repeal of the Test and Corporation Acts in March 1790 and Burke made the issue a central feature of his speech on that occasion.[69] As Pitt's supporter John Rolle warned, after attending an agricultural meeting in Devon, 'altho' the Question of a Compensation might appear simple & feasible in itself yet [it] might be construed by those who might love Mischief to be a Contest between the Dissenters & the Church & thereby disturb the Peace of both & the Tranquillity of the Country'.[70] There was a strong underlying fear of secularization, furthered by the suspicion that Pitt's ministry was at best indifferent to the dangers posed by the notion that clerical property had originally been the property of the state and as such was reclaimable by the state.[71] Secondly, there were fears that, in some parishes, a corn rent would prove an inadequate substitute for tithes in kind, for all

[61] Morgan Cove, *An Inquiry into the Necessity, Justice & Policy of a Commutation of Tithes* (1800), pp. 68ff.

[62] *C.J.*, XLVIII, 226–7, 613, 634, 667, 687, 819–20, 826, 833, 845, 874; Cove, *Inquiry*, p. 102.

[63] Evans, *The Contentious Tithe*, p. 80.

[64] P.R.O., 30/8/170/1, ff. 176: John Mitford to Pitt, 31 Aug. 1798.

[65] Lambeth Palace Lib., Moore papers, item 9; A. W. Rowden, *The Primates of the Four Georges* (1916), pp. 373ff.

[66] *Anecdotes of the Life of Richard Watson, Bishop of Llandaff, written by himself at different intervals* (2nd edn., 2 vols., 1818), pp. 56–60.

[67] See the documents in P.R.O., 30/8/10; and Jupp, *Lord Grenville*, pp. 274, 277.

[68] Cove's attack on the Board of Agriculture may be found in his *Inquiry*, p. 36.

[69] See G. M. Ditchfield, 'Parliament, the Quakers and the Tithe Question, 1750–1835', *Parliamentary History*, IV (1985), 103; W. Cobbett, *Parliamentary History of England* (36 vols., 1806–20), XXVIII, 437–8.

[70] P.R.O., 30/8/173, ff. 34–5: John Rolle to Pitt, 17 Nov. 1791.

[71] Cove, *Inquiry*, p. 102; Evans, *The Contentious Tithe*, p. 109.

the difficulties involved in the collection of the latter. The economic benefits to the clergy, obvious with hindsight, had to be fought for fiercely, and their full extent could not be predicted.

Hence the 'temperate accommodation' over the tithe question which Pitt hoped that the episcopate might propose did not materialize, let alone take legislative form. Undoubtedly Pitt wished to avoid the political damage which would accompany an anglican outcry should the ministry pursue a unilateral initiative, instead of legislating along lines proposed by the bishops: 'Even the appearance of concession which might be awkward in Government, could not be unbecoming if it originated with them.'[72] Hence, too, the Church Court Bill of 1786 had to be purged of its tithe clauses before it could become law the following year, while James Adair's two bills to extend the summary legal procedures for the recovery of tithes from quakers were lost in 1796 and 1797.[73] Mildmay's initiative for the leasing of clerical tithes did not emerge until the ministry's eleventh hour in March 1801.[74] Pitt's ministry, however, did not share all these clerical concerns and had as its priorities economic efficiency (reinforced by the need for maximizing agricultural production in years of warfare and dearth) and the avoidance of a political backlash against the clergy which could only harm the interests of government. It looked with benign approval, though without direct participation, upon the succession of private enclosure bills which were gradually promoting at a parish level that which Pitt had wished to achieve on a national basis.

2

When one turns to the matter of the Church's relations with non-anglican religions, it is not surprising to find a substantial measure of legislative continuity. There was no interruption, for instance, in the series of the Indemnity Acts, passed annually from 1758, and taking a virtually identical form except for the extension to deputy lieutenants and officers of the militia from 1788. Similarly, successive Militia Acts continued to stipulate that quakers provide certificates of their religious allegiance and provide a substitute if chosen by ballot to serve.[75] In 1785 the Registration Act (25 Geo. III, c. 75) extended the stamp duty, already applicable to quakers, to dissenting births, marriages and burials.

On the question of the Test and Corporation Acts, the evidence that Pitt was influenced against repeal by the reprint of Thomas Sherlock's *Vindication of the Corporation and Test Acts* (1718) is slender indeed.[76] It is characteristic of the ambivalence of the ministry's attitude to repeal in 1787 that the re-issue of Sherlock and of Benjamin

---

[72] Stanhope, *Pitt*, I, 319.

[73] Ditchfield, 'Parliament and the Tithe Question', pp. 90–91, 103–4.

[74] Mildmay's initiative for the leasing of clerical tithes ended when the order for the committal was discharged on 12 May 1801. *C.J.*, LVI, 399.

[75] 26 Geo. III, c. 107; and 39 Geo. III, c. 90.

[76] J. C. D. Clark, *English Society 1688–1832. Ideology, Social Structure and Political Practice during the Ancien Regime* (Cambridge, 1985), p. 341 and n. 248. The only direct evidence is offered by Theophilus Lindsey, hardly a witness disposed in Pitt's favour; see H. McLachlan, *Letters of Theophilus Lindsey* (Manchester, 1920), p. 64. The original letter (from Lindsey to William Tayleur, 2 Mar. 1787), in which Lindsey claimed that he was 'well assured' of the truth of his claim, without specifying any source, is in John Rylands University Library of Manchester.

Hoadly's *Refutation of Bishop Sherlock's Arguments against a Repeal of the Test and Corporation Acts* were both dedicated to Pitt, claiming to identify the principles of each with him.[77] In May 1794 the appearance of a parliamentary motion by Sheridan for the repeal of military and naval tests gave Pitt the opportunity to declare privately to Canning that the Test was 'comparatively speaking of very little importance'.[78] Allowance will no doubt be made for the tactical advantage of seeking to win over an effective young supporter, but the willingness to contemplate repeal in principle is beyond doubt. More explicit, as well as more public, was the response of the master of the rolls, Pepper Arden, to William Smith's amendment to the Regency Bill on 12 February 1789 which sought, in Smith's words, 'to prevent any new difficulty being placed by the Regency bill, in the way of the repeal of the Test Act, if application should be made for such a repeal hereafter'. Arden replied:

> It was true, that there were, in the statute of Charles the Second, many severe penalties and unjust disabilities, several of which had been since repealed by the Act of Toleration in favour of the Protestant dissenters, and he thought there were others remaining that ought to be repealed; but then, it should be done regularly, directly and avowedly. At a fit time, he should have no objection to assist in framing a proper bill of repeal.[79]

When Pitt, rejecting the first repeal motion moved by Beaufoy, on 28 March 1787, declared 'The members of the Church of England, a part of our constitution, will be seriously injured; and their apprehensions are not to be treated lightly',[80] he referred, again, to those same perils of an anglican backlash which had served as a cautionary influence in the time of Walpole.

For whatever may be said about the allegedly repressive legislation of the 1790s against radical societies and seditious meetings, notably the 'Two Acts' of 1795, such legislation was never extended to religious activity. The failure of the unitarian petition in 1792 made little practical difference to the continuity of non-trinitarian worship. It is notable that Pitt's ministry did not seek to suppress unitarianism, despite the barrage of anti-unitarian propaganda, mainly (albeit not exclusively) from clerical sources. At no time was such propaganda pitched at a higher level than during the 1790s. Yet the act of 1799 (39 Geo. III, c. 79), which proscribed radical societies by name and outlawed certain forms of oath-taking, with implications, for example, for freemasonry, did not include the Unitarian Society (1791) in London nor any of its provincial offshoots. It is of some significance that this measure does not fall within the category of ecclesiastical legislation, however widely defined. Similarly, following the Priestley riots in July

---

[77] See the title pages of *Bishop Sherlock's Arguments against a Repeal of the Corporation and Test Acts* (1787); and *Bishop Hoadly's Refutation of Bishop Sherlock's Arguments against a repeal of the Test and Corporation Acts* (1790).

[78] *The Letter-Journal of George Canning, 1793–1795*, ed. Peter Jupp (Camden Soc., 4th ser., XLI, 1991), p. 98. Sheridan's motion for repeal of military and naval tests was negatived without a division on 26 May 1794. *C.J.*, XLIX, 632.

[79] Debrett, *Parliamentary Registry*, XXV, 478. There is a brief discussion of Pitt's attitude towards repeal of the Test and Corporation Acts in Jennifer Mori, *William Pitt and the French Revolution 1785–1795* (Edinburgh, 1997), pp. 36–8.

[80] Cobbett, *Parl. Hist.*, XXVI, 826.

1791, while opposing Whitbread's motion for an inquiry, the ministry acquiesced in the passage of the bill to pay compensation to Priestley and other victims. It was a measure which originated in applications from unitarian victims themselves, as well as the parliamentary initiative of the M.P.s for Warwickshire and, while not a government bill, it could not have been carried, especially without challenge in any division, in the absence of ministerial consent.[81] It was a consent given in a spirit best summarised by Grenville: 'I do not admire riots in favour of Government much more than riots against it.'[82]

When restrictions on non-anglican preaching were seriously considered in the late 1790s, they were prompted more by anxiety about unlettered itinerant preachers than alleged blasphemers against the Trinity. The researches of Ian McCalman, among others, suggests that there was some justice in Horsley's complaint that political subversives whose campaigns had been frustrated by the limitations on public meetings imposed by the acts of 1795 were evading the law by masquerading as religious teachers.[83] There was a sense of near-panic among some bishops in the later 1790s over the rising numbers of dissenting meeting houses, for which registration under the Toleration Act was sought and obtained. As Bishop Cleaver of Chester lamented:

> I have reason of late within the last two, or three years to believe, the increase of these Meeting Houses is chiefly owing to the facility which they afford of privately discussing Political Topics and of forming Political combinations. Indeed the applications for them have frequently come from Persons better known by their Democratical principles, than by a Religious zeal.[84]

The interests of political tranquillity led Grenville at least to sympathise with Cleaver's demand for 'some exertion on the part of the legislature'[85] to ward off the threat of sectarian attack. But the ministry resisted strong demands for legal restrictions upon itinerant dissenting preachers. Wilberforce, admittedly, claimed that Pitt had contemplated an abridgement of the Toleration Act, but he probably exaggerated his own role in dissuading him.[86] In fact, Pitt was effectively lobbied from elsewhere against such a course, notably by Thomas Coke, who lauded the respectability of his fellow-methodists, warned against any measure which would 'soon fill the Jails with numbers of as loyal and virtuous People as any in his Majesty's dominions', and ended with the plea 'O Sir, I pray you, that no restriction may be laid on the present state of Toleration, at least before the next Session of Parliament.'[87] Crucial to this question is

[81] P.R.O., 30/8/174, ff. 218–9: William Russell to Pitt, 24 Aug. 1792; *C.J.*, XLVII: 823 (23 May 1792), petition of Russell and other trustees of New Meeting House, Birmingham; for the progress of the bill, see *C.J.*, XLVII, 191, 203, 682, 713, 720, 762, 766, 778, 800, 827. The Compensation Bill passed as 33 Geo. III, c. 39.

[82] H.M.C., *Fortescue MSS,* V, 136.

[83] Ian McCalman, *Radical Underworld. Prophets, Revolutionaries and Pornographers in London, 1795–1840* (1988); Michael Watts, *The Dissenters. Volume II: The Expansion of Political Nonconformity* (Oxford, 1995), p. 368.

[84] P.R.O., 30/8/123, f. 114: Cleaver to Isaac Hawkins Browne, 5 Feb. 1799. The letter was intended to be communicated to Pitt.

[85] *Ibid.*, See also H.M.C., *Fortescue MSS,* VI, 7, 20–21.

[86] *The Life of William Wilberforce,* II, 360–5.

[87] P.R.O., 30/8/124, f. 151: Thomas Coke to Pitt, 10 Feb. 1800. For a similar appeal, see B. L., Add. MS 59307, ff. 197–99: Coke to Grenville, 15 Jan. 1807.

that anglican pressure, even when supported by someone as close to Pitt as Pretyman, did not result either in government legislation or government-sponsored legislation. When such legislation was (unsuccessfully) proposed, its sponsor was the Foxite whig Michael Angelo Taylor.[88] Although Horsley denounced Sunday Schools as centres of jacobinism, there was no move to suppress them.[89] That which was not legislated for could be just as significant as that which was.

Although there was also a measure of institutional continuity with regard to the catholic question, evident, for instance, in the successive acts for granting extra time for the enrollment of Papist deeds and wills,[90] the principal theme was one of change. There was a widespread acceptance in parliament of the desirability of some form of Catholic Relief Act, to allow the English (and from 1793 the Scottish) catholic community a legally tolerated worship which was similar to, although not identical with, that available to protestant dissenters since 1689. The sharp controversy which followed largely concerned the precise form which such a measure might take. Charles Butler believed that Tomline in his biography gave Pitt insufficient credit for the passage of the act. It was the prime minister who composed differences over the formulation of the oath, eased parliamentary doubts and 'unfeignedly participated in the joy of the Catholics at its ultimate success'. Hence the catholic, added Butler, 'desires nothing more, than that all who glory in his name, should inherit his principles, and imitate his conduct in their regard'.[91] Pitt also overcame episcopal reservations, notably those of Moore: Hurd, too, would have preferred a more gradual approach.[92] Pitt did not accept Watson's suggestion that the oath be buttressed with yet another declaration, and three bishops voted against the clause repealing restrictions upon catholics practising at the bar.[93] Nigel Aston has identified a strong sympathy with catholicism as a factor which distanced Burke from some high Church clergy. That factor operated all the more powerfully in the case of Pitt, who was actually in a position to legislate, and not merely to aspire.[94]

Although supporting the appeal fund for the French *emigré* clergy, however, Pitt's ministry did not go anything like so far as Burke and such high churchmen as Horsley in applauding them; in particular, there was no question of Pitt's sharing Horsley's theological sympathy with the *emigrés*.[95] And at the same time, the ministry was unmoved by the anti-catholic, anti-Roman rhetoric of another type of high Church opinion.[96] It held aloof from what Professor Mather calls the 'the backlash of Protestant fury' against the *emigrés* in 1799–1800.[97] Hence it remained lukewarm

---

[88] There are manuscript drafts of M. A. Taylor's bill in B.L., Add. MS 59307, ff. 47–52.

[89] Lawrence Stone, 'Literacy and Education in England, 1640–1900', *Past & Present*, No. 42 (1969), p. 86.

[90] 27 Geo. III, c. 42; 28 Geo. III, c. 47; 29 Geo. III, c. 36; 30 Geo. III, c. 19; 35 Geo. III, c. 99.

[91] *Reminiscences of Charles Butler, Esq., of Lincoln's Inn* (4th edn., 2 vols., 1824–7), II, 68.

[92] Rowden, *Primates of the Four Georges*, pp. 372–3; Kilvert, *Memoirs of Hurd*, pp. 178, 322.

[93] *Anecdotes of the Life of Richard Watson, Bishop of Landaff; Written by Himself* (2nd edn., 2 vols., 1818), I, 397; *Whitehall Evening Post*, 7–9 June 1791. The three bishops were Moore, Horsley and John Warren.

[94] Nigel Aston, 'A "Lay Divine": Burke, Christianity and the Preservation of the British State, 1790–1797', in *Religious Change in Europe 1650–1914. Essays for John McManners*, ed. Nigel Aston (Oxford, 1997), pp. 198–200.

[95] Mather, *High Church Prophet*, p. 109.

[96] Aston, 'A "Lay Divine" ', pp. 198–9.

towards the Monastic Institutions Bill, even though it was introduced by one of Pitt's own supporters, Sir Henry St John Mildmay. Fuelled by anxieties over proselytizing, and especially by the establishment of two convents in Winchester, the bill proposed a series of resolutions which would have laid severe restrictions upon catholic institutions of that type. Though consenting to the resolutions, thereby ensuring that the bill passed the Commons (in a thin house) on 22 May 1800, Pitt placed the most tolerant possible gloss upon them, in contrast, for instance, to Spencer Percival's warm endorsement of the anti-catholic spirit of the bill.[98] In the Commons, ministerial spokesmen, notably Windham, found themselves on the same side as some of the more anti-clerical members of the opposition, such as Hobhouse and Sheridan, although Windham's comment, 'If conversion be the evil complained of, why is that greater in this case than in that of the sectaries?',[99] showed that they were not always drawing upon the same arguments. In the Lords, the postponement, and effective defeat, of the bill probably owed more to the effective defence of the *emigré* clergy offered by Grenville than to the passionate intervention of Horsley.[100]

Although it would be impossible to argue that Pitt himself took a detailed interest in Irish affairs, the ministry in general saw no objection of principle when the winning of catholic loyalty seemed a political necessity. It was on Pitt's orders that pressure was put on the Irish parliament to pass the measure known as Hobart's Act in 1793, which conferred a limited enfranchisement upon catholic freeholders. Fitzwilliam's error as lord lieutenant in 1795 was a matter of tactics and timing, not one of principle. His objective, to grant further concessions in order to promote a greater degree of national security at the height of the French wars, was one which the ministry fully endorsed. After the rebellion in 1798 Pitt and a slender majority in cabinet wished to achieve precisely the same objective with a post-union measure of emancipation. In each case, inadequate preparation had been made and key elements, notably, of course, the king's susceptibilities over the coronation oath, had not been won over. When, on 30 April 1800, Holland proposed in the Lords a motion to allow catholics to sit in parliament, ministers were embarrassed precisely because they agreed with its substance: they did not answer it.[101] Holland's justification for his proposal was one which at least half of the cabinet had held for several years: 'The only way . . . to give the Catholics of Ireland a direct interest in the union was, to hold out to them a certain advantage, and it was at the same time the only means of securing that tranquillity which was admitted to be essential to the success of the measure of union.'[102] There were also, of course, both cabinet divisions and episcopal objections, as well as the royal veto, over emancipation: both Moore and Porteus were convinced that emancipation would violate the coronation oath.[103]

---

[98] Cobbett, *Parl. Hist.*, XXXV, 345.

[99] *Ibid.*, p. 352.

[100] *Ibid.*, pp. 368–86; Mather, *High Church Prophet*, pp. 109–12; Peter Nockles, " 'The Difficulties of Protestantism": Bishop Milner, John Fletcher and Catholic Apologetic against the Church of England in the Era from the First Relief Act to Emancipation, 1778–1830', *Recusant History*, XXIV (1998), 193–236. I am most grateful to Dr Nockles for allowing me to consult this article before publication.

[101] Cobbett, *Parl. Hist.*, XXXV, 161–5.

[102] *Ibid.*, col. 165.

[103] Stanhope, *Pitt*, III, 267; Rowden, *Primates of the Four Georges*, p. 376; Aston, '"A Lay Divine"', p. 200 n. 87.

It was in large part because of the legislative record of Pitt's ministry that the king's speech on 27 April 1807, after the fall of the Talents, could express the conviction 'that after so long a Reign, marked by a Series of Indulgences to his Roman Catholic subjects, they, in common with every other Class of his people, must feel assured of his Attachment to the Principles of a just and enlightened toleration'.[104] But Pitt had wished to go much further than toleration: when Hurd reassured George III at the time of the impending resignation that 'Toleration should be allowed to those who dissent from an Establishment & that such Establishments should be guarded by a Test Law. Both these things are provided for in our happy Constitution, & it is not easy to see what should incline wise & good men to think otherwise',[105] he emphasized the width of the gulf which had opened between the minister and much of the bench. Pitt did not believe that emancipation, or its equivalent for dissenters, would necessarily work to the disadvantage of the interests of the Church of England. Given that parliamentary support for emancipation vastly exceeded support for it outside parliament, Pitt had brought the issue to the point where little more than one man's longevity stood between it and enactment.

3

There is something paradoxical in the way in which a ministry whose dedication to the Church of England was far from absolute received the regular political support of the bench in the house of lords. On only four occasions did bishops sign Lords', protests during Pitt's administration, and one of those was an episcopal dissent from Fox's Libel Bill of 1792.[106] But this absence of the kind of 'episcopal opposition' identified by William C. Lowe and Michael McCahill for the 1760s and early 1770s[107] is deceptive. Resistance to unfavourable legislative initiatives was more effectively conducted by private solicitation, as with the Test and Corporation Acts in 1787, than by passionate oratory in debate. Moreover, bishops and anglican clergy in general were in effect pushed into support of Pitt by the anti-clericalism of the opposition. They needed to shelter behind the image, if not the reality, of a champion of the Church, and thus had a vested interest in creating and sustaining such an image. Hence Archbishop Moore could thank Pitt for 'the able and effectual support which on all occasions you have given to our Church establishment'.[108] He certainly had reason to acknowledge a willingness to defer, on tactical grounds, to episcopal opinion, if expressed in sufficient

---

[104] *L.J.*, XLVI, 202.

[105] *The Later Correspondence of George III*, ed. Aspinall, III, 501.

[106] The protests may be found in *L.J.*, XXXVII, 568 (7 July 1786); XXXVIII, 334 (29 Dec. 1788); XXXVIII, 339–40 (23 Jan. 1789); and XXXIX, 483 (11 June 1792). A total of only five episcopal signatures were appended to these four Lords' protests between 1784 and 1800; three were by Christopher Wilson (Bristol) and the other two by Watson and John Warren (Bangor).

[107] William C. Lowe, 'Bishops and Scottish Representative Peers in the House of Lords, 1760–1775', *Journal of British Studies*, XVIII (1978), 86–106; Michael W. McCahill, 'The House of Lords in the 1760s', in *A Pillar of the Constitution. The House of Lords in British Politics, 1640–1784*, ed. Clyve Jones (1989), pp. 165–98.

[108] P.R.O., 30/8/161, ff. 9–10: Moore to Pitt, 9 Jan. 1792, quoted in Mori, *Pitt and the French Revolution*, p. 38.

numbers. A more realistic verdict was provided by Bishop Butler of Hereford, writing to his patron Lord Onslow in 1799: 'If we had a different King or different Ministers, your Lordship and I might at this time have all our faculties at work, in contriving an escape out of a French prison.'[109] Butler only admired Pitt's part in the Act of Union because of the absence of catholic emancipation.[110] Similarly, the high churchman Jonathan Boucher wrote of Pitt in 1794, 'Little as I like the Man, I like my Country, & public Tranquillity so much, that I should dread a Change of Ministry now – perhaps I ought at any Time.'[111]

That the administration treated clerical resistance with extreme caution cannot be doubted. That caution helps to explain why, by 1801, there had been no general commutation of tithes, no repeal of the Test and Corporation Acts and – to some extent – why there were no provisions for emancipation in the Act of Union. The ministry retreated from some of its own initiatives. On the other hand, there remained a chasm between anglican pressure, amounting almost to panic, in the 1790s and the government's lack of legislative response. As far as ecclesiastical legislation was concerned, there was a far greater response to negative than to positive clerical agitation. The value of the Church's material perquisites and of its clergy as agents of political stability was well recognized, but the preservation of its near monopoly of public life and the enhancement of its role as a teacher of theological truth for the saving of souls meant comparatively little.

Pitt has appropriately been compared to an improving landlord. His attitude to the Church of England belongs far more obviously to that category than to that of a theologically-inspired anglican. The Church was an estate, to be judged by standards of economy and usefulness; it was to be protected, so that it could be made to yield better returns. Pitt would have removed a privilege which obstructed that end in much the same way that an improving landlord would have removed a village or altered the scenery. For all its internal divisions, Pitt's ministry was not driven by any specifically 'anglican' agenda to defend the confessional state. The record of ecclesiastical legislation indeed shows that Pretyman and the other 'christianizers' of Pitt's reputation sought to mislead; but his radical and dissenting critics were equally in error. Ecclesiastical legislation forms a striking exception to the image of a 'repressive' administration in the 1790s. Pitt can indeed be rescued from his detractors, who denounced him as an ecclesiastical tyrant, but only by further tarnishing that very anglican image which they themselves helped to perpetuate and which has already been undermined by James Sack. In subsequent years, the authority commanded by Pitt's name conferred a respectability upon reform of the anglican constitution, as well as upon its preservation. This was a ministry which, by its legislative enactments, and, at times, by its refusal to legislate, contributed in no small degree to religious pluralism and thus to the long-term decline both of the ideology and the practical implementation of the confessional state.

[109] Surrey History Centre, 173/2/2, no. 113: Butler to Onslow, 16 Feb. 1799.

[110] *Ibid.*, no. 122: Butler to Onslow, 26 Apr. 1800.

[111] Earl Gregg Swem Library, Williamsburg, Virginia, Boucher papers: Jonathan Boucher to Sir Frederick Morton Eden, 8 Jan. 1794. I am grateful to the Earl Greg Swem Library for permission to quote from this document.

The Costs and Benefits of Establishment:
Clergy-Discipline Legislation in Parliament,
c. 1830–c. 1870

ARTHUR BURNS

During the early 1830s, the clergy and churchgoing laity of the Church of England suffered a collective loss of confidence. Despite their increasingly bitter internal theological divisions, churchmen of all hues shared a sense of crisis as they attempted to assess the implications of the constitutional changes of the late 1820s and early 1830s. It was not only the nascent Oxford movement or evangelicals touched by contemporary millenarianism who foresaw momentous consequences: the liberal Thomas Arnold pronounced the stark verdict that 'The church as it now stands, no human power can save.'[1] Combined with the accession of what many regarded as a hostile whig administration, the admission of Roman catholics to parliament and the electoral benefits expected to accrue to the dissenting interest from the 1832 Reform Act could be interpreted as jeopardizing the reformation settlement in Church and state. If few shared Hurrell Froude's belief that events had already rendered that settlement void,[2] many judged that previous levels of state support for the established Church would not be matched in future.

One can exaggerate the extent to which the Church had been able to achieve its own ends as a centrepiece of the Church-state nexus sometimes characterized as an 'ancien regime'.[3] Even statesmen such as Sidmouth had recognized that there were limits beyond which it would be politically unwise to extend their backing for the established Church.[4] Yet there is no doubting the increased state commitment to the Church which had followed the Napoleonic wars, most obviously in the form of subventions

---

[1] T. Arnold to J. E. Tyler, 10 June 1832, quoted in A. P. Stanley, *The Life and Correspondence of Thomas Arnold, D.D.* (2 vols., 1844), I, 287.

[2] See R. H. Froude, 'Remarks on State Interference in Matters Spiritual', in *Remains of the Late Reverend Richard Hurrell Froude*, ed. J. Keble and J. H. Newman (4 vols., London and Derby, 1838–9), III, 184–269. 'The joint effect of . . . (1.) the Repeal of the Test and Corporation Acts, (2.) the Concessions to the Roman Catholics, (3.) the late Act for Parliamentary Reform, has most certainly been to efface in at least one branch of our Civil Legislature, that character which . . . qualified it to be at the same time our Ecclesiastical Legislature, and thus to cancel the conditions on which it has been allowed to interfere in matters spiritual.': *ibid.*, p. 185.

[3] Most influentially in J. C. D. Clark, *English Society 1688–1832. Ideology, Social Structure and Political Practice during the Ancien Regime* (Cambridge, 1985).

[4] As emphasized in D. Hempton, *Religion and Political Culture in Britain and Ireland. From the Glorious Revolution to the Decline of Empire* (Cambridge, 1996), pp. 22–3. See also the important article by S. J. C. Taylor, 'Whigs, Bishops and America: The Politics of Church Reform in Mid-Eighteenth-Century England', *Historical Journal*, XXXVI (1993), 331–56.

for church-building: a commitment, as Stewart J. Brown has emphasized, which extended to the established Churches in Scotland and Ireland.[5] After 1832 the atmosphere was very different, with churchmen's fears first being realized in the government's approach to the Church in Ireland. For all the importance attached to the establishment by both whig and Conservative administrations after 1832, and the experiment with constructive reform represented by the ecclesiastical commission, the religious reconfiguration of parliament and electorate combined with radical interest in the Church as a bastion of 'old corruption' to frustrate schemes such as plans for factory education under the supervision of the established Church, and precluded further state grants for church-building.[6] Moreover the reformed parliament became the venue for further assaults on the privileges of the established Church, as the conflict of Church and chapel over the future of church rates, dissenters' civil rights and the Liberation Society's campaign for disestablishment gathered pace.[7]

The erosion of the privileges of establishment was not the only source of concern to churchmen, however. Some feared that the new political and constitutional context rendered the Church increasingly vulnerable to hostile interference in its internal affairs. The reformed parliament remained a key component in the government of the Church as the source of legislation vital to equip the Church for the pastoral challenges of a rapidly expanding population and also to disarm anticlerical critics by eradicating embarrassing abuses; yet parliament could now be more easily infiltrated by the Church's declared enemies. The difficulties the Church faced in this respect were considerably eased by the mechanism established through the ecclesiastical commission made permanent in 1836 for proceeding by orders-in-council in the redeployment of the Church's financial resources and the rearrangement of jurisdictions, although not before the parameters of its operations had been set along lines unacceptable to many in the Church.[8] There still remained, however, significant matters of concern to reforming churchmen which required more direct legislative attention if any improvement was to be effected. The fact that they often had no immediate constitutional or theological implications relevant to the discussion of the relationship of Church and state or Church and chapel did not make them any less important to the Church's future prospects. Indeed, as understood from the parochial and diocesan perspective of churchmen and clergy seeking to reinvigorate the Church's pastoral mission at the grass roots, who saw only too clearly the obstacles to their project represented by shortcomings in the Church's internal administrative and disciplinary structures, they might well appear to be of especial importance.

---

[5] See S. J. Brown, 'Tribunes of the People? The Struggles for National Establishments in the Three Kingdoms 1832–41' (unpublished paper, 1996), pp. 2–3.

[6] For good brief summaries of these developments see G. I. T. Machin, *Politics and the Churches in Great Britain 1832 to 1868* (Oxford, 1977), chs. 2–5, or W. O. Chadwick, *The Victorian Church: Part I* (3rd edn., 1971), chs. 1–2.

[7] See two important recent essays on the politics of dissent in this period: J. P. Ellens, *Religious Routes to Gladstonian Liberalism. The Church Rate Conflict in England and Wales, 1832–1868* (University Park, PA, 1994); T. Larsen, *Friends of Religious Equality. Nonconformist Politics in Mid-Victorian England* (Woodbridge, 1999).

[8] For the ecclesiastical commission, see the classic study by G. F. A. Best, *Temporal Pillars. Queen Anne's Bounty, the Ecclesiastical Commissioners, and the Church of England* (Cambridge, 1964), esp. ch. 7.

Such issues have inevitably attracted less historical interest than the set-piece battles over constitutional principles provoked by more obviously controversial initiatives. This essay therefore seeks to shed light on the extent to which the post-reform parliament in practice proved to be a difficult environment for legislation concerned primarily with the internal affairs of the established Church and without direct ramifications for the lives of non-anglicans. It will focus on legislative initiatives intended to establish an effective form of clergy discipline which were introduced into parliament between the 1832 Reform Act and 1874, the point at which the issue became inextricably bound up with the ritual question in the Public Worship Regulation Act. This aspect of ecclesiastical reform has a number of recommendations for addressing the larger theme. First, save for the origins and passage of the Public Worship Regulation Act, it has hitherto received little historical attention.[9] Secondly, clergy discipline was identified as an issue needing attention at the time of the Reform Act, and remained a continued source of concern for the next 40 years, provoking a plethora of legislative initiatives. Thirdly, it was an issue on which the Church's leadership was agreed on the need for legislation, if not on its detailed provisions. Fourthly, concerned as they were solely with the professional standards of anglican ministers, clergy-discipline bills did not impact directly on the lives of non-anglicans. This is not to suggest that they had no wider ramifications. After 1850 the issue of the shape and nature of the final court of appeal in discipline cases became increasingly controversial. Not only was this less central to earlier discussions, however, but even in the later period it was far from the only concern of prospective legislators. Finally, the story of the Church's efforts to secure a more effective clergy discipline in this period was largely one of failure. Alongside a desire to address the rise of ritualism, this was an important justification for the Public Worship Regulation Act (itself hardly a stunning success). This failure would not have been anticipated by those who expressed considerable confidence at the outset of the period that an effective solution was near at hand. It therefore prompts two questions in the context of the present inquiry. Was the failure a direct consequence of the requirement that the Church leadership pursue a solution in the parliamentary context? And to what extent was the manner of the solution attempted itself shaped by the need there to pursue it?

1

Before proceeding further it is necessary to outline the convoluted history of efforts to secure an effective system of clergy discipline over the period. At the outset, two connected impulses set the campaign in motion. The first defined the problem: the extraordinary case of Dr Edward Drax Free.[10] Free was a clerical delinquent of

---

[9] For the Public Worship Regulation Act and its origins, see J. Bentley, *Ritualism and Politics in Victorian Britain. The Attempt to Legislate for Belief* (Oxford, 1978); P. T. Marsh, *The Victorian Church in Decline. Archbishop Tait and the Church of England, 1868–1882* (1969), chs. 5–9; G. W. Graber, *Ritual Legislation in the Victorian Church of England. Antecedents and Passage of the Public Worship Regulation Act, 1874* (San Francisco, 1993). For the period from the 1820s to the late 1850s see A. Burns, *The Diocesan Revival in the Church of England, c. 1800–1870* (Oxford, 1999), ch. 7.

[10] For the case of Dr Free, see R. B. Outhwaite, *Scandal in the Church. Dr Edward Drax Free, 1764–1843* (London and Rio Grande, 1997).

antiheroic proportions. A quick-tempered brawler as a fellow of St John's College, Oxford, his colleagues could think of no more suitable candidate for the college living of Sutton in Bedfordshire when it became vacant in 1808. Employing a combination of sexual harassment and carefully selected readings from *Aristotle's Masterpiece*, this single and apparently singularly unattractive parson managed to seduce four of the five women he employed as housekeepers, fathering three illegitimate children and inducing a miscarriage through a brutal assault on one victim. Proceedings were finally instituted in the ecclesiastical courts in 1823. Despite the weight of evidence against him, Free was able to exploit the inadequacies of the existing system of clerical discipline to evade a definitive judgment against him until February 1830, having meanwhile continued to draw his income from the living and involved his prosecutors in some £1,500 of expense. The scandal the case aroused helped to provoke the second impulse, which initially appeared to have defined a solution: a royal commission established by the Wellington administration, which paid particular attention to the issue of clergy discipline while investigating the whole system of ecclesiastical courts. The commission's report, largely written by the liberal ecclesiastical lawyer Stephen Lushington,[11] condemned the existing practice by which the inefficiency of consistory courts, too often in the hands of sinecurists, encouraged the referral of discipline cases to the provincial court of arches, staffed by the *élite* civilian lawyers of Doctors Commons. Both consistory and provincial courts admitted only written evidence and fostered protracted and expensive litigation. Instead, as part of a wide-ranging reform of the ecclesiastical courts, the commissioners proposed that future discipline cases should be heard personally by the bishop assisted by an expert legal assessor; that oral evidence be admitted; and that delinquents should be suspended pending appeals (in future only to be admitted against definitive sentence rather than intermediate acts, the means Free had employed to prolong proceedings in his own case).

When made public in 1832, this aspect of the royal commission's report could be interpreted as an example of the benefits that might accrue to the Church from its established status. The commission had brought together bishops and professional lawyers to produce a clear-cut set of proposals acclaimed by almost everyone bar the civilians of Doctors Commons. Those hailing its recommendations ranged from Henry Brougham to the orthodox high church and ultra-tory bishop of Exeter, Henry Phillpotts, a keen disciplinarian who reckoned that the report promised both 'prodigious slaughter' and 'much practical good'.[12]

Yet eight years were to pass before any successful general legislation on clergy discipline resulted. The Church Discipline Act of 1840 (3–4 Vict., c. 86) in fact owed less to the 1832 report's proposals than some historians have assumed.[13] In the interim, a succession of failed initiatives had been wrecked on the parliamentary shore. In 1833 a bill incorporating the report's proposals in a wider measure for reforming the ecclesiastical

[11] For the report, see *Parl. Papers*, 1831–2, XXIV (no. 199), *Reports made by His Majesty's Commissioners Appointed to Inquire into the Practice and Jurisdiction of the Ecclesiastical Courts in England and Wales.* For Lushington, see S. M. Waddams, *Law, Politics and the Church of England. The Career of Stephen Lushington, 1782–1873* (Cambridge, 1992).

[12] Devon R.O., Exeter Diocesan Papers, Moger Basket D12, f. 175: H. Phillpotts to R. Barnes, 26 Feb. 1832.

[13] E.g., Graber, *Ritual Legislation*, p. 20.

courts obtained only a first reading; in 1835, two more focused bills got no further. In 1836, a quite different measure reached a third reading; in 1838, a further and substantially new bill was abandoned at the same stage. This was modified before being reintroduced in 1839, when it actually escaped its chamber of origin before expiring. Finally, in 1840, another new bill reached the statute book as the Church Discipline Act. After a few years working with this new measure, the bishops concluded that it would not do. In 1845 they began a second legislative initiative. Bills were presented in 1845, 1846, 1847, 1848, 1849 and 1850 without ever passing beyond the committee stage. A hiatus followed. By early 1853 the bishops were once more gearing up for action, securing a draft bill from the newly restored convocation. In 1856, however, it was the government which emerged with a new initiative, which was defeated on its second reading. The bishops attempted to formulate a new measure, but by the end of the decade were growing resigned to resting content with the unsatisfactory measure of 1840. After 1860 the focus of discussion of clerical discipline increasingly shifted towards the problem of ritualism, with the introduction by private members and lay peers of bills concerned to prohibit specific ritualistic practices, the bishops themselves not reentering the legislative arena until 1869, when Tait's Clergy Discipline and Ecclesiastical Courts Bill was introduced alongside Shaftesbury's Ecclesiastical Courts and Registries Bill.[14] The latter, modified in important respects to accommodate the bishops' views, became an annual fixture until 1872. And thus we arrive at the preliminaries of the 1874 episcopal bill which, this time amended to satisfy Lord Chancellor Cairns and others, became law as the Public Worship Regulation Act.[15]

2

If the origins of the attempt to reform clergy discipline showed the establishment functioning effectively, did this long saga of abortive or unsatisfactory legislative initiatives demonstrate its drawbacks in the context of the post-1832 parliament?

Certainly, the explanations accounting for the failure of so many bills include some which illustrate the often prosaic difficulties besetting parliamentary initiatives aimed at reforming the Church's internal structures. A good example can be drawn from the years when the project was buoyed up by the widespread acclaim for the proposals of the royal commission. Reform was accepted by the episcopate; it also had cross-party support. In 1835, bills derived from the 1832 report were introduced both in the Commons by Peel's attorney-general, Frederick Pollock, and in the Lords by the former whig lord chancellor, Henry Brougham. On this occasion, however, the measures were lost when Peel called a general election. In 1839, as a result of a ministerial crisis, a bill introduced in the Lords with government support on 12 April was only embarking on its second reading in the Commons by the early hours of 3 August. By then, significant amendments with which the government was unhappy having been introduced by the Lords, there was no possibility of the bill being enacted before the end of the session.

---

[14] For a fuller account of these initiatives, see Burns, *Diocesan Revival*, ch. 7.
[15] For the passage of the Public Worship Regulation Act, see Marsh, *Victorian Church in Decline*, ch. 7.

If parliamentary and ministerial instability could thus spell the end for relatively uncontentious legislation, so could the everyday press of other parliamentary business. However urgently churchmen regarded the need for a more effective system of clergy discipline, measures could never successfully compete for time in the increasingly crowded parliamentary timetable with numerous more politically significant issues. A reader attempting to track the parliamentary career of any clergy-discipline bill of the period through the Lords' and Commons' Journals is invariably embroiled in an unrewarding chase from page to page as readings and committees are repeatedly postponed. The problem was exacerbated by the fact that ecclesiastical legislation was frequently introduced only towards the end of a parliamentary session, when it had to jostle for space with measures which the government hoped to pass before the session expired. By an unhappy coincidence, the instances already mentioned of political instability injuring discipline bills' prospects occurred on the only two occasions in the 1830s on which measures were introduced before mid-June; in 1845 Blomfield did not secure a first reading until 22 July. Late introduction had other drawbacks. Should a measure be amended to a significant degree, sponsors faced a stark choice between accepting the alterations or losing the bill completely. Thus the expiry of the 1836 bill was closely linked to the reluctance of Lord Chancellor Cottenham to accept or contest amendments to the measure he had jointly promoted.[16] We have already seen how amendments killed off the bill of 1839. The comparatively smooth passage of the 1840 bill is partly explained by the fact that the difficulties encountered in parliament by the 1838 and 1839 measures had encouraged the most extensive consultation procedure and active compromise yet seen before legislation was introduced.[17]

Such circumstances made the degree to which a measure secured government backing a crucial factor in determining its prospects. Leading churchmen had higher expectations of Conservative than whig administrations. After the bishops had agreed in 1845 that the act of 1840 needed reworking, Bishop Blomfield of London introduced new measures annually in the later 1840s without significant support from the whig government, one reason why bills introduced in some cases as early as mid-February on only one occasion (in 1847) progressed as far as a committee stage. The advent of a Conservative government under Lord Derby in 1852 encouraged the bishops,[18] who asked convocation to consider a prospective measure, but before they were ready to proceed the ministry had fallen and had been replaced by the Aberdeen coalition. When the second Derby administration took office in February 1858, Bishop Wilberforce put out feelers only to be told that there was no prospect of the government sponsoring a measure: Derby offered sympathy, but insisted that any bill should emanate from the bench of bishops.[19] Given their prior experience the bishops decided not to attempt to secure legislation without government support.[20] Prospects deteriorated further with the accession

---

[16] See Hansard, *Parl. Debs.*, 3rd ser., XXXV, 7; XLIV, 628–9.

[17] See Burns, *Diocesan Revival*, pp. 167–73.

[18] See Bodl., Wilberforce papers, MS Wilb. d 35, f. 114: W. E. Gladstone to S. Wilberforce, 3 Mar. 1852; also the letter from Wilberforce to Blomfield cited in A. R. Ashwell and R. G. Wilberforce, *The Life of the Right Revd. Samuel Wilberforce D.D., Lord Bishop of Oxford and Afterwards of Winchester* (3 vols., 1880–2), II, 136 n.

[19] Bodl., Wilberforce papers, MS Wilb. c. 5, ff. 221–2: Derby to Wilberforce, 2 and 9 Mar. 1858.

[20] The bishops' discussion of clergy discipline bills in these years can be traced in Bodl., Wilberforce papers, MS Wilb. e. 13, the minutes of private meetings of the bishops.

of Palmerston's ministry the following year, and no further episcopal measure appeared until the late 1860s. Yet whig governments were not necessarily antithetical to clergy-discipline measures: the bills introduced in 1836, 1838, 1839 and 1840 were all introduced by Lord Chancellor Cottenham, and in 1856 it was Lord Chancellor Cranworth who piloted a bill introduced promisingly early in a session on 14 March. This raises the important matter of the extent to which the effort to secure clergy-discipline legislation in collaboration with such ministries itself shaped the character of the bills concerned, a question to which we will later return.

3

Before doing so, however, it is worth raising the issue of whether the changing composition of the house of commons after 1832 itself was a significant factor in the failure of clergy-discipline legislation. In fact of the bills under consideration, all of which originated in the Lords, only the government-backed initiatives of 1839 and 1840 ever reached the Commons. Moreover in the former case, after the first and second readings had passed without debate, Lord John Russell made it clear in moving the bill's committee stage that there was no intention of proceeding to legislation.[21] It was only in 1840 that the Commons discussed a bill which had a prospect of making it to the statute book.

The debates and divisions which occurred on this occasion are, however, at least suggestive of the manner in which the post-1832 Commons handled legislation concerned solely with the internal affairs of the Church, and their evidence can be supplemented by that of other Commons debates on bills with no obvious ramifications for Roman catholic or dissenting interests, such as the Pluralities Act of 1838, and the Ecclesiastical Commissioners Act of 1850.[22] These bills were all discussed in a house of commons in which Roman catholic and dissenting M.P.s constituted a significant minority of members, and in which all M.P.s had to be increasingly conscious of the religious opinions of their constituents. Although Roman catholic M.P.s and some protestant dissenters were subject to oaths abjuring any intention of damaging the interests of the established Church,[23] as indicated earlier many churchmen feared that the new constitutional arrangements in place after 1832 would allow the religious minorities to exploit their new position to interfere with the Church.

It is apparent from the division lists on these measures that neither Roman catholic nor nonconformist members felt precluded from participation in the parliamentary consideration of legislation concerning the internal affairs of the Church of England. The 94 M.P.s involved in the two Commons divisions on the Church Discipline Bill in

[21] Hansard, *Parl. Debs.*, 3rd ser., L, 262.

[22] The Pluralities Act of 1838 (1–2 Vict., c. 106) was a clergy-discipline measure which placed strict restrictions on the holding of livings in plurality and non-residence, as well as regulating clerical participation in trade and farming. The Ecclesiastical Commissioners Act of 1850 (13–14 Vict., c. 94) altered the terms on which the commission could take over and manage the endowments of canonries, established an estates committee, and merged the hitherto distinct 'episcopal' and 'common' funds of the commissioners.

[23] See the test rolls for both the Lord and Commons preserved in the H.L.R.O.

1840 included four Roman catholics (all Irish repealers) and up to four English dissenters;[24] some eight dissenters and ten Roman catholics (including some representing English constituencies) had participated in at least one division on substantial issues concerning the Pluralities Bill two years before.[25] Given that just over 40 Roman catholic M.P.s signed the test rolls during the 1837–41 parliament, this was a reasonable showing in divisions at most involving some 150 members, while the nonconformists were disproportionately well-represented. A decade later, a much better attended division on the Ecclesiastical Commissioners Bill similarly suggests that nonconformist M.P.s were more inclined to intervene in the affairs of the established Church than their Roman catholic counterparts. While only some six of 45 Roman catholic members then sitting voted, more than half of the nonconformists identified did so.[26]

While non-anglicans voted, however, they did not speak. That this reflected more than the fact that only a small proportion of members ever did, and rather indicates some sense of impropriety attached to such interventions, is suggested by the care taken by leading anticlerical speakers to establish that they were indeed members of the established Church. Thus in 1838 Joseph Hume, moving a motion to prohibit all pluralities, spoke of his aim as that of 'those who consider themselves sincere friends of the Church, and who, though they might be friends of an establishment, were not friends of the establishment as now maintained'. Among the results he anticipated from his motion, he informed the Commons, was the diminution of dissent.[27] In the debates on the Ecclesiastical Commissioners Bill, Benjamin Hall carefully presented himself as the friend of the working anglican clergy and stressed his anglican credentials.[28] It may also be suggestive that when in later years nonconformists did intervene in discussion of the Public Worship Regulation Bill, W. E. Forster confessed that 'speaking generally, it was a question on which, perhaps, he had no right to trouble them by giving any opinion', but pointed out that he at least attended the services of the established Church. The voluntarist Henry Richard was more aggressive, yet still took his stand on the fact

[24] The Roman catholics D. Callaghan, A. H. Lynch, W. Roche and R. L. Sheil; the nonconformists E. Baines, J. Brotherton, B. Smith (?) and J. A. Yates (?). For the divisions, see *C.J.*, XCV, 586, 599. Determining the number and names of nonconformist and Roman catholic M.P.s and peers is difficult in the absence of definitive published lists, and the findings presented here must therefore be treated with caution pending the completion of the relevant volumes of the History of Parliament. In the case of Roman catholics I have made use of the test rolls for the Commons and Lords preserved in the H.L.R.O., which also identify quakers and moravians. For other English nonconformists I have referred to the discussions of parliamentary representation in M. Watts, *The Dissenters. Volume 2: The Expansion of Evangelical Nonconformity* (Oxford, 1995), *passim*; R. G. Cowherd, *The Politics of English Dissent* (1959), p. 215; D. W. Bebbington, 'Baptist MPs in the Nineteenth Century', *Baptist Quarterly*, XXIX (1981). G. F. Muntz, who according to Cowherd's list would add another to the list of voting nonconformists, was in fact an anglican.

[25] Dissenters: E. Baines, J. Brotherton, J. Fielden, C. Hindley, M. Philips, G. R. Philips, G. W. Wood, J. A. Yates (?). Roman catholics: R. Archbold, G. S. Barry, H. Bridgeman, H. Chester, J. O'Connell, R. M. O'Ferrall, W. Roche, W. M. Stanley, J. H. Talbot, the earl of Surrey. For the divisions, Hansard, *Parl. Debs.*, 3rd ser., XLII, 920–5, 931–2, 934–5, 955–62.

[26] *Commons Divisions, 1850*, pp. 392–4, no. 220. Roman catholics: R. M. Bellew, M. J. Blake, Lord Edward Howard, Viscount Mahon, G. H. Moore, R. L. Sheil. Nonconformists: M. T. Baines, J. Bright, J. Brotherton, C. Cowan, W. G. Craig, H. Drummond, W. J. Fox, J. Heald, J. Heywood, J. Kershaw, J. G. Marshall, J. Pilkington, W. Scholefield, J. B. Smith, T. Thornely, J. P. Westhead, J. Wilson.

[27] Hansard, *Parl. Debs.*, 3rd. ser., XLII, 906, 910.

[28] *Ibid.*, CXII, 1088, 1091.

that as far as the law was concerned he was still defined as a member of the Church, and thus entitled to voice his opinions.[29]

If all this suggests that measures of primarily internal Church reform had little to fear from organized phalanxes of non-anglicans operating in the reformed house, this implication is confirmed by voting patterns. Non-anglicans were never present in sufficient numbers to sway the outcome of debates, and nor were they in any case always inclined to vote *en bloc*, any more indeed than the political parties. In their worst defeats, the Church party might be reduced to a rump of just over a dozen conservatives perhaps led by Inglis or Gladstone.[30] But in more even divisions Liberals and Conservatives were to be found on both sides, and especially where an amendment or motion carried an anticlerical tinge, catholics were likely to divide, with the English and those Irish with closer links to the whig leadership opposing it. The predominantly unitarian nonconformist M.P.s were more solidly anticlerical in their votes, although the two most assiduous opponents of the Church were Edward Baines and Joseph Brotherton, a congregationalist and a Bible Christian respectively.[31] By 1850, when the House divided on the clauses in the Ecclesiastical Commissioners Bill which would determine whether a separate fund would remain for endowing bishoprics, however, the addition of methodist M.P.s had broken the nonconformist line: J.P. Westhead voted for the preservation of an episcopal fund, although his fellow methodist James Heald voted against.[32] In fact even during the 1830s nonconformists would not necessarily oppose measures favouring those aspects of the internal organization of the Church of England to which they, as anti-episcopalian nonconformists, most objected: thus in 1838, the majority of 69 to five which carried the third reading of the bill to preserve the see (and thus the bishop) of Sodor and Man from merger with Carlisle under the leadership of Lord John Russell included both Baines and Brotherton.[33]

If the Church's internal business was therefore unlikely to suffer directly from the presence of dissenters and Roman catholics in the Commons, it was still the case that bishops remained nervous of the reception their measures would receive there. The hard-core Church party in the Commons was matched by a hard-core opposing lobby. This could rally around the pre-1832 'old corruption' critique of the Church as a platform for amendments and intervention on matters concerned with clergy discipline. The Commons opposition to the Church Discipline Bill of 1840 was led by the radical reformer Henry Warburton who, along with the veteran Joseph Hume and Benjamin Hall, sought tougher restrictions on clerical behaviour than the episcopate thought practical and resisted provisions calculated to increase 'episcopal tyranny' over the 'working clergy'. In the only significant amendment to the 1840 bill carried in the Commons, an episcopal veto over prosecutions of the clergy was struck out.[34] It is clear that such sentiments, if in a diluted form, were gaining ground, not least as the 'old corruption' critique of the episcopate metamorphosed

---

[29] *Ibid.*, CCXXI, 38–9, 56.

[30] See, e.g., one of the divisions on the Pluralities Bill: *ibid.*, XLII, 931–2.

[31] Brotherton was a member of the Bible Christians of Manchester, who had broken away from the Swedenborgians and are not to be confused with the Methodist Bible Christians of the south-west. I owe this information to Dr Clyde Binfield.

[32] See *Commons Divisions, 1850*, pp. 392–3.

[33] See Machin, *Politics and the Churches*, p. 64; Hansard, *Parl. Debs.*, 3rd ser., XLIII, 783–4.

[34] Compare *Parl. Papers, 1840*, I (479), 299, with *ibid.*, (567), 315.

into an ostensibly more theological and partisan position. For many laymen, the rise of the Oxford movement encouraged an assumption that the defence of episcopal authority was a reliable indication of unacceptably catholic conceptions of Church hierarchy. In 1840, although they scored a significant success in removing the episcopal veto, the opponents of the Church Discipline Bill could only muster a few supporters to oppose a bill which promised a significant increase in episcopal power. By the late 1850s, however, bishops were being warned by Roundell Palmer that 'the majority would take care that no bill favourable to episcopal authority became law. I fear that it would be really mangled before it entered the House of Lords.'[35] A key factor encouraging the bishops' growing caution was probably their reading of the significance of the debates on the Ecclesiastical Commissioners Bill of 1850.[36] The Lords, led by the bishops, had rejected the government's proposal to merge the ecclesiastical commission's episcopal and common funds, which – since the episcopal fund had represented a resource reserved for revamping the episcopate as opposed to increasing parochial provision and endowment – seemed calculated to frustrate plans for additional sees agreed in 1847. The Commons reinstated the merger after several speakers had stressed that the interests of the 'working clergy' should always receive priority over those of bishops, and a number of interventions describing in graphic and highly misleading detail the financial affairs of named leading prelates. On its return to the Lords, the bishops could no longer rally sufficient numbers to prevent the amalgamation, and the episcopal fund was lost.

In comparison, as this example illustrates, the Lords remained a comparatively friendly environment for Church-sponsored reform legislation. The presence of the episcopal bench on the face of it provided the basis for a reliable Church party; Roman catholic peers were few in number and less in evidence in divisions than their Commons counterparts,[37] while nonconformity was in practice represented in the religious affiliations of some Scottish peers. For clergy-discipline bills the Lords offered the additional advantage of legal expertise. Debates on clergy discipline were in fact dominated by the episcopate, the lord chancellor and peers with legal experience (not least ex-lord chancellors), occasionally augmented by others such as Harrowby with a particular interest in Church affairs. On the two occasions when discipline bills were dispatched to select committees, in 1839 and 1847, these contained an episcopal majority, with the remainder being made up of lawyers and others with keen Church interests and in some cases close episcopal kinsmen, such as William Courtenay, earl of Devon, son of a bishop and an ecclesiastical commissioner, and Thomas Brand, Lord Dacre.[38] These

---

[35] Bodl., Wilberforce papers, MS Wilb. c. 12, f. 97: R. Palmer to S. Wilberforce, 8 Apr. 1858.

[36] For these debates, see Hansard, *Parl. Debs.*, 3rd. ser., CX–CXII, *passim*.

[37] The Lords test rolls for this period (101–10), preserved in the H.L.R.O., contain the signatures of between six and 17 Roman catholic peers.

[38] The membership of the select committees was as follows. In 1839 Bishops Allen, Bethell, Blomfield, Butler, Denison, Howley, Kaye, Longley, Maltby, Monk, Murray, Musgrave, Phillpotts, Stanley, C. R. and J. B. Sumner, Vernon Harcourt (with Copleston added at a later date); lay members Ashburton, Bexley, Brougham, Dacre, Dartmouth, Devon, Ellenborough, Kenyon, Langdale, Lansdowne, Lyndhurst, Wellington, Wrottesley (with Bute added at a later date). In 1847 Bishops Bethell, Blomfield, Denison, Lonsdale, Pepys, Phillpotts, Short, Stanley, C. R. and J. B. Sumner, Thirlwall, Wilberforce (with Whately added at a later date); lay members Brougham, Campbell, Cottenham, Dacre, Devon, Langdale, Lansdowne, Lyndhurst, Monteagle, earl of Suffolk and Berkshire (with Denman added at a later date). *L.J.*, LXXI, 369–70, 388; LXXIX, 280, 296.

conditions make it all the more necessary to explain why so many measures failed to complete their passage through the Lords.

4

This consideration takes us back to the question of the extent to which clergy-discipline measures were themselves shaped by the fact that they needed to be presented in parliament, and whether this in turn helped determine the bills' failure and indeed the parliamentary and subsequent fortunes of the Church Discipline Act of 1840.

As we have seen, perhaps the two most significant aspects of the parliamentary context confronting those seeking improved clergy discipline in the 1830s were the need for government backing, perforce from a whig administration, and the powerful legal constituency in the Lords, often common lawyers rather than members of the civilian *élite* of Doctors Commons. The episcopate were also conscious that a workable and effective discipline system once enacted would in practice require the acquiescence of the chief constituency whose interests it would affect, the parochial clergy. By the late 1830s the episcopate and Church reformers had found by experience in the Diocesan Revival that the best way to present reform to this latter constituency was to offer it clothed in historical legitimation. The most effective rhetoric situated Church reforms in an anglican tradition which was not partisan in its appeal to particular periods of ecclesiastical history and which spoke to the widespread clerical desire for unity by directing it to the historic institutions of the Church rather than theological affinities.[39] In contrast, the most effective rhetoric deployed by those seeking Church reform in parliament tended to be the pragmatic utilitarianism best encapsulated in Blomfield's speeches in the debates on the ecclesiastical commission, reflecting his belief that the true beauty of the Church lay in its 'holy usefulness'.[40] A successful clergy-discipline measure, perhaps requiring clerical acceptance to a greater extent than other Church reforms, would therefore need to strike a balance between the two approaches.

In its emphasis on the immediate personal authority of the bishop, the aim of accelerating litigation and introducing oral evidence, the 1832 royal commission report had indeed managed to strike such a balance between the concerns of professional lawyers and clergy. It may not be insignificant, however, that the legal constituent of the commission had been drawn from tory ranks, for in 1836 the whig lord chancellor, Cottenham, secured the cooperation of the archbishop of Canterbury in a rather different approach. The new bill featured provision for the case to be heard by a clerical jury rather than by a bishop and assessor alone.[41] That this was in no small respect an attempt to bring the system more into line with a whig understanding of the constitution is apparent from Cottenham's language in introducing the change: bishops could not sit alone for 'it was not congenial with the other establishments of the country to vest such

[39] See A. Burns, ' "Standing in the Old Ways": Historical Legitimation of Church Reform in the Church of England, *c.*1825–65', in *The Church Retrospective*, ed. R. N. Swanson (Studies in Church History, XXXIII, 1997), pp. 407–22; Burns, *Diocesan Revival*, esp. ch. 10.
[40] A phrase coined in C. J. Blomfield, *A Charge Delivered to the Clergy of the Diocese of London* (1834), pp. 16–17.
[41] *Lords Sessional Papers*, 1836, II (162), 231–42.

power and influence in the hands of an individual'.[42] It is clear that this proposal, together with other novelties designed to expedite proceedings, was unacceptable to many bishops, and if Howley's later comments are to be trusted, his own commitment to the bill was severely shaken by a mass clerical petition objecting to juries as incompatible with the constitution of the Church.[43] The amendments that resulted, combined with the late date and Cottenham's own disillusion with the clerical response, ensured that the initiative petered out. That which appeared two years later similarly reflected Cottenham's politics, and greatly surprised many of those involved in the royal commission by abandoning its proposals altogether in favour of a system of centralization, with the provincial court of arches hearing all cases subject to an appeal to the judicial committee of the privy council. Its own judges would sentence and suspend clergy; the bishop was sidelined. This time debate was much fiercer, as it was when a similar bill, slightly modified in an attempt to preempt opposition, was introduced the following year.[44] Phillpotts, in one of his finest parliamentary speeches, fatally holed the measure, which he denounced as 'the greatest blow that was ever struck against the Church of England as a church'.[45] The case against it was neatly summarized in a pamphlet whose title gestured unconvincingly towards objectivity: *The 'Church Discipline Bill' Anti-Episcopal, Unprofessional, Unconstitutional, Insulting, Inefficient, Impolitic. The Church's Discipline Episcopal, Professional, Seemly, Efficient, Desirable. The Premises Investigated, Established, Exhibited, for the Reader to Draw his Own Conclusion.*[46] Phillpotts sought to show that it undermined episcopal authority, the cornerstone of the Church, and that this overruled other considerations; as the *British Critic* put it, the danger was 'of taking too practical a view of the subject'.[47] But even from a practical view, the return of the court of arches with its unsatisfactory procedure was of no interest to Brougham, aghast to see his earlier measure tossed aside.[48] The 1838 bill was abandoned at the end of the only debate without a vote. In 1839, it weathered a bombardment of clerical petitions [49] and hostile amendments which together with the ministerial crisis ensured that it was stillborn in the Commons. A similar scenario was to be enacted when a later whig government sponsored a discipline measure in 1856, again proposing centralization in order to secure legal expertise and seeming to undermine episcopal authority by authorizing diocesan chancellors to hear non-doctrinal cases without the bishop; questions of fact would be submitted to a lay jury. This time a whole phalanx of bishops rose in protest at the measure when it was introduced in the Lords (the last surviving commissioner, Christopher Bethell, describing it as a monstrous abortion), undoubtedly provoked by the underlying anticlericalism which Lord Chancellor Cranworth carelessly allowed to colour his speech. When Lord Derby, who had originally intended to support the measure, stated that he could no longer do so, the writing was on the

---

[42] Hansard, *Parl. Debs.*, 3rd. ser., XXXIV, 999.
[43] *Ibid.*, XLIV, 616.
[44] *Lords Sessional Papers*, 1837–8, II, 373–8; *ibid.*, 1839, II, 197–206.
[45] Hansard, *Parl. Debs.*, 3rd ser., XLIV, 603.
[46] F. R. A. Glover, *The 'Church Discipline Bill'* (1839).
[47] *British Critic*, XXV (1839), 448.
[48] Hansard, *Parl. Debs.*, 3rd ser., XLIV, 618.
[49] See *L.J.*, LXXI, 341, 369–70, 380, 387–8, 395, 402, 413, 422, 428, 435, 445, 452, 464, 478, 512, 519, 528, 544, 557; *C.J.*, XCIV, 295, 306, 322, 488, 523.

wall, and a motion that the bill be read in six months time was carried against the lord chancellor by a majority of 41 to 33, all the English bishops voting against.[50]

Thus whig insistence that measures broadly match with their constitutional preferences was indeed one factor in the failure to find a satisfactory basis for discipline legislation. The successful act of 1840, which might appear at first to belie this observation, was more than a minor modification of Cottenham's centralizing scheme of the year before: it was rather a skilful if nevertheless shotgun marriage between Cottenham's plans and an alternative draft prepared by Phillpotts which paid much more attention to episcopal authority and which provided new mechanisms to assist the bishop in investigating delinquency in his diocese. Indeed the main survival from the lord chancellor's scheme was the preservation of an opportunity for diocesans to send cases to the court of arches in the first instance.[51] Cottenham himself was no doubt driven to accept modifications to his scheme in the light of the sustained opposition it had provoked, and thus this measure achieved the vital combination of government backing and acceptability to clerical reformers concerned that measures should be compatible with diocesan structures.

These conflicts of interest might suggest that the parliamentary context was the major obstacle facing the Church leadership in their ambition of establishing a workable model of Church discipline, but this would be an oversimplification. Equally important were divisions within the Church. The episcopate itself, although agreed on the need for reform, was divided as to the shape it should take. In 1836 and 1838–9 Phillpotts was taking on not only Cottenham, but also Archbishop Howley and Bishop Blomfield, both of whom claimed that Phillpotts and other bishops who found fault on ecclesiological grounds were possibly not without a case, but one which the paramount necessity of overhauling clergy discipline overruled. In 1856, although all the English bishops opposed the government measure, the Irish bishops supported it, in part because they saw in the bill's provisions a means of strengthening their ties with the English Church. There were desperate but unsuccessful attempts to resolve the differences between English and Irish in private meetings of bishops, but to no avail. After one such meeting Phillpotts moaned to Wilberforce: 'will it be necessary to let in the Irishmen? After their last performance I can hardly stomach it.'[52] Phillpotts, however, was on weak grounds when it came to episcopal meetings. One of the most intriguing aspects of the 1838 parliamentary debate is the extent to which Howley was clearly wrong-footed by Phillpotts's intervention, poised as he was to claim the backing of the bench on the basis of preliminary episcopal meetings. And perhaps Phillpotts protested too much in the excuses he offered to explain why his objections had not been stated earlier: turning up late, unavoidably absent from meetings, being unaware of the intention of legislating and so having gone down into the country, only to discover what was afoot and to make a mad dash back to London to take part in the debate.[53] It is not

[50] For the bill, see *Lords Sessional Papers*, 1856, III, 337–70; for the debate, Hansard, *Parl. Debs.*, 3rd ser., CXLI, 1251–1324.

[51] For a discussion of the genesis of the 1840 act, see Burns, *Diocesan Revival*, pp. 167–73.

[52] For discussions, see Bodl., Wilberforce papers, MS Wilb. e. 13: minutes for 26 Apr., 9 and 27 May, 27 June 1856; *A Letter to the Lord Bishop of Exeter from the Lord Bishop of Armagh on the Church Discipline Bill* (1856); Bodl., MS Wilb. c. 5, f. 184: Phillpotts to Wilberforce, 16 Aug. 1856.

[53] Hansard, *Parl. Debs.*, 3rd ser., XLIV, 613.

impossible that Phillpotts had calculated that his rhetorical skills offered him a better prospect of seeing off an unsatisfactory measure within the parliamentary arena than in a private meeting of bishops where he might be overruled or outnumbered, and had consequently kept his powder dry. Parliament also offered him the prospect of making more of the clerical support he could obtain in national petitions than would have been possible in a private meeting of diocesans. Thus for some bishops, and not necessarily those whom one would have expected to favour it, a parliamentary context for the discussion of Church affairs could sometimes be a positive advantage.

After this experience, the English bishops were never again to allow their differences on the topic such public expression. By the mid-1840s, however, the lower clergy began to adopt an agenda which could conflict with that of the bishops. As party tensions increased, and their involvement in the Diocesan Revival gave clergy increased experience of participatory diocesan institutions, opposition to clerical juries gave way to a demand for a role for lower clergy in clergy discipline. By the late 1840s the bishops' own proposals acknowledged this changing mood by embracing clerical juries for non-doctrinal cases – initially selected by the bishop, later chosen from a panel elected by the parochial clergy. But by then whig and legal interests formerly favourable to clerical juries were unenthusiastic, as anticlerical sentiments were fanned by the Oxford movement's clericalism, and this helps explain the absence of significant government support for the episcopal bills of the late 1840s. A further disincentive to any government contemplating lending backing to episcopal measures came with the revival of convocation. Bishops felt obliged to consult the lower House in order to demonstrate that they had clerical support, but too often this simply served to expose the wide differences between Church parties now being generated over the matter of the final court of appeal, making it almost impossible to design a measure acceptable to the full spectrum of clerical opinion.[54]

Something of a similar process occurred with anglican laity. If never as anticlerical in general as its most outspoken ostensible representatives in parliament, it would be misleading to suggest that the opposition to episcopal authority which helped dissuade bishops from attempting legislation towards the end of the period was simply a parliamentary phenomenon. As with the lower clergy, anglican laity were becoming increasingly involved in formal Church organizations by the 1850s and 1860s, which also saw the rise of the Church Institution and other lay pressure groups. The bishops found themselves forced to consider including a lay element in any jury when they considered a possible parliamentary initiative in 1858, and by 1874 Tait in his original bill would contemplate a panel half of whom would be laymen elected by churchwardens.[55] Such a demand was already being voiced by evangelicals 20 years before, fearing that clerical panels might be too soft on Romanizers. As the issue of ritual gained prominence such concerns only deepened.

5

What conclusions follow from this consideration of parliamentary initiatives to reform clergy discipline? First, it is apparent that the necessity to pursue reform in a

---

54 See Burns, *Diocesan Revival*, pp. 175–81 for further discussion of these points.
55 See Marsh, *Victorian Church in Decline*, p. 169.

parliamentary context did indeed have serious disadvantages: bills shipwrecked through unrelated parliamentary circumstances, the need to accommodate whig constitutional preferences difficult to reconcile with the characteristics of reform required to gain clerical support or reassure the episcopate, and at times a fear of the mutilation of any measure in the Commons. Indeed the parliamentary context was partly responsible for the fact that the 1840 act was something of a mishmash which proved to be poorly drafted and inconsistent when applied in practice, for it was a quickly arranged compromise between two contrasting models of reform. Even the Commons' removal of the episcopal veto in a burst of anticlerical zeal was not without serious consequences.

On the other hand, even before the changing nature of Church disciplinary problems produced a different type of defendant, divisions within the Church's leadership, sometimes exposed only within parliament, had an equally important role in frustrating reform. Moreover, if the attitudes of lay M.P.s were part of the problem with the parliamentary context, any alternative venue for decisions about Church government which would have secured sufficient legitimacy to function effectively by the late 1860s would of necessity have had to incorporate a lay element itself, as was the case with the diocesan conferences then being founded.[56] It was only from a position positing a narrow clerical conception of the Church, less widespread among even high churchmen than subsequent literature would suggest, that this consideration could be ignored.

Finally, the difficulties experienced by reformers over the previous 40 years provide an important backdrop for understanding some striking aspects of the passage of the Public Worship Regulation Act. For in ultimately acquiescing in the measure as finally passed, the majority of the episcopate abandoned the very principles of diocesan and provincial integrity on which they had set such store in the 1830s and 1850s and which had still figured prominently in their original proposals of 1874.[57] Here, perhaps, we see that the parliamentary context was a decisive factor. We have noted, and the episcopate had learnt, the importance of government backing, effectively on offer once Lord Cairns's objections to the original scheme had been met; the bishops were conscious of the long history of failed legislation preceding the act and sensed that prospects had tended to become less rather than more favourable; and perhaps decisive was the fear that a less sympathetic measure might be brewing in the Commons should the current one fail. Roundell Palmer's warning might still have been ringing in some of the older ears.

---

[56] For the foundation of diocesan conferences, see Burns, *Diocesan Revival*, ch. 9.

[57] The act established a single tribunal presided over by a professional lawyer in place of the diocesan tribunals proposed in Tait's original bill. On the other hand, an episcopal rebellion against Tait and the government this time managed to reinstate an episcopal veto struck out in the Commons.

Disraeli, the Conservatives and the National Church, 1837–1881*

ALLEN WARREN

Mid-nineteenth century political historians have become used to seeing the connexions between religion and politics within the emerging Liberal party. Among students of mid Victorian conservatism, on the other hand, the focus is still very much upon personal, parliamentary or organizational manoeuvring in the years after 1846. This is surprising, since a significant number of front-bench Conservatives – Walpole, Cairns, Gathorne-Hardy, Cranborne, Carnarvon to name merely the best known – were active churchmen with highly developed opinions and prejudices on ecclesiastical policy.[1]

This historiographical bias is explicable in a number of ways. The lack of any modern biography of the 14th earl of Derby remains a major gap, given his stern resistance to any serious alteration in the constitutional position of the Church of England. Secondly, historians still know relatively little about the role of Church questions in the electoral politics of the period. In particular, the general elections of 1865 and 1874, in each of which the Conservatives had high hopes, still await systematic treatment. Thirdly, historians have tended to accept unquestioningly that a curious political and ecclesiastical compromise would emerge between 1865 and 1880, whereby a modified established Church, respectful of most of the sensitivities of other denominations and

* Versions of this paper have been delivered at the staff-graduate seminar at the University of York, the Parliamentary History Conference on 'Parliament and the Church', July 1998, and at the modern church history seminar at the Institute of Historical Research, November 1998. The author would like to thank Dr John Wolffe and Dr Arthur Burns, in particular, for their comments. He would also like to thank the owners or custodians of the following manuscript collections: Bodleian Library, Oxford (Beaconsfield MSS, Wilberforce MSS), Christ Church, Oxford (Phillimore MSS), British Library (Gladstone MSS, Disraeli MSS, Carnarvon MSS), Lambeth Palace Library (Tait MSS, Longley MSS), Hatfield House, Herts. (Salisbury MSS), Liverpool City Record Office (Derby MSS), Gloucestershire County Record Office, Gloucester (Sotheron Estcourt MSS), Suffolk County Record Office (Cranbrook MSS), Somerset County Record Office, Taunton (Jolliffe MSS).

[1] For background, John Vincent, *The Formation of the Liberal Party, 1857–1868* (1966); J. P. Parry, *Democracy and Religion. Gladstone and the Liberal Party, 1867–1875* (Cambridge, 1986); idem, *The Rise and Fall of Liberal Government in Victorian Britain* (1993); E.D. Steele, *Palmerston and Liberalism, 1855–65* (Cambridge, 1991); D.W. Bebbington, *The Nonconformist Conscience. Chapel and Politics, 1870–1914* (1982); G.I.T. Machin, *Politics and the Churches in Great Britain 1832–1868* (Oxford, 1977); *Politics and the Churches in Great Britain, 1869–1921* (Oxford, 1987); Eugenio F. Biagini, *Liberalism, Retrenchment and Reform. Popular Liberalism in the Age of Gladstone, 1860–1880* (Cambridge, 1992); Robert Blake, *The Conservative Party from Peel to Thatcher* (1985); Bruce Coleman, *Conservatism and the Conservative Party in the Nineteenth Century* (1988); Robert Stewart, *The Foundation of the Conservative Party, 1830–1867* (1978); Angus Hawkins, *Parliament, Party and the Art of Politics in Britain, 1855–59* (1987).

faiths, would be allowed to remain with its constitutional powers, its wealth and social and educational role largely intact.

Finally, and the focus of this article, there is the figure of Disraeli, the historiography of whose career remains fixed in the opportunistic and pragmatic interpretative schema established by Lord Blake in 1966. Church questions play only a small part in that study. Even so, it can be argued that the Church of England played a major part in Disraeli's political thinking throughout the 1860s, only becoming largely subordinated to other doctrinal strategems after the electoral defeat in 1868. Earlier historians recognised this; Buckle, for instance, devoted a whole chapter in his official life to Disraeli and the Church, 1860–5. This paper examines Disraeli's relations with the Church from the beginning of his parliamentary career until his death. It concentrates on the 1860s and tries to redirect our understanding away from a narrow concentration on the politics of parliamentary reform and its consequences. It suggests that two models of the relationship between Church and politics were being fought over during the decade. In the Gladstonian version, a reformed establishment would bring anglicanism and dissent together, creating a true unity of nations in the ecclesiastical sphere, and integrating and enthusing men from both religious traditions within the Liberal party. Alternatively, Disraeli offered a political and constitutional framework which linked the established Church to the historic identity of the English nation. Associated with this was the claim that only an established Church could guarantee the state's moral and spiritual purposes, acting thereby as an institutional bulwark against a denominational struggle to control the state for sectarian ends, and also providing a shield against the corrosive atheism of German theological scholarship, Enlightenment secularism, and evolutionary science.[2]

Disraeli's Church thinking can be divided into four main phases. First are his early years in politics, his contacts with Young England and his later distancing himself from their medievalism to espouse a vigorous protestantism in attacking Peel and his disciples. Second is the period from the late 1840s, during which Disraeli tried to find some broader political basis for the protectionists. Particularly after the papal aggression in late 1850, this aimed at combining protestant enthusiasm with a softness towards Irish catholics, a policy which achieved little in the short term. Third, throughout much of the 1860s, was the attempt to create a distinctly Conservative ecclesiastical politics, through which the reforming energies of the Church at the parochial and diocesan level would

[2] For ecclesiastical background, Owen Chadwick, *The Victorian Church* (2 vols., 1966–70); E.R. Norman, *Church and Society in England, 1770–1970* (Oxford, 1976); *idem, The Catholic Church in the Age of Rebellion, 1859–1873* (1965); D. Bowen, *The Idea of the Victorian Church. A Study of the Church of England, 1833–1889* (Montreal, 1968); John Wolffe, *The Protestant Crusade in Great Britain, 1829–1860* (Oxford, 1991); Olive Brose, *Church and Parliament. The Reshaping of the Church of England, 1828–1860* (1959); M.A. Crowther, *The Church Embattled. Religious Controversy in Mid-Victorian England* (Newton Abbot, 1970); K.A. Thompson, *Bureaucracy and Church Reform. The Organisational Response of the Church of England to Social Change, 1800–1965* (Oxford, 1970); Frances Knight, *The Nineteenth-Century Church and English Society* (Cambridge, 1995); J.P.B. Kenyon, 'High Churchmen and Politics, 1845–1865', University of Toronto Ph.D., 1967 (an important and underconsulted study). For studies of Disraeli, Robert Blake, *Disraeli* (1966); Paul Smith, *Disraeli. A Brief Life* (1996); John Vincent, *Disraeli* (1990); Ian Machin, *Disraeli* (1995); Jane Ridley, *The Young Disraeli, 1804–1846* (1995); William Flavelle Monypenny and George Earle Buckle, *The Life of Benjamin Disraeli, First Earl of Beaconsfield* (new and revd. edn. in 2 vols., 1929); *Disraeli, Derby and the Conservative Party. Journals and Memoirs of Edward Henry, Lord Stanley, 1849–69*, ed. John Vincent (Hassocks, Sussex, 1978) [subsequently referred to as *Stanley Journal*].

be harnessed to the party's electoral advantage. The overwhelming defeat of 1868 showed that such a doctrinal politics could not be sustained. The final phase can be seen more as a epilogue than as a culmination to Disraeli's career, in which his second government preserved an arms' length relationship with the Church, modestly defending its interests, but no longer seeing it as fundamental to the future progress of the party or the nation.

Disraeli and the Church, 1837–45

Disraeli's early life and political career was little touched by contemporary ecclesiastical or religious excitement. Born into a Jewish family which formally converted to anglicanism in 1817, his upbringing was in an urbane and sceptical literary atmosphere, something confirmed by his private schooling and non-attendance at Oxford or Cambridge. His father's occupation of a gentleman's country house at Bradenham in 1829 seems to have made little difference (despite the change in life style, including the right to present to the local living), and Disraeli's early letters and novels contain little of ecclesiastical interest. On a visit to York Minster in 1825, Disraeli was impressed by its gothic majesty, and thought it superior to the cathedrals on the Rhine, but added no further reflections. Recent biographical studies have highlighted the importance of Disraeli's Jewishness, but this was an underground political stream at this point, only to surface in significant ways in the mid-1840s. Disraeli's opinions on the Church of England came almost certainly from the historical work of his father, whose studies of the reigns of James I and Charles I had the specific intention of rehabilitating the latter's reputation. These family interests found expression in Disraeli's *Vindication of the English Constitution* (1835), with its anti-whig interpretation based on a rereading of seventeenth century political and ecclesiastical history. In that essay Disraeli introduced two arguments that he was to use throughout his career – that the historic experience of the English showed that the existence of an established Church was not incompatible with the growth of religious liberty, and, secondly, that the history of the anglican Church was intimately and profoundly identified with the development of the nation, even if it had often been submerged beneath the waters of the whig Venetian oligarchy during the long century after 1688.[3]

Disraeli did not follow up his essay in conservative theory in the years that followed. His main concerns were political, literary, social and financial. Elected for Maidstone in 1837, his address and his early parliamentary speeches, notably that on the Charter in 1839, contain no reference to ecclesiastical reform or religious renewal, and it is clear

---

[3] For Disraeli's early life and writing, Monypenny and Buckle, *Disraeli*, I, 3–396; Blake, *Disraeli*, pp. 3–142; Ridley, *The Young Disraeli*, pp. 1–203; for his Jewishness, Paul Smith, 'Disraeli's Politics', *Transactions of the Royal Historical Society*, 5th ser., XXXVII (1987), 65–86; Benjamin Disraeli, *Vindication of the English Constitution in a Letter to a Noble and Learned Lord* (1835); for Isaac D'Israeli's historical writings, *An Inquiry into the Literary and Political Character of James I* (1816); idem, *Commentaries on the Life and Reign of Charles I* (1828–30) (a second edition of which was published by Disraeli in 1850); on York Minster, *Benjamin Disraeli Letters*, ed. J.A.W. Gunn, John Matthews, Donald Schurman and M.G. Wiebe (The Disraeli Project, Queens University at Kingston, 6 vols. so far, Toronto, 1982–97), I, 26 [subsequently referred to as *Letters*]: Disraeli to John Murray, 17 Sept. 1825.

that he moved little in the company of churchmen, clerical or lay. Similarly, the political novels of the 1840s and Disraeli's association with the Young England group contain little that is directly ecclesiastical. While *Coningsby* (1844) and *Sybil* (1845) might have a 'high Church' atmosphere, Disraeli did not share Lord John Manners' ecclesiological medievalism, or his desire to come closer to the Roman catholic church in both Great Britain and Ireland. In his speech on the acquisition of knowledge at the Manchester Athenaeum in October 1844, Disraeli made no reference to Christian or religious values, or to their role in underpinning state or voluntary education. Despite its religious theme, *Tancred* (1847) contains little reference to the Church of England as a historic national institution, only including an unflattering caricature of Bishop Blomfield of London as the ecclesiastical equivalent of 'arch-mediocrity'. As the editors of Disraeli's letters note, his political concerns at this time centred on the nature of the territorial constitution, the condition of England, and hostility to Peel, along with some rather inconsistent views about Ireland.[4]

Disraeli and Popular Protestantism, 1845–1860

Disraeli's prospects were dramatically changed by the protestant reaction to the proposed increase in the Maynooth grant in April 1845. Even so, and despite the enthusiasm of Irish protestants like the Rev. Tresham Gregg, and the energetic extremism of backbenchers like Inglis, Spooner and Newdegate, he needed to take care in positioning himself.[5]

In the first place, although many of the later leading Protectionists were protestant enthusiasts, they were not united ecclesiastically, and many found the doctrinairism of some backbenchers distasteful and impolitic. Stanley and Manners had both voted in favour of the increase in the Maynooth grant and had well developed, if differing, ecclesiological views. For Stanley, the most important issue was the maintenance of the constitutional settlement of 1828–30, while Manners wanted to preserve and develop the specifically anglo-catholic nature of the national Church. Disraeli trimmed as a result, writing rather disingenuously to Manners that the 'dreadful Tresham Gregg' had dedicated a 'furious Protestant volume' to him. Disraeli also found his position carefully scrutinized locally when he sought election for Buckinghamshire in 1847. Again, his loyalties seemed unclear. In his address, he simultaneously defended the continued existence of an established and endowed Church, political opposition to the increase in the Maynooth grant, and support for civil and religious equality for Roman catholics. Church/state relations had become part of established tradition with the state as the main beneficiary, and which 'for long series of years, happily secured to us the blessings alike of orthodoxy and religious freedom'. It was the argument of the *Vindication*

---

[4] *Letters*, II, 632: Disraeli to the freemen and electors of Maidstone, 8 July 1837; on the early novels, *Letters*, IV, intro., xxvii; on the Charter, Hansard, *Parl. Debs*, 3rd ser., XLIX, 246: 12 July 1839; at Manchester, *The Times*, 5 Oct. 1844, p. 5f; Benjamin Disraeli, *Tancred, or The New Crusade* (1847) (Bradenham Edition of the Tales and Novels of Benjamin Disraeli, 1st Earl of Beaconsfield, X, 1927).

[5] On the Maynooth grant, Hansard, *Parl. Debs*, 3rd ser., LXXIX, 555: 11 May 1845; *Letters*, IV, 1398: Disraeli to Tresham Gregg, 1 Apr. 1845; Bodl. (Beaconsfield MSS), Dep Hughenden, 129/3, f. 93: Tresham Gregg to Disraeli, 7 Apr. 1845.

repeated. On the other hand, election cards appeared in the constituency under his name with the caption 'Opponent of Popery' in rather bolder type than 'Friend of Agriculture', an emphasis he was forced to defend in a speech at Buckingham, and in letters to John Delane and the Rev. Daniel Baxter Langley, the local vicar of Olney.[6]

Secondly, Disraeli found himself uncomfortable because of his deeply held views on the rights of Jews to sit in parliament. These were feelings surprisingly shared by his leader, Lord George Bentinck, who also had no time for protestant zealots, but strongly opposed by Stanley and Manners. Disraeli had first written on the Jewish question in a letter to the editor of the *Morning Post* in August 1845 on the philosophy of Young England, in which he emphasized the historic contribution of the Jews to the development of Christian Europe. It was for this reason that he supported admission rather than from any principle of religious equality.[7]

Thirdly, Disraeli's acquisition of a country house and estate at Hughenden, and his election for Buckinghamshire, gave him important new insights into the diocesan and parochial operations of the Church. At Westminster, he had struggled to comprehend the factious political tensions between what Manners called the Church party and the Exeter Hall zealots. Once settled at Buckinghamshire, he began to see the clergy in a new light as he came into contact with their pastoral and ecclesiastical concerns for the first time. Most importantly, he met Samuel Wilberforce, recently arrived as bishop in the newly extended diocese of Oxford and committed to its total transformation as part of the Church of God. They were first introduced at Wimpole, the home of Lord Hardwicke in late 1848, and Disraeli was impressed. Writing to Manners, a few weeks later, after attending Wilberforce's two day county gathering in Oxford to raise funds for his clerical seminary at Cuddesdon, Disraeli described how they had come to 'a cordial understanding', and had decided to form 'a compact alliance between Church and State and are henceforth to work together'. For the future, Disraeli concluded, 'I expect to find him a pillar of the Church in our sense'. Manners was also pleased, adding that it was useful to have such an important ally in 'The Chamber of Stagnation' (the house of lords). At the same time, Disraeli was also being encouraged by polemicists, like the Rev. Francis Merewether, to form a Church party.[8]

---

[6] For Stanley, Hansard, *Parl. Debs*, 3rd ser., XLVIII, 578; LXIX, 897; LXXX, 72; LXXXI, 105; LXXXVII, 1283; XCIII, 283: 14 June 1839, 25 Mar. 1843, 2 May, 4 June 1845, 20 July 1846, 10 June 1847; for Manners, *ibid*, LXXIX, 823, LXXXIII, 499, LXVII, 933, LXXXVII, 1254, XCI, 778: 16 Apr. 1845, 5 Feb., 24 June, 17 July 1846, 14 Apr. 1847; *Letters*, IV, 1519, 1573A, 1567A, intro., lxiv, 1551: Disraeli to Manners, 19 Sept. 1846, Baxter Langley, 24 June 1846, John T. Delane, 14 June 1846, electoral address and cards, 22 May 1847.

[7] On the Jewish question, *Letters* IV, 1433: Disraeli to the editor, *Morning Post*, 16 Aug. 1845; Hansard, *Parl. Debs*, 3rd ser., XCV, 1321: 16 Dec. 1847; Stanley, *ibid.*, XCVIII, 1390: 25 May 1848; Bodl., Dep Hughenden 106/1, f. 42: Manners to Disraeli, 17 Nov. 1847; Somerset R. O., Jolliffe MSS, DD HY 44, f. 66: Bentinck to Jolliffe, 24 Dec. 1847; Benjamin Disraeli, *Lord George Bentinck. A Political Biography* (1852), ch. 24.

[8] For ecclesiastical tensions in the Conservative party, Bodl., Dep Hughenden 106/1, ff. 34, 42, 38, 44, 48, 53, 66: Manners to Disraeli, 8, 17, 19 Nov., 29 Dec. 1847, 19 Jan., 2, 21 Feb. 1848; for Samuel Wilberforce, Standish Meacham, *Lord Bishop. The Life of Samuel Wilberforce, 1805–1873* (Cambridge, 1970); A.R. Ashwell and R.G. Wilberforce, *Life of the Right Reverend Samuel Wilberforce, D.D., Lord Bishop of Oxford and Afterwards of Winchester; With a Selection From his Diaries and Correspondence* (3 vols., 1880–2); Ronald K. Pugh, 'The Episcopate of Samuel Wilberforce (Bishop of Oxford, 1845–1869, and of Winchester, 1869–1873) with special reference to the Diocese of Oxford', Oxford D.Phil., 1957; for Disraeli and Wilberforce and the Oxford diocesan meetings, *Letters*, V, 1745: Disraeli to

Having found church politics difficult to fathom, Disraeli's meeting with Wilberforce was to be of great importance in the longer term – even though their relationship was based on a mutual misreading of the other's character and intentions, and was to end in tears some 20 years later. Writing a new introduction to the fifth edition of *Coningsby* in 1849, Disraeli gave a prominence to the role of the Church for the first time.[9]

Religious issues played only a small part in Disraeli's efforts to refashion the Conservative party after 1846. But the papal aggression and Russell's Durham letter of December 1850 in response made them, at least temporarily, much more critical. With Russell putting anti-catholicism at the centre of the political debate, Disraeli found it difficult to gain maximum advantage, and was forced to concentrate on the detail of how the government had handled the papal threat. He accused Russell's government of a volte-face in its relations with the Holy See, and represented the ecclesiastical titles legislation as simply an exercise in political opportunism. On the other hand, Russell's impetuous action had also provided a political opportunity, since it seemed that the prime minister had forgotten catholic Ireland, something which Naas, the Conservatives' manager in Ireland, drew to Disraeli's attention. Disraeli had a delicate balancing act to perform so as to retain as much protestant feeling on the Conservative side, while seeming to be sympathetic to Irish catholic aspirations. This meant keeping his ultra protestant supporters under control, while continuing to attack the government.

Appointment to office in February 1852 made the situation even more tricky, if the Conservatives were to improve their parliamentary position at the forthcoming election. As a result, Disraeli agreed to an enquiry into the Maynooth grant, but not its abolition. But on the question of Irish national schooling he accepted the advice of the viceroy that it would be unwise to aid the efforts of the Church of Ireland directly, at the risk of alienating the hierarchy. Meanwhile, so as not to alienate high churchmen at home, he declined to interfere in the Frome vicarage case, one of the first *causes célèbres* of ritualistic controversy in the parishes, arguing that sufficient clerical disciplinary powers were already available. He also supported the covert revival of the convocation of Canterbury. Disraeli's task was not easy, especially as he had come under clerical suspicion as a result of his celebrated and idiosyncratic twenty-fourth chapter in his life of Bentinck. Many believed, as Stanley reported, that Disraeli had no true religious opinions of his own, a charge which he tried to meet (not altogether convincingly) in his letter to the electors of Buckinghamshire in June 1852.[10]

[8] *continued* Manners, 19 Nov. 1848; Bodl., Dep Hughenden 106/1, f. 89: Manners to Disraeli, 21 Nov. 1848; *Oxfordshire Chronicle and Berkshire and Buckinghamshire Gazette*, 18 Nov. 1848; on Merewether, *Letters*, IV, 1745 n.6: Manners to Disraeli, 24 Nov. 1848; Francis Merewether, M.A., *A Letter to Charles W. Pake, Esq., M.P., on the Desireableness and Necessity of a Church Association in Parliament* (1849); Francis Merewether (1784–1864), rector of Cole Orton, Leics., (1815–1864), ecclesiastical controversialist, see F. Boase, *Modern English Biography* (6 vols., Truro, 1892–1921).

[9] On 5th edn of Coningsby, Monypenny and Buckle, *Disraeli*, I, 849.

[10] For politics, the papal aggression, and the first Derby ministry, Wolffe, *Protestant Crusade*, pp. 243–6; Machin, *Politics and the Churches, 1832–1868*, pp. 219–51; Disraeli on Ecclesiastical Titles Bill, Hansard, *Parl. Debs*, 3rd ser., CXIV, 256, CXV, 597: 7 Feb., 25 Mar. 1851; on the governing of Ireland, Allen Warren, 'Disraeli, the Conservatives and the Government of Ireland: Part 1, 1837–1868', *Parliamentary History*, XVIII (1999), 45–64; on the conversion of Manning, Robert Wilberforce and James Hope, *Letters*, V, 2117, 2122: Disraeli to Sarah Disraeli, 13 Apr. 1851, Lady Londonderry, 20

Disraeli and the Defence of the Church, 1855–65

The years that followed, including Derby's second government and the general election of 1859, hardly improved Conservative morale. It seemed impossible to secure an electoral majority, and the attempt at building bridges with moderate whigs through reforms of the franchise and Church rates had failed. Gladstone's decision to join Palmerston appeared to make the situation worse. Disraeli, however, seems to have drawn the opposite conclusion. In particular, Gladstone's departure weakened his personal position as the leading defender of the Church in politics, a change which his later conduct did nothing to diminish. Protestant high churchmen had always been suspicious of the 'popish' inclinations of the Peelites, and younger anglo-catholics in particular were becoming less certain that Gladstone's political ambitions would continue to coincide with their vision for the Church. Disraeli saw an opportunity to renew an uncomplicated connexion between the Conservative party and the Church.[11]

There were other encouraging aspects. The general election of 1859 had marked a modest Conservative advance in England and a significant success in Ireland as anti-catholic fears died down. Both could be built on. Secondly, the final admission of Jews to parliament removed a painful division between Disraeli and Derby, who had now to accept that the issue was dead, and that the Church had to be defended from other redoubts. This is not to say that the Conservatives were united. Stanley, Pakington and Sotheron Estcourt each had fads on particular Church issues, which made united action difficult in relation to the Irish Church, education and the Church rates respectively. The increasing vigour of the Liberation Society suggested that there were new Church battles ahead. Some leading Conservatives desired compromise in order to preserve the Palmerstonian consensus. Disraeli, on the other hand, demanded a firm adherence to the constitutional settlement of 1828–30, and the revival of the old cry of the 'Church in danger'.

At first sight, Disraeli's new role as the vigorous defender of the Church of England may seem perverse and a cause that was bound to fail. But he did not see it that way. On the one hand, the radical pressures for further ecclesiastical change, pressures that Palmerston and Russell also now recognized, gave the Conservatives a better chance to appeal to moderate M.P.s anxious about the impending post-Palmerstonian era. Secondly, it seemed that the Church was ready to engage in the battle for its own defence. Critical in this respect was the apparent public hostility to the campaign to abolish the Church rates. Despite support from the Liberal

[10] *continued* 1850; on the Maynooth grant, *ibid.*, CXX, 85, 582, 798: 25 Mar., 2 Apr., 3 June 1851; on the Frome vicarage case, *ibid.*, CXX, 916; CXXI, 685: 20 Apr., 17 May 1852; on the suspicions of the clergy, *Letters*, VI, 2236, 2242: Disraeli to Rev. William Partridge, 25 Feb. 1852, address to the electors of Buckinghamshire, 1 Mar. 1852. In October 1851 Wilberforce made a full episcopal visit to Hughenden accompanied by a retinue of 12 advisors and servants, which prompted much refurnishing and amused comment by Disraeli, *Letters*, V, 2189–90, 2195: Disraeli to Sarah Disraeli, 23, 27 Oct., 7 Nov. 1851.

[11] For the high politics of the late 1850s, Angus Hawkins, *Parliament, Party and the Art of Politics in Britain, 1855–59* (1987), esp., pp. 118–279; for changing complexion of ecclesiastical politics, Kenyon, *High Churchmen*, ch. 6; for Disraeli's analysis, Liverpool City R. O., Derby MSS, 920DER14, 146/1A: Disraeli to Derby, n.d. Aug. 1863.

leadership, the Commons' majorities for Trelawny's annual attempt at abolition disappeared in the early 1860s. Disraeli was much impressed, and especially by the weight of parliamentary petitioning in defence of the rates, believing that members were responding to changes in public opinion, which could be the basis for a re-invigorated Conservative politics. Accordingly he conceived a new strategy. This would bring together a reformed and re-invigorated Church of England and a re-fashioned Conservative ideology; an alliance that would emphasise the Christian nature of the state, alongside a proclamation of the historic identity of the nation with the Church of England, both united politically and ecclesiastically against dissenting voluntarism and alien theological liberalism.[12]

The strategy operated at a number of levels. In summary, it involved a vigorous defence of the Church's constitutional rights in parliament, a programme of diocesan speeches brought together as an electoral manifesto in 1865, an identification with the movements for parochial and diocesan reform, and an encouragement to those wanting to unseat Gladstone within Oxford University.[13]

In all of this Disraeli was associated with Samuel Wilberforce, who by the late 1850s was seen as the leading reforming diocesan bishop, and as the most active and potentially influential member of the episcopal bench. For much of the previous decade, Disraeli's enthusiasm about Wilberforce had lain dormant, overwhelmed by the outfall from the papal aggression. But then their mutual regard seems to have revived. Wilberforce tried to engage Disraeli's interest in diocesan affairs, briefing him about Oxford University reform, and he probably noticed Disraeli's contacts with the committee of laymen, the parliamentary grouping formed in 1858 to defend the Church rates. Wilberforce had also become a more vigorous defender of Church interests, as is shown by comparing his triennial episcopal charges of 1857, 1860, and 1863, his membership of Marlborough's select committee on the Church rates, and his stand on *Essays and Reviews*. On the other hand, always more concerned with the defence of the Church than with political alliances, Wilberforce was personally and temperamentally more inclined to exercise his influence through Gladstone. Hopeful that his 'friend's' joining Palmerston's cabinet would increase their joint influence on Church policy, and especially on episcopal appointments, Wilberforce was disappointed to find their ways diverging, feelings that encouraged a re-appraisal of his relations with Disraeli and the

---

[12] For the history of the Church rates question, J.P. Ellens, *Religious Routes to Gladstonian Liberalism. The Church Rates Conflict in England and Wales, 1832–1868* (University Park Pa., 1994); *The Parliamentary Diaries of Sir John Trelawny, 1858–1865*, ed. T.A. Jenkins (Cambers Soc.,4th ser. XL, 1990); for a general discussion on the Church party, Machin, *Politics and the Churches, 1832–1868*, I, 311–19.

[13] Disraeli's principal parliamentary speeches, Hansard, *Parl. Debs*, 3rd ser., CLVI, 672; CLVII, 2046; CLVIII, 291; CLXI, 1039; CLXVI, 1721; CLXXI, 642; CLXXX, 52: 8 Feb., 20, 27 Apr. 1860 (Church rates), 27 Feb. 1861 (Church rates), 14 May 1862 (Church rates), 9 June 1863 (Act of Uniformity), 12 June 1865 (Roman catholic oaths); for his Oxford diocesan speeches, *The Times*, 8 Dec. 1860, p. 10b (on the Church rates to the rural deanery of Amersham at Prestwood), 15 Nov. 1861, p. 7a (to the Oxford Diocesan Board of Education at Aylesbury), 30 Oct. 1862, p. 5a (to the Association for the Augmentation of Small Benefices at Aylesbury), 26 Nov. 1864, p. 7d (to the Society for Increasing the Endowment of Small Livings in the Sheldonian Theatre, Oxford), 22 May 1865, p. 5e (address to the electors of Buckinghamshire). A selection of the speeches were published in 1865 as, B. Disraeli, *Church and Queen. Five Speeches delivered by the Rt. Hon. B. Disraeli, M.P., 1860–1864*, ed. with a Preface by a member of the University of Oxford [Hon. F. Lygon, M.P.] (1865).

Conservatives. From 1860 onwards he was keen to involve Disraeli in his own campaigns of church reform.[14]

Disraeli had trimmed on the Church rates question whilst in government in 1859, and had not highlighted Church questions in his electoral address. In opposition, he quickly moved to a more militant position, vigorously opposing Trelawny's Abolition Bill, and making two speeches on the subject in the House. The work of Archdeacon Hale of London in organising the archdeacons across the country in the campaign to defend the rates through parochial petitioning seems to have particularly impressed him, and he remained in close contact with Archdeacons Hale, Bickersteth (of Buckingham in his own diocese) and Denison (of Taunton) throughout the early months of 1860. At the same time, Disraeli agreed to address the rural deanery of Amersham later in the year. In his speech on 7 October, he defended his firm stand on the Church rates, arguing that members of parliament of all parties were closer to popular opinion than the Conservative peers on Marlborough's select committee had been in their report on the subject earlier in the year. He defended the existing parochial system in national life and the Church's social and educational role within it, and urged the clergy and the committed laity to unite in its defence through the petitioning of parliament, and by the forming of Church unions in every parish. Following the meeting, a lay and clerical conference was held at Hughenden including Disraeli, Wilberforce, Phillimore, Manners and Stanley to plan the next move. Derby was not altogether happy at Disraeli's hard line, arguing that it would increase the party's difficulty in the Commons, although he recognized the political sense of Disraeli's recommendation 'to make this a prominent question in the exercise of their influence at Elections'. That was the point; Disraeli's stance was designed to encourage a popular response and to stimulate the archdeacons and the parochial clergy to redouble their efforts.[15]

[14] For relations between Wilberforce and Disraeli, Bodl., Dep Hughenden 147/2, ff. 29, 31, 35, 37, 47, 49, 55, 57: Wilberforce to Disraeli, 18 Apr., 15 Oct. 1860, 2 Jan., 27 Sept., 15 Dec. 1862, 24 Jan. 1863, 8 Mar., 23 Sept. 1864; Lambeth Palace Library, Wilberforce MSS, c. 12, f. 236, c. 13. ff. 124, 185, 189, 207, 217: Disraeli to Wilberforce, 9 Nov. 1860, 21 July, 3, 28 Oct., 30 Nov., 16 Dec. 1862; for Wilberforce and Gladstone, B.L., Add. MS 44344, ff. 91, 95, 108, 120, 122, 188, 192, 219, 241, 296; 44345, f. 15; 44344, f. 209, 235, 248, 276; 44345, f. 24: Wilberforce to Gladstone, 20, 24 Feb., 27 June, 20 Aug., 20 Sept. 1860, 8, 9 Sept., 4 Nov. 1862, 24 Mar. 1863, 24 Oct. 1864, 18 July 1865, Gladstone to Wilberforce, 2 Oct. 1862, 21 Mar., 26 Apr. 1863, 3 June 1864, 25 July 1865. See also Samuel Wilberforce, *A Charge Delivered at the Triennial Visitation of the Diocese* [of Oxford] (1857); *idem*, *A Charge Delivered at the Triennial Visitation of the Diocese* (1860); *idem*, *A Charge Delivered to the Diocese of Oxford at his Sixth Visitation* (1863); *idem*, 'The Church of England and her Bishops', *Quarterly Review*, CXIV (1863), 538–79. For Wilberforce on Essays and Reviews, Chadwick, *The Victorian Church*, II, 83.

[15] For Disraeli's 1859 speech on the Church rates, Hansard, *Parl. Debs*, 3rd ser., CLIV, 1175: 13 July 1859, and his address to the electors of Buckinghamshire, *The Times*, 3 May 1859, p. 6a, and for 1860 speeches see footnote 14 above; for Disraeli and the archdeacons' campaign, Bodl., Dep Hughenden 119/3, ff. 95, 97, 99, 103: Archdeacon Bickersteth (of Buckingham) to Disraeli, 26 Jan., 9, 10 Feb., 10 Apr. 1860; 130/1, ff. 8, 13, 18, 26, 28, 30: Archdeacon Hale (of London) to Disraeli, 3, 13 Apr., 13 July, 19 Oct. 1860, Hale circular to M.P.s, 23 Apr. 1860; 124/3, ff. 34, 36, 38: Archdeacon Denison (of Taunton) to Disraeli, 23 Apr., 17, 27 Nov. 1860; for political reactions to Disraeli's tough line, *ibid.*, 110/1, f. 206; 106/2, f. 66; 96/3, f. 143: Derby to Disraeli, 12 Oct. 1860, Manners to Disraeli, 13 Dec. 1860, Ralph Earle to Disraeli, 28 Dec. 1860; also Gloucestershire R. O. (Sotheron Estcourt MSS), D1570–1: Sotheron Estcourt diaries, 1859–60 (many entries); for the conference at Hughenden after Disraeli's diocesan speech, Bodl., MS Wilberforce, c. 12, f. 236: Disraeli to Wilberforce, 9 Nov. 1860 ('I hear Manners will be with us, and therefore, we may settle our next Church campaign with the chief of our "ecclesiastical laymen" – perhaps we may convert Stanley, who is also here.').

The debate in 1860 over the Church rates was Disraeli's first sustained foray into the politics of the Church of England. The contacts made through Wilberforce and Archdeacon Hale convinced him that there was a groundswell of opinion on which a parliamentary and popular politics could be based. Thereafter, he gave close attention to church affairs in Commons' debates and through further diocesan orations, culminating in the major meeting in the Sheldonian Theatre in Oxford in November 1864. Disraeli broadened his political argument through these speeches, increasingly concentrating on Church reform and renewal, rather than simply Church defence, and expressing the hope that the Church might renew its historic mission to the English people. While owing much to the conditions of the 1860s, Disraeli's propositions had their roots in the *Vindication*, nearly 30 years before, and involved four main arguments.

The first was that the Church of England was indissolubly linked historically to the English experience and the development of national character, and that any reduction in its established position would also demean the nation.

> The Church of England is not a mere depository of doctrine. The Church of England is part of England – it is a part of our strength, and a part of our liberties, a part of our national character. It is a chief security for that local government which a Radical Reformer has thought to denigrate as an 'archaeological curiosity'. It is a principal barrier against that centralising supremacy which has been in all other countries so fatal to liberty.[16]

The second, also illustrated in the above quotation, involved a re-commitment to the parochial system of ecclesiastical and local government. Disraeli was digging deep here into the tradition of civic liberty as situated in the localities, and which expressed itself through hostility to a centralizing and modernizing government. Usually deployed against the secular state, it could be applied no less to the Church. Disraeli was playing on the fears of the clergy and the educated anglican laity about a centralizing tendency on the part of the episcopal as well as the civil authorities. In the 1861 and the 1862 debates on the Church rates, Disraeli was keen to undermine the authority of the bishops, either by suggesting that they were in the hands of 'finical faddists' like Beresford Hope or Roundell Palmer with their desperate attempts to find some compromise with the government; or, more strongly, that the issue was not a narrow ecclesiastical one to be settled by prelates, but was a major constitutional question about the place of establishments, the system of local government, and the right to self-taxation.[17]

---

[16] Disraeli, Hansard, *Parl. Debs*, 3rd ser., CLXI, 1039: 27 Feb. 1861.

[17] Disraeli on parochial system and anti-episcopal tendencies, *ibid.*, CLVI, 672; CLVIII, 291; CLXVI, 1721: 7 Feb., 27 Apr. 1860, 14 May 1862; Liverpool R. O., Derby MSS, 920DER 14, 146/1 (substantially reprinted in Monypenny and Buckle, *Disraeli*, II, 92): Disraeli to Derby, 28 Jan. 1861; for Cecil's attacks on the bishops, *Saturday Review*, 148, 152 (16, 30 Mar. 1860); Manners on the parochial system, Hansard, *Parl. Debs*, 3rd ser., CLXII, 1345: 1 May 1861 (speaking against Locke King's Religious Worship Bill), also Toulmin Smith, *The True Points on the Church Rates Question* (1856), in which he expounds fully the idea of the ecclesiastical parish as at the core of English liberties. Toulmin Smith later gave evidence to the Marlborough Lords select committee on the Church rates. Marlborough's select committee (of which both Derby and Wilberforce were members and to which Hale and Estcourt gave evidence) reported in February 1860 and recommended that exemptions to the payment of Church rates should be allowed, but that legal redress for non-payment should be sought through the civil rather than the ecclesiastical courts: PP 1859 (170-sess 2) v. 15, and PP 1860 (154) xxii. 159.

Thirdly, Disraeli continued to argue that the existence of an established Church had been a precondition for liberty, one of the glorious paradoxes of English history, and that the Church rates were merely one element in a unique constitutional system. It was an argument he had used in the *Vindication* and he would use it again in the defence of the Irish Church in 1868 and 1869, anchored as it was in his reading of seventeenth and eighteenth century English history. Not surprisingly, Disraeli found the dissenters difficult to place in such an interpretation, usually suggesting that their grievances were largely sentimental, and distinguishing old and new dissent. Recently Frances Knight has shown that the separation of anglican and methodist worship was by no means complete in rural areas at mid-century, and it is also true that the number of disputes over the Church rates was small. In that sense Disraeli's comments had some plausibility. But old dissent had no place in his explanatory schema of English history. It was simply outside his experience.[18]

Finally, Disraeli appealed for unity among the clergy and laity in the face of the common assault from dissenting radicalism at home and atheistical theology abroad. In his second major public speech on Church affairs to the Oxford Diocesan Board of Education on 14 November 1861, with Wilberforce again in the chair, he made this his centrepiece. Already frustrated by the disputes within his own party, and aware of the tensions stimulated by ritualistic practice and theological liberalism, Disraeli waxed lyrical about the 'true' anglican tradition. 'Happy the land where there is an Institution which prevents the enthusiasm from degenerating into extravagance, and the ceremony from being downgraded into superstition.' The public, he continued, were perplexed by the clerical disputatiousness and confusion following the publication of *Essays and Reviews*. It could not understand the enthusiasm for Germanic scholarship, representing as it did 'a revival of Pagan Pantheism'. Attacked as it was on all sides – Church rates, burials, amendments to the Act of Uniformity, the laws of marriage and divorce, and the integrity of the formularies of the Book of Common Prayer – the Church had now to defend itself with energy. In particular, the clergy had to remain united if traditional institutions were to be protected, 'institutions which ensure liberty by securing order'.[19]

By the summer of 1861 it seemed that the defence of the Church rates had been largely won, with numbers evenly divided on Trelawny's critical division. But this success did not lead to a clear conclusion. Most leading Conservatives were uneasy about Disraeli's stance. They remembered their own attempts to secure a compromise in 1859, and that the recommendations of Marlborough's select committee were still on the table. For men like Sotheron Estcourt in particular, for whom the whole question was something of a fad, the weight of petitioning provided a better environment in which to achieve a satisfactory cross-party agreement. At times he exceeded his brief, incurring Derby's wrath, and in the end no solution was found. Disraeli saw the issue differently. Largely influenced by Archdeacon Hale and his colleagues, Bickersteth and Denison, and encouraged by Wilberforce, he saw the

[18] Disraeli on liberty and dissent (attacking Bright), Hansard, *Parl. Debs*, 3rd ser., CLVIII, 291; CLXI, 1039: 27 Apr. 1860, 27 Feb. 1861; for Cecil's views, *ibid.*, XLVIII, 1560: 17 Feb., 1858; Knight, *Nineteenth-Century Church* pp 24–32.

[19] Disraeli, *The Times*, 15 Nov. 1861, p. 7a.

Church rates question as part of a wider campaign to revitalise the clergy in the political defence of the Church Established, and to revive the alliance between the Church and the Conservative party.[20]

The following year saw a further development of the strategy. Within the Commons, support for Trelawny continued to decline. Outside parliament, Archdeacon Denison founded a new journal, *The Church and State Review*, to encourage and inform the Church party in the Commons and the country. He was in touch with Disraeli, seeking comment and a contribution, and it is possible that Disraeli wrote something for him. In its leaders (almost certainly written by Denison himself), Gladstone was attacked in particular, and Disraeli named as the leader of the Church party since his Aylesbury speech the previous November. The successes of the parliamentary session were lauded. The objective was clear – put the clergy to work in the parishes. As Archdeacon Bickersteth wrote to Disraeli, 'I can see on every side the proof that where the Church System is adequately administered, the people unconsciously become Conservative'.[21]

Bickersteth was trying to persuade Disraeli to move beyond a campaign simply focused on the Church rates – in this case, urging him to support an increase in the episcopacy to effect the Church's work – and it may have been Bickersteth who encouraged Disraeli to develop his Church views in his third diocesan speech at High Wycombe on 29 October 1862. Not that Wilberforce was in any way opposed as the year marked a low point in his relations with Gladstone. Stung by his failure to secure the reversion to the archbishopric of York on Longley's translation to Canterbury, Wilberforce lashed out. Gladstone responded in kind, accusing Wilberforce of being 'a most able prelate getting all you can for the Church, asking more, and giving nothing'. Three weeks later, the night before his own meeting, Disraeli wrote to Wilberforce, rubbing salt into an open wound,

> I hope that we may have a good meeting. It is now or never, with the Laity. If they move, all will be right, but we have troublous times before us. I wish you could have induced Gladstone to have joined Lord Derby's government when Ellenborough resigned in 58. It was not my fault, he did not. I almost went down on my knees to him. Had he done so the Church and everything else would have been in a very different position.[22]

[20] For the continuing differences between leading Conservatives over the Church rates, see Gloucestershire R.O., Sotheron Estcourt MSS, D1571, F412, X86: Sotheron Estcourt diary 1862, Derby to Sotheron Estcourt, 20 June 1862; Bodl., Dep Hughenden 127/1 ff. 62, 66, 72, 74: Sotheron Estcourt to Disraeli, 23 Nov. 1861, 15 Jan., 2 Feb., 17 May 1862.

[21] For Disraeli's continuing links with the archdeacons, Bodl., Dep Hughenden 130/1, ff. 32, 34, 36, 38, 40, 42, 46: Archdeacon Hale to Disraeli, 2, 21, 26, 31 Jan., 4, 12 Feb. 1861, 11 Nov. 1862; 119/3, ff. 107, 113, 117, 119, 123: Archdeacon Bickersteth to Disraeli, 31 July, 24 Oct. 1861, 21 Mar. (from which quotation taken), 4 Oct., 1 Nov. 1862; 124/3, ff. 40, 42, 46, 48, 60: Archdeacon Denison to Disraeli, 25 July 1861, 12 Feb., 31 Mar., 29 May, 16 Sept. 1862. For Denison in the *Church and State Review*, 1/3 (Aug. 1862), p. 111, 1/4 (Sept. 1862), pp. 159–62, 1/7 (Dec. 1862), p. 299. Disraeli was also keen to improve his own coverage in the press, Bodl., Dep Hughenden 88/2, ff. 50, 65: Thomas Hamber (editor of the *Standard*) to Disraeli, 26 Feb. 1861, 27 Feb. 1862.

[22] Bodl., Dep Hughenden 119/3, f. 117: Bickersteth to Disraeli, 21 Mar. 1862; B.L., Add. MS 44344, ff. 188, 192, 209: Wilberforce to Gladstone, 8, 9 Sept. 1862, Gladstone to Wilberforce, 2 Oct. 1862; Bodl., MS Wilberforce, c. 13, f. 189: Disraeli to Wilberforce, 28 Oct. 1862 (from which the quotation is taken).

In the speech, in addition to the usual phrases on the importance of Church and state, and the ringing rhetorical phrase, 'Industry, liberty, religion – that is the history of England', Disraeli most uncharacteristically concentrated on five specific proposals for Church reform and renewal. These measures would enhance the Church's role as educator of the people, increase the episcopate (building on the experience of the diocese of Manchester), extend lay involvement so that the national Church should not appear simply as a clerical corporation, strengthen the parochial system especially in the large towns, and make the clergy themselves more efficient.[23] The following session seemed to confirm Disraeli's strategy, with the defeat of radical Church bills and a growing division between Gladstone and his Church friends. Disraeli made just one major speech opposing any change in the Act of Uniformity, thereby adding a plank to his programme of Church defence by re-affirming that the Church was the Church of the Book of Common Prayer, that its use for the last 200 years had represented a triumph of 'orthodoxy with tolerance', and that greater flexibility in its use would merely encourage the priestly invention of doctrine. 'I prefer to stand as we are – on a Church which lives in the historic conscience of the country, which comes down with the title deeds of its great Liturgy which we can all understand, because our fathers and forefathers have contributed to its creation.'[24]

Disraeli was also generally politically optimistic. Derbyism could never produce more than about 300 members, but the party's prospects had improved, as a result of Liberal differences with the Roman catholic community over Italian nationalism, through the formation of a Church party, and because there seemed to be little pressure from the towns for further parliamentary reform. In fact, he was being over sanguine; the session may have been a success, but there was little evidence that Church defence was making much impact in the country. Parliamentary by-elections failed to send any clear message, the *Church and State Review* had few subscribers, and the Church Institution was hardly a mass movement. Furthermore, while the Church rates policy had been a success, radical moves to concentrate on the Church of Ireland did not bode well in electoral terms. Moreover the 'Church party' was not very coherent. Certainly, there was a closer identity between the Conservative party and Church defence, but just as over Church rates, there was little agreement as how best to conduct the campaign in the future.[25]

---

[23] Disraeli, *The Times*, 30 Oct. 1862, p. 5a. Disraeli was rather unspecific about how the Church was to become more efficient.

[24] *Annual Register* (1863), p. 69, and for the increasing self-confidence and anti-episcopal tone of the Church party, Cecil in *Saturday Review*, 345, 365 (3 Jan., 28 Feb. 1863), pp. 6, 258, Denison in *Church and State Review*, 2/9, 2/11, 2/12, 3/15, 3/16 (Feb., Apr., May, Aug., Oct. 1863); for Hardy and Manners on the Church rates (Disraeli did not speak), Hansard, *Parl. Debs*, 3rd ser., CLXX, 932, 965: 29 Apr. 1863, for Disraeli on the Act of Uniformity, CLXXI, 642 (quotation col. 655): 9 June 1863; for Disraeli's tactical response to the issue of Roman catholic chaplains in prisons in order to secure the support of Irish members on Church rates, CLXX, 429: 20 Apr. 1863; but see also his strong support for resistance on dissenting burials, CLXX, 163: 15 Apr. 1863; on the threat to Gladstone's position in Oxford, B.L., Add. MS 44344, f. 248: Gladstone to Wilberforce, 26 June 1863; Bodl., Dep Hughenden 101/4, f 65: Hon. F. Lygon to Disraeli, 6 June 1863.

[25] For Disraeli's general political analysis, Liverpool R.O., Derby MSS, 920DER 14, 146/1A: Disraeli to Derby, nd. Aug. 1863. For his part, Derby was satisfied with the party's recent performance in borough by-elections (Coventry and New Windsor) but feared they lacked money and men in the counties. Bodl., Dep Hughenden 110/2, f. 53: Derby to Disraeli, 5 Nov. 1863. It is striking that in two

Little of this seems to have affected Disraeli directly, and the next 18 months saw a development of his ecclesiastical electoral strategy, which centred on the Oxford university constituency and the growing campaign to unseat Gladstone there. With the provision of postal voting since 1861 and the increasing political distrust of Gladstone by the younger anglo-catholic clergy, there seemed to be a real prospect of victory. The detailed history of the campaign has still to be written, but it is clear that Disraeli kept closely in touch with events, principally through the enthusiastic high churchman, the Hon. Frederick Lygon, recently returned as member for West Worcestershire and a fellow of All Souls. Quite how Disraeli and Lygon came together is not clear, but by late 1864 their relations were emotionally close, with Lygon enabling Disraeli to re-enact his role as Sidonia to an intelligent and enthusiastic sprig of the English aristocracy. Essentially, Lygon became Disraeli's amanuensis, staying with him at Hughenden as he prepared his speech for the Oxford meeting, an occasion again orchestrated by Wilberforce. Once delivered, Lygon brought Disraeli's Church speeches together for publication immediately prior to the election, writing the introduction himself, in which he outlined Disraeli's triumphant progress since 1859 as the defender of the Church against the whig dissenter alliance.[26]

In the speech itself, Disraeli built explicitly on his earlier addresses, using the story of the Church rates as proof that dissent and an established Church could successfully co-exist within an historic national tradition. To his earlier five point plan of ecclesiastical reform, he added three others – that convocation should be more representative of the parish clergy, that the colonial Church should be put on a better foundation, and that there should be a tribunal of last appeal in spiritual matters. But the centrepiece of the speech was that the Church still presented itself as divided and perplexed in the face of liberal theology and Darwinian science. In the debate on evolution, he put himself firmly on Wilberforce's side and on that of the angels. There was no conflict in his mind between the teachings of the Church and of science. He concluded, 'In fact, society must decide between these and the acceptance of that Divine truth of which the Church is the guardian, and on which all sound, sensible, coherent legislation depends – the only security for civilization, and the only guarantee of real progress.'[27]

[25] *continued* county contests in late 1863, the first for Disraeli's partner in Buckinghamshire, and the second for West Worcestershire, where the unopposed candidate was Frederick Lygon, neither Conservative candidate put the battle for the Church to the forefront of their public statements. For increasing financial difficulties of *Church and State Review*, Bodl., Dep Hughenden 124/3, ff. 68, 72, 94, 96, 98: Denison to Disraeli, 10 July, 11 Dec. 1863, 28 Nov. 1864, 3 Jan, 20 Mar., 9 June 1865. It ceased publication in July 1865. The Church Defence Institution had only recruited 400 members by 1862, Crowther, *Church Embattled*, p. 196; M.J.D. Roberts, 'Pressure Group Politics and the Church of England: The Church Defence Institution, 1859–1896', *Journal of Ecclesiastical History*, XXXV (1984), 560–82. Finally, as attention began to focus on the Irish Church, Cecil commented that no sane person would have established the Church of Ireland, *Saturday Review*, 391 (23 May 1863), p. 646.

[26] University Postal Elections Act 1861 (24 and 25 Vic, c. 53); for the attitudes of the younger anglo-catholic clergy, Kenyon, *High Churchmen and Politics*, ch.6; for Lygon, B.L., Add. MS 61892, ff. 9, 30, 32, 36, 41: Disraeli to Lygon, 28 Sept. 1864, 11 Apr., 24 July, 5 Oct., 27 Nov. 1865 (for the tone of the relationship, Disraeli writing from Hughenden in the autumn of 1864 and asking Lygon about his new life, 'It is a life precious to me. I have lost D'Orsay and George Smythe, who were the delights of my existence, and I cannot afford to lose you, who alone remain.': f.9); Bodl., Dep Hughenden 101/4, ff. 68, 65, 70: Lygon to Disraeli, 1 Nov., 4 Dec 1864, 5 Apr. 1865.

[27] Disraeli, *The Times*, 26 Nov. 1864, p. 7d.

The Conservative whip, Jolliffe, along with others pressed him to publish his Church speeches, so it is not surprising that Church defence provided the centrepiece to Disraeli's electoral address five months later. Disraeli represented himself as having pursued a consistent and successful policy since 1859, concluding,

> The maintenance of the National Church involves the question – whether the principle of Religion shall be an element in our Political Constitution: whether the State shall be consecrated, or, whether, dismissing the sanctions that appeal to the higher feelings of man, our scheme of government should degenerate into a mere system of police. I see nothing in such a result but a corruption of nations and the fall of empires.[28]

The general election of July 1865 was to be the acid test. However, the results were disappointing, and showed the geographical and denominational limits of Disraeli's political and religious intelligence. True, the Conservatives made up some ground in English constituencies with an estimated 290 members as against 260 in 1857, but Conservative strength in Scotland and Ireland declined significantly, and the party had secured little support in the metropolis. Derby thought that the party had been overconfident and had shown insufficient vigour. As a result the Conservatives' minority position remained largely unchanged. The Church cry had failed to alter the balance of popular politics, and all that could be hoped for was a reconstruction of parliamentary politics, something that would only be possible after Palmerston's departure.[29]

The Attack Renewed – 1865–70

When Palmerston died in October 1865, few were confident about the political future. Historians have concentrated on the battle for parliamentary reform and Gladstone's subsequent electoral victory, giving the impression that little else mattered between 1865 and 1868. But it needs to be remembered that parliamentary reform dominated only the 1867 parliamentary session, and that the real stuff of political argument and debate, as this new political world emerged, were the interconnected issues of Ireland and the Church.

Amid all the political convolutions over franchise and redistribution, Gladstone was gradually fashioning an alliance of Irish catholics and English nonconformists around the issue of reform of the Irish Church. For him the issues of the government of Ireland,

[28] Disraeli's addresses to the electors of Buckinghamshire, *ibid.*, p. 5e: 22 May 1865; *Oxford University Herald*, 3 June, 15 July 1865, pp. 7a, 10b.

[29] For 1865 general election and reactions to it, Parry, *The Rise and Fall of Liberal Government*, pp. 193–4; *The Annual Register* (1865), pp. 152–9; Liverpool R.O., Derby MSS, 920 DER 14, 146/1: Disraeli to Derby, 28 July, 16 Aug 1865 (in which Disraeli offered to retire from the leadership in the Commons). There had been some tension between Derby and Disraeli in the run-up to the election with Derby feeling that Disraeli was not taking a sufficiently robust stance on ecclesiastical questions in relation to oaths and the Irish Church. Disraeli, who did not speak in the debate on Dillwyn's motion on the Irish Church, leaving the lead to Gladstone's Oxford University rival, Gathorne-Hardy, doubtless was more concerned than Derby to maintain at least the chance of some catholic support in Ireland: Bodl., Dep Hughenden 110/2, ff. 100, 104: Derby to Disraeli, 10 Mar., 24 July 1865; Disraeli on oaths, Hansard, *Parl. Debs*, 3rd ser., CLXXX, 52: 12 June 1865.

the future of the established Church and the future shape of parliamentary politics were inextricably bound together.

For Derby and Disraeli, the political challenge was how to disentangle the two issues, so that the new electorate would rally to Church defence at home, while in Ireland voters and those influencing them would be more attracted by reform of ecclesiastical endowments, the provision of university education, and improvements in the socio-economic infrastructure, all combined with a firm handling of the Fenian threat. With Gladstone making the running, the Derby and Disraeli governments needed a more conciliatory approach, which would suggest to the new electorate that Irish disestablishment was simultaneously a sentimental grievance in Ireland and a constitutional danger at home. In so doing, and especially in the immediate run up to the 1868 election, all the tensions and differences on church questions within the Conservative leadership were exposed, and Disraeli's attempt to rally the Church in its own defence fell apart in acrimony over patronage policy, destroying his association with Wilberforce in its wake. Even so, Disraeli clearly believed that electoral opinion was working in his direction, with the result that his overwhelming defeat at the polls caused him to reflect bitterly on how the Church had engineered its own downfall, sentiments powerfully put in the general preface to the collected edition of his novels published in 1870.[30]

Despite the prominence of the parliamentary reform question in 1867, it was clear that the Conservatives would have to develop a position on the various religious issues which were attracting attention. As a result the Derby government began to prepare its own Church policy as an alternative to Gladstone's focus on the Irish Church. While standing firm on the university tests, it decided to compromise on the Church rates, it established the royal commission into ritualism, and tried to develop policies and executive structures for the state provision of elementary education.[31]

As far as Irish policy was concerned, as I have argued elsewhere, Disraeli was largely happy to leave its development and articulation to Naas (who succeeded to the earldom of Mayo in August 1867), only occasionally intervening in the complex web of negotiations with the Roman catholic hierarchy.[32]

[30] For background, Vincent, *The Formation of the Liberal Party*; Parry, *The Rise and Fall of Liberal Government*; Machin, *Church and Politics, 1832–1868*; F.B. Smith, *The Making of the Second Reform Bill* (Cambridge, 1966); Maurice Cowling, *1867. Disraeli, Gladstone and Revolution: The Passing of the Second Reform Bill* (Cambridge, 1967); Warren, 'Disraeli, the Conservatives and the Government of Ireland', pp. 45–64.

[31] During the 1866 session the Conservatives had opposed amendments to parliamentary oaths, the abolition of university tests, and the abolition of Church rates; Disraeli on parliamentary oaths, Hansard, *Parl. Debs*, 3rd ser., CLXXI, 1712: 8 Mar. 1866; Gathorne-Hardy on Church rates and university tests, CLXXX, 1679: 3 Mar. 1866; CCLXXXII, 699: 21 Mar. 1866. On forming a government in late June 1866, the Derby ministry, while continuing to oppose abolition of university tests, agreed to a royal commission on ritualism (partly to slake Shaftesbury's fire), and began to formulate compromise policies in relation to elementary education, Church rates, the increase in the episcopate, and reform of the endowments of the Irish Church: Bodl., Dep Hughenden 106/2, f. 113: Manners to Disraeli, 24 Oct. 1866. See in particular, P.J. Chilcott, 'British Politics and the Elementary Education Question, 1850–1870', University of Oxford D.Phil., 1990, ch.4; also Ellens, *Religious Routes to Gladstonian Liberalism*, ch. 5; Olive Anderson, 'Gladstone's Abolition of Compulsory Church Rates: A Minor Political Myth and its Historiographical Career', *Journal of Ecclesiastical History*, XXV (1974), 185–98.

[32] 'Disraeli, the Conservatives and the Government of Ireland', pp. 45–64; Mayo on the state of Ireland, Hansard, *Parl. Debs*, 3rd ser., CXC, 1353: 10 Mar. 1868.

On becoming prime minister in late February 1868, Disraeli had immediately to concentrate on Church affairs, with Gladstone determining the political agenda through his resolutions on the Irish Church. Stanley's amendment to put off the question until the new parliament, as well as covering the ministry's own lack of agreement on the issue, was a recognition that the election would be fought on the Irish Church. Disraeli saw his task as directing public attention to the threat to Church and state rather than continuing to concentrate on the privileges of the Church in Ireland (an issue which the government was addressing by an enquiry into its endowments and through a search for a solution to the university question). He presented Gladstone as the 'thief in the night', plundering the Irish Church without a mandate, and of pursuing a policy that would increase sectarian divisions in Ireland by the establishing of a papal supremacy, undermining thereby the spiritual foundations of the state. He concluded with the accusation that the campaign against the Irish Church was simply a conspiracy of ritualists and romanists, aiming to destroy the conciliatory policies pursued for the previous quarter century. Ten days later, Disraeli repeated this last jibe in an open letter to *The Times*, which represented the Liberation Society as simply a cover for ritualists and romanists.[33]

In this atmosphere of an undeclared election campaign, it was over questions of Church appointments that Disraeli's relations with Wilberforce finally broke down. On the one hand, Disraeli had agitated the high churchmen by his public attacks on ritualism, and on the other, he was thought by low churchmen to be in the pocket of Wilberforce. As far as Wilberforce was concerned, the large number of Church appointments falling vacant in 1868 was the opportunity to reward moderate high churchmen (above all, Dr Leighton, warden of All Souls and active in the campaign to unseat Gladstone), long starved of patronage under the whigs. He used every opportunity on the country house circuit to get his message across. For Disraeli, the overriding consideration was to secure the defence of the Church through united action at the election. As he wrote to Wilberforce the day after his attack on the ritualists, 'The fate of the Established Church will depend on the opinion of the country, as it is directed, formed, organised during the next eight months. Don't let any of us flatter ourselves that it will last our time. We live in a rapid age, and if there be apathy now, it will not last my time.'[34]

Disraeli resisted Wilberforce's (and Gathorne-Hardy's and Beauchamp's) pressure to give Leighton the see of Hereford, preferring another moderate high churchman,

---

[33] Disraeli on the Irish Church, Hansard, *Parl. Debs*., 3rd ser., CXC, 1771; CXCI, 893, 920, 1667: 16 Mar., 3, 30 Apr. 1868; Disraeli's open letters to the secretary of the National Union of Conservative Associations, and 'On High Church Ritualists and Irish Romanists: A Reply to the Rev. Arthur Baker', *The Times*, 27 Mar. 1868, 14 Apr. 1868, pp. 9f., 7f.; Bodl., MS Wilberforce, c 16, f.77: Disraeli to Wilberforce, 15 Apr. 1868.

[34] For Disraeli and Church patronage, Wilberforce, *Life of Wilberforce*, III, 245: Disraeli to Wilberforce, 15 Apr. 1868; on Wilberforce's suggestions, Bodl., Dep Hughenden 157/1, ff. 41, 147: Wilberforce to Disraeli, 24 Apr., 11 Aug. 1868; for comment on the relations of Wilberforce and Disraeli, Lambeth Palace Lib., Tait MSS, 84, f. 299: John Hassard (principal registrar in the province of Canterbury) to Tait, 3 June 1868 ('Is he [Disraeli] really a great genius – or one of the most profound humbugs the world has ever produced? . . . I wish your Lordship could have seen the B[ishop] of Oxford and Mr. Disraeli sitting alone, under a tree near Halton Manor House, for an hour, enjoying the shade and the quiet. Each seemed to know his man, and it filled me with amusement.').

Atlay. But Wilberforce's lobbying was increasingly agitating the low church evangelical party, particularly after the cabinet had had to trim on Shaftesbury's attempt to introduce legislation against ritualism. Already aware that the promotion of the militant evangelical canon of Liverpool, Hugh MacNeile, would be a popular move, Disraeli became convinced in August 1868 that his earlier appointments were doing real electoral damage. Particularly important was the letter of the Conservative agent for Berkshire, in which he expressed the fear that the sitting county members would lose, because the farmers and dissenters were so agitated over appointments and Wilberforce's influence.[35]

Disraeli acted swiftly, and, on the sudden death of the dean of Ripon, appointed MacNeile to the vacancy without any further consultation. Wilberforce was sore, but kept his own counsel in public. Not so Dean Hook of Chichester, who was seen as working against the government interest, prompting an outburst of frustrated anger in Disraeli, marooned at Balmoral,

> I read it [Dean Hook's letter] with great pain. It seemed to me so violent, and written in such complete ignorance of the times and what is happening. It is the spirit of a provincial Laud.
>
> Not withstanding this fine sentiment in which it is very easy to indulge for those not responsible, it is all over with the Church of England, if she is to be disconnected with the State.
>
> Even the Roman Catholic Church without Rome would be weakened. . . .
>
> Certainly, I hold that the long pent up feeling of this nation against ultra Ritualism will pronounce itself at the impending election. The feeling has been long accumulating; its expression might have been retarded: circumstances have brought an unexpected opportunity; and what I presumed to foretell at one [of] our Church meetings, some years ago, in Bucks has come to pass. The questions of labour and liberty are settled, the rise of religious questions may be anticipated in an eminently religious people, undisturbed in their industry and secure in their freedom.
>
> It will be a Protestant Parliament, though it may not be a Church Parliament.
>
> But there can be no doubt, that every wise man on our side should attract the Protestant feeling, as much as is practicable to the Church of England. . . .
>
> It appears to me, that if we act in the spirit of the Dean of Chichester, we may all of us live to see the great Church of England subside into an episcopalian sect.

For Disraeli, the constitutional relationship of Church and state was the fundamental historic doctrine to be defended, an object to be realized by an alliance of the Church and Conservative party. He had hoped that a revived and energized Church could recreate what he imagined to have been the community of Church and party in the eighteenth century, but without the whig hegemony at Westminster. What he found was an increasingly energized Church mainly interested in its own corporate

---

[35] Bodl., Dep Hughenden, 157/1, ff., 28, 125; 91/1, f. 151: James Barnes (Conservative agent for Berks.) to Disraeli, n.d.[Aug] 1868, Cairns to Disraeli, 30 Aug., 17 Sept. 1868. Barnes concluded his letter, 'Public report says you are completely in the Bishop of Oxford's hands on these matters – you could not possibly have a more one-sided adviser, if it is true, however I cannot believe it.'

life, nationally and locally, which could not simply be mobilized for party political ends.[36]

Even so, Disraeli remained optimistic about the elections, feelings not shared by Derby, and it was not until the last week in November that he realized the disaster facing the Conservative party.[37]

The general election of 1868 is usually interpreted in relation to Disraeli's opportunism over the Second Reform Act. But it also reflected a rejection of the politics that he had been pursuing since 1860. With admittedly varying degrees of engagement and consistency, Disraeli had tried to put the established Church at the centre of popular as well as parliamentary politics. The failure of the Church to combine in its own political defence, its inability to agree on issues, its factionalism, and above all the divisive impact of the ritualists had made this task impossible as he faced the much more serious political challenge posed by Gladstone's campaign against the Irish Church. As a result, overwhelming electoral defeat forced Disraeli simply to defend the Irish Church in a half-hearted way by defending simply its material interests rather than the principles underlying its establishment.[38]

The following year, Disraeli showed his attachment to the ideas he had been putting forward over the previous ten years in the general preface to the collected edition of his novels. The Church was its most prominent theme. Disraeli portrayed his career since the 1840s as an attempt to persuade the Church to re-adopt its role as trainer of the nation, to dilute its tendency to become a clerical sect, in order that a society could be built on the principles of 'loyalty and religious reverence'. But he had fallen foul of the utilitarian spirit of the age. No doubt, he continued, all would have been different if a churchman equal to the occasion had arisen to give a lead in ecclesiastical affairs. But,

[36] On appointment of McNeile, Bodl., Dep Hughenden 157/1, f. 91; 95/2, f.24: bishop of Ripon to Disraeli, 13 Aug. 1868, Disraeli to M. Corry, 14 Aug. 1868. Dean Hook (of Chichester) had particularly irritated Disraeli, partly on account of his denial of the Church being in danger in his sermon at the consecration of Atlay as bishop of Hereford, and partly because he was suspected of working against the re-election for Chichester of another of Disraeli's young aristocratic favourites, Lord Henry Lennox: see, W.R.W. Stephens, *The Life and Letters of Walter Farquhar Hook, D.D., F.R.S.* (7th edn., 1885), pp. 557–8. For Wilberforce's and Disraeli's reactions, Bodl., MS Wilberforce, c 16, f. 87: Disraeli to Wilberforce, 9 Sept. 1868; Wilberforce, *Life of Wilberforce*, III, 260–1, 266–7: Wilberforce to Disraeli, 11 Sept. 1868, Disraeli to Wilberforce, 23 Sept. 1868; for Wilberforce's disillusion with Disraeli, Christ Church, Oxford, Phillimore MSS: Wilberforce to Sir Robert Phillimore, 31 Dec. 1868, in which he talks of Disraeli's 'shuffling trickiness'; also Samuel Wilberforce, *The Break-up of Dame Europa's School* (1871); 'He was always playing his own game, and he liked to talk big words like an African mystery man, . . . still nobody really trusted Ben, for they saw that he always threw everyone over . . . no matter what promises he had made him – if he ever thought he could get anything by doing so,' quoted in Meacham, *Lord Bishop*, p. 289.

[37] On electoral prospects, *Stanley Journal*, pp. 336: 14 Sept., 9 Oct. 1868, Bodl., Dep Hughenden 112/3, f. 75; 95/2, f. 54; 107/3, f. 95; 110/3, ff., 311, 317: Stanley to Disraeli, 29 Sept., 1868, Disraeli to Corry, 21 Sept. 1868, Pakington to Disraeli, 8 Nov. 1868, Derby to Disraeli, 14, 22 Nov. 1868; Suffolk R. O., Ipswich, Cranbrook MSS HA 43, T501/262: Cairns to Gathorne-Hardy, 29 Oct. 1868.

[38] With electoral defeat already obvious, Disraeli made his last ecclesiastical appointment, Tait of Canterbury, who recorded in his diary, 'Then he harangued me on the state of the Church; spoke of the rationalists, explained that these now so-called did not follow Paulus. He spoke at large of his desire to rally a Church party, which, omitting the extremes of rationalism and ritualism, should unite all sections of the Church . . . Remarked that, whether in office or not, he had a large Church party', printed in Randall Thomas Davidson and William Benham, *Life of Archibald Campbell Tait, Archbishop of Canterbury* (2 vols., 1891), I, 535.

instead, these matters had fallen into the hands of 'monks and schoolmen', and a little over a year after the publication of *Coningsby*, the secession of Dr Newman had dealt a blow to the Church from which it was still reeling. Rather than concentrating on Christianity's early history and Judaic origins, the seceders had sought refuge in medieval superstitions, which in general were only the embodiments of 'pagan ceremonies and creeds'. More recently, German scholarship and the discoveries of science had further assaulted the historic and doctrinal foundations of the faith. 'But,' Disraeli concluded, 'there is no reason to believe that the Teutonic rebellion of this century against the Divine truths entrusted to the Semites will ultimately meet with more success than the Celtic insurrection of the preceding age.'[39]

In blaming churchmen and the spirit of the age for his mission's failure, Disraeli conveniently ignored two other critical factors. One was the ability of Gladstone to infuse the new and existing electorate with a moral enthusiasm for the reform of the Church establishment in Ireland, in the ancient universities and in the provision of schooling. Secondly, in attacking the factiousness of churchmen, Disraeli had ignored the deep divisions among his own Conservative supporters. Indicative of the vigour in the debate over the future of the Church, these differences made any simple conjuncture of Church, state and the Conservative party impossible to achieve. Disraeli had hoped in 1865 and 1868 that the Church in danger would be the basis for a popular Conservative renewal. By 1870 he realized that this could not be so, and as a result the 1868 election proved to be the last in which the established status of the Church of England would be a central issue.

The Epilogue – 1870–1881

Thereafter, Conservatives had to find some new doctrinal and organizational approach to the expanding political system. Disraeli had little idea where such a new direction might be found. We now know that he would touch on some of the elements of that renewed conservatism in the last decade of his career – through his assumption of the Palmerstonian mantle in foreign and colonial affairs, through articulating the anxieties of propertied opinion, and by a more generalized defence of national institutions and ideals. Church defence would be part of that agenda, but it would no longer take pride of place. As Gladstone's government increasingly ran into difficulties, Disraeli hinted darkly about the future but there was no suggestion of putting the clock back.[40]

His electoral address in early 1874 concentrated on the general radical threat posed by the re-election of a Liberal government rather than the cry of the Church in danger. On becoming prime minister, Disraeli's support for increasing legislative control of ritualistic practice through the Public Worship Regulation Bill did not form a part of any broader political strategy; it was a largely tactical response to the desire of the bishops to

[39] Benjamin Disraeli, *Collected Edition of the Novels and Tales of the Right Honourable Benjamin Disraeli* (1870), general preface, pp. xiv–xvi.
[40] For Disraeli's speech on disestablishment in May 1871 and on refusing office in March 1873 including his views on the Church, Hansard, *Parl. Debs*, 3rd ser., CCVI, 548; CCXIV, 1929: 9 May 1871, 20 Mar. 1873.

increase their own authority over parochial practice and was in preparation before the dissolution. Disraeli was well aware that it would be a divisive issue for the cabinet, but that there was a general protestant desire that something should be done, views vigorously expressed by the queen. A wide spectrum of Conservative opinion, including Salisbury, Hardy, Cairns, Marlborough and Shaftesbury, were anxious about any increase in episcopal authority, and ritualists like Beauchamp and Bath were likely to be extremely disruptive. Gladstone's response was unpredictable. It was like the reform debates all over again, a matter of party and parliamentary tactics with Disraeli wanting to win the game, simply in order to put the question at rest.[41]

In Scotland, the government attempted rather crudely to attract popular support through reforms of the patronage system in the established Church, but in England had to limit its activity to minor amendments to the reforming process in the endowed schools. Later efforts to broker a settlement of the question of dissenting burials was an attempt to reach a compromise, like that over the Church rates, for fear of something worse. Even the re-organisation of the diocesan system, the most extensive since the Reformation, was a series of *ad hoc* responses to the wishes of high churchmen and the interest of the home secretary, R. A. Cross. The government made it clear that official backing for legislation had to come from the Church knowing what it wanted to achieve and how to pay for it. The dioceses created (St Albans, Truro, Liverpool, Southwell, Wakefield and Newcastle) were the result of ecclesiastical brokering and local resourcing, and not part of any directly politically inspired programme. Consequently, there was no attempt to recreate the pre-1868 settlement with Disraeli's declining Beresford Hope's invitation to make a great speech on Church affairs in May 1875. Church rates and university tests remained abolished; the 1877 Oxford and Cambridge legislation was largely concerned with endowments. The 1870 Education Act was modified but not wholly reworked, and the Church of Ireland was left to get on as best it could. In each case, the government was fully aware that the Church constituted an important Conservative pressure group, whose support was important electorally, but it was no more than that.[42]

[41] Disraeli's address to the electors of Buckinghamshire, Monypenny and Buckle, *Disraeli*, II, 615. On Public Worship Regulation Act, J. Bentley, *Ritualism and Politics in Victorian Britain. The Attempt to Legislate for Belief*, (Oxford, 1978); Peter Marsh, *The Victorian Church in Decline. Archbishop Tait and the Church of England, 1868–1882* (1969), pp. 158–92; Machin, *Politics and the Churches, 1869–1921*, pp. 70–86; Monypenny and Buckle, *Disraeli*, II, pp. 653–71. For Disraeli's speech on the bill, Hansard, *Parl. Debs*, 3rd ser., CCXXI, 76. For the essentially tactical nature of the question, Bodl. Dep Hughenden, 56/4, f. 1; 92/3, ff. 3, 7, 25, 30, 32: Bishop Ellicott of Gloucester to Disraeli, 24 Jan. 1874, Salisbury to Disraeli, 22 Feb., n.d., 2 Mar., n.d.; the marquess of Salisbury, Hatfield House, Herts., Salisbury MSS HH/3M/E: Disraeli to Salisbury, 23 Mar. 1874; Lambeth Palace Lib., Tait MSS, 203, ff. 189, 230: Salisbury to Tait, 25 Feb., 19 Mar. 1874; for Disraeli's equanimity in the face of Salisbury's making difficulties, B.L., Add. MS 60763, f. 43: Disraeli to Carnarvon, 8 Aug. 1874. Interestingly, Disraeli was staying at Longleat as the parliamentary crisis over the legislation was finally resolved, paying a visit to the parish church at Frome to view the Rev. Bennett's decorative excesses and which he enjoyed: Monypenny and Buckle, *Disraeli*, II, 680–1. The following year there was continuing squabbling between the government and the Church over who should pay Lord Penzance's salary under the legislation. For continuing episcopal gloom, Lambeth Palace Lib., Tait MSS 95, f. 9: Archbishop Thomson of York to Tait, 5 Aug. 1875.

[42] For Disraeli's Church policy, 1875 to 1880, Marsh, *The Victorian Church in Decline*, pp. 193–263; Deborah Wiggins, 'The Burials Act of 1880, The Liberation Society and George Osborne Morgan', *Parliamentary History*, XV (1996), 173–90. For Beresford Hope's attempt to persuade Disraeli to make a great Church speech, Bodl. Dep Hughenden 157/3, f. 25: Beresford Hope to Corry, 10 May 1875.

Conclusion

This exploration of Disraeli's political involvement with the Church of England has developed a number of themes. It has shown that, while he may have acquired an early historical interpretative framework from which to view the Church of England, it was not until the 1860s that he tried to give any substance to those historical assumptions. Secondly, it has argued that Disraeli had almost no interest in the ecclesiological side of Young England and only a little in the concerns of high churchmen generally before 1860. Disraeli's preoccupations at this time were largely tactical in order to preserve unity among the protectionists while capitalizing on protestant enthusiasm, balanced with apparent sympathy for Irish catholic voters. Thirdly, it has presented Disraeli as trying to construct a parliamentary and popular politics after 1860 around the defence of the Church of England, whereby the reforming energies of the clergy and the enthusiasm of the anglican laity would be harnessed electorally to create a Conservative majority. In this endeavour, Disraeli worked closely, if intermittently, with Samuel Wilberforce who was himself trying to find an alternative to Gladstone's increasing rapport with political liberalism. Initially optimistic as a result of the defence of the Church rates, Disraeli found himself in a much weaker position in supporting the Irish Church. His attempts in 1865 and 1868 failed, not just because he totally misunderstood the strength of dissenting opinion among the new electorate, and had little understanding of the electoral politics of Scotland and Wales and to a lesser extent, Ireland, but also because neither the Church nor his leading political allies were prepared to sign up to such a political enterprise. Disraeli might blame the short-sightedness and the scheming of churchmen, but he was in fact equally hobbled by the deep ecclesiastical divisions within his own party, both locally and nationally. As a result his return to office with a majority in 1874 was a recognition that the cry of the Church in danger could never be the route to power. Church defence might remain one of the planks out of which the Conservative platforms might be built, but it could no longer provide a unifying politico-religious ideology, if indeed it ever had. Finally, it has been suggested that historians might like to look more closely at the politics of the 1860s from an ecclesiastical point of view. The disputes between Gladstone and Disraeli which came together over the Irish Church had been developing distinctively from the moment Gladstone joined Palmerston's final government. Gladstone was the victor, but in fact the worst fears of Conservative churchmen were not realized. The disestablishment of the Irish Church and the other ecclesiastical reforms of Gladstone's first government proved more of an end than a beginning. The future shape of the Church in the years after 1880 would depend more on churchmen, believers and supporters, than on national politicians.

George Osborne Morgan, Henry Richard, and the Politics of Religion in Wales, 1868–74

MATTHEW CRAGOE

At the general election of 1868, the Liberals won no fewer than 23 of the 33 seats in Wales. In December 1868, the most famous Welsh-language journalist of the day, John Griffith, better known by his pen name 'Y Gohebydd' hailed the result as destined to demonstrate to English public opinion 'that there is such a nation on the face of the earth as Wales; that this nation has its notables, has its views on matters of politics – in a word, that we are here, and are determined to live'.[1] The following year, the editor of the leading English-language newspaper in North Wales, the *Carnarvon and Denbigh Herald*, celebrated the first session of the new parliament: 'Wales for once is truly represented by her own sons, and the voice and moral power of the Welsh constituencies have been asserted'.[2] With the shackles of toryism broken, it seemed, Wales had entered a new era.

The triumphalist and nationalist euphoria evidenced by these contemporary comments has not, however, been shared by modern historians. In the key work on late nineteenth-century Wales, Kenneth O. Morgan played down both the 'Welshness' of the electoral triumph itself and of the men sent to parliament. The election, he argued, was simply a referendum on the position of the Church in Ireland: nonconformist Welsh voters, in supporting Liberal candidates, indicated their support for the principle involved, but no more. Far from expressing any 'nationalist' sentiment, they were simply taking part in a 'British-wide radical assault on privilege'. As for the men returned to parliament, Morgan pointed out that, 'Twenty-four of the thirty-three Welsh MPs were still landowners; most of the Liberal members returned were undeniably Whiggish (only three were nonconformists); the bulk of the Welsh electorate, let alone the Welsh people, remained unrepresented'.[3] If any additional evidence were needed to indicate how slight the changes effected by the election were in practical terms, the history of the next parliament provided it: the Welsh M.P.s who served in the 1868–74 parliament, said Morgan, had 'little to show for their efforts' by its end.[4]

---

[1] *Baner ac Amserau Cymru*, 16 Rhagfyr 1868, pp. 3–4: 'Llythr y Gohebydd', 'Yr Ymdrechfa Etholiadol'. There were many such effusions at this time, i.e. *ibid.*, 9 Rhagfyr 1868, pp. 6–7, 'Etholiad Swydd Fynwy' by 'Un o Fynwy'; *ibid.*, 19 Rhagfyr 1868, p. 7: letter of 'G'. For Gohebydd, M. Cragoe, 'John Griffith, "Y Gohebydd", and the General Election of 1868 in Wales', *Transactions of the Honourable Society of Cymmrodorion*, new ser., IV (1998), 48–64.

[2] *Carnarvon and Denbigh Herald*, 28 Aug. 1869, editorial.

[3] K. O. Morgan, *Rebirth of a Nation. Wales, 1880–1980* (Cardiff and Oxford, 1981), p. 12.

[4] *Ibid.*, p. 12. In the best of the recent text-books on the principality, the parliamentary performance of Welsh M.P.s in the 1868–74 parliament is not even mentioned: P. Jenkins, *A History of Modern Wales, 1536–1990* (1992).

Nothing was more characteristic of the Welsh M.P.s' slight impact than the fate of a motion introduced on 17 May 1870, by Watkin Williams. The newly elected M.P. for Denbigh proposed nothing less than that the Church in Wales be disestablished and disendowed after the fashion of the Church in Ireland. Although this issue had been widely discussed throughout Wales during the 1860s,[5] and was indeed an important matter for comment on many platforms during the 1868 election campaign, Williams's motion took the rest of the Welsh members by surprise.[6] It seems he had not revealed his intention of proposing the resolution to them, and they were thus left with very little opportunity to organize any demonstration of extra-parliamentary support. The brief debate reflected this lack of preparation.[7] Williams himself outlined the current, alienated state of the Welsh Church, drawing the parallel with Ireland, and the motion was seconded by the Denbighshire M.P., Osborne Morgan. The prime minister, William Gladstone, however, argued that there was no congruity between the situations of the Church in Ireland and Wales and refused to support the motion. The debate was cut short by cries for a division, where the motion was predictably lost, going down by 209 votes to 45. Only ten Welsh M.P.s supported the measure, whilst 18, including several Liberals, voted against. Williams had, to quote K. O. Morgan, 'failed ignominiously',[8] and the episode revealed both the disunity and lack of ambition of those M.P.s returned to this parliament from Welsh constituencies under the Liberal banner.

In this article, a rather different view of the activities of the Welsh M.P.s in the parliament of 1868–74 will be offered. By examining the involvement of two Welsh M.P.s returned for the first time at the general election of 1868, Henry Richard (M.P. for Merthyr Tydfil) and George Osborne Morgan, in a range of religious measures in parliament, it will be argued that Welsh interests were championed in a way unknown before this parliament. If the specific legislative outcomes were limited, the self-conscious effort discernible in the speeches of key members such as Morgan and Richard to make a reality of Welsh representation, mark the years between 1868 and 1874 as a turning point in the history of Wales in parliament.

Using Richard and Morgan as the focus for this study also presents an opportunity to challenge another piece of received wisdom concerning the 1868–74 parliament, the implicit assumption that the limited legislative success visible between 1868 and 1874 reflected the fact that 30 of the principality's 33 M.P.s were members of the anglican Church. In fact, as this article will demonstrate, such an emphasis on religious allegiance is misleading: Henry Richard and George Osborne Morgan, though both strong advocates for Wales, came from opposite sides of the religious divide.

Henry Richard was an archetypal Victorian, middle-class Welshman. His father was a well-known calvinistic methodist preacher in Cardiganshire,[9] and Richard himself was ordained as a congregationalist minister after completing his training at Highbury College in London. For 15 years he was pastor of the Marlborough Street chapel on the

[5] I. G. Jones, 'The Liberation Society and Welsh Politics', in *Explorations and Explanations. Essays on the Social History of Victorian Wales* (Llandyssul, 1981), pp. 236–68.

[6] National Library of Wales, Gee MS 8308D, f. 297: Henry Richard to Thomas Gee, 17 Aug. 1869; f. 307: E. M. Richards to Thomas Gee, 21 Aug. 1869.

[7] Hansard, *Parl. Debs*, 3rd. ser., CCI, 1274 ff., for the debate, 5 Aug. 1869.

[8] Morgan, *Rebirth*, p. 12.

[9] E.W. and H. Richard, *Bywyd y Parch Ebenezer Richard* (1839).

Old Kent Road, only giving up that position in 1850 to devote himself to the work of the Peace Society, whose secretary he had become in 1848.[10] Although no longer formally connected with the chapel, Richard continued to fight hard for nonconformist causes, writing on education and becoming a member of the Liberation Society in the early 1860s.[11] Although backed by the society, he withdrew from a contest for the parliamentary representation of his native Cardiganshire in 1865 at the last minute; in 1868, however, he answered the call of the nonconformists of Merthyr Tydfil, and entered parliament for the borough.[12] He quickly became known, as his biographer recorded, as 'the Member for Wales', a keen advocate of a 'thoroughly liberal' policy on issues such as the claims of dissenters to civil equality.[13]

George Osborne Morgan's background and career were quite different.[14] The son of an anglican clergyman from Conway, he pursued a glittering career at Oxford and was called to the bar in 1852. Despite his background, he held liberal opinions on religious issues, and was favourably disposed towards the disestablishment of the anglican Church, although he was not a member of the Liberation Society.[15] His career as a chancery barrister required that he live in London, but he was well known to radical leaders within the principality, and was spoken of as a possible candidate for the Caernarfon Boroughs seat in 1859.[16] His campaign for Denbighshire in 1868 was remarkable: he only declared his candidature for the seat some ten days before the poll, thereby catching his opponents unaware.[17] Backed by the influential Welsh-language press and with the strength of feeling in favour of disestablishment at his back, he sailed into parliament.[18] Notwithstanding his anglican loyalties, Morgan became a leading champion of Welsh dissent in the parliament of 1868–74, as this article will demonstrate. Indeed, in 1873, he confided to Thomas Gee, proprietor of Wales's most influential Welsh-language radical newspaper, *Baner Ac Amserau Cymru*, that the tories believed his defeat in Denbighshire at the next election, if it could be effected, would be 'the greatest triumph the Church Party has achieved since Miall was turned out of Bradford'.[19]

[10] This aspect of his career is well charted: L. Appleton, *Henry Richard, The Apostle of Peace* (1889); J. Goronwy Jones, *Wales and the Quest for Peace, 1815–1939* (Cardiff, 1969); G. A. Williams, *Peace and Power. Henry Richard, a Radical for our Time* (Cardiff, 1988).

[11] Jones, 'The Liberation Society and Welsh Politics', p. 262.

[12] Nat. Lib. Wales, Richard Family Letters, 14021D, f. 180: C. H. James to Henry Richard, 16 Aug. 1867; I. G. Jones, 'The Election of 1868 in Merthyr Tydfil', in *Explorations and Explanations*, pp. 193–214.

[13] C. S. Miall, *Henry Richard, MP. A Biography* (1889) p. 151.

[14] This paragraph is based upon J. B. Edwards, 'Sir George Osborne Morgan, M.P. (1826–97): Nineteenth-century Mould Breaker', *Old Denbighshire. Transactions of the Denbighshire Historical Society*, XLVI (1997), 91–108.

[15] Deborah Wiggins, 'The Burial Act of 1880, The Liberation Society and George Osborne Morgan', *Parliamentary History*, XV (1996), 181.

[16] *Carnarvon and Denbigh Herald*, 23 Apr. 1859: editorial; for an excellent summary of Morgan's views at this stage, see his speech in support of David Williams at Towyn, Merioneth: *ibid.*, 30 Apr. 1859: 'Towyn – The Election'.

[17] Powys R. O., M/D/Sandbach/1/15: diary of H.R. Sandbach 1868. Sandbach, one of Sir Watkin Williams Wynn's principal electoral agents, only learned of Morgan's candidature on Saturday 21 Nov. The poll was taken on Friday 27 November.

[18] J. Morgan, 'Denbighshire's Annus Mirabilis: The Borough and County Elections of 1868', *Welsh History Review*, VII (1974–5), 63–87.

[19] Nat. Lib. Wales, Gee MS 8307D, f. 197: G. O. Morgan to Thomas Gee, 17 Mar. 1873.

In this article, the religious issues championed by the two men between 1868 and 1874 will be examined in detail. It will be suggested that both Richard and Morgan brought into parliament with them a determination to represent the interests of Welsh nonconformity in a way that had not been true before. The anglicanism of the one made him no worse a representative than the other. The paper, divided into two sections, begins by exploring the ideas about representation articulated during the 1868 election campaign itself, which, as will become clear, marked a real shift from what had been the norm in Wales. The second section analyses the contribution to the representation of Welsh interests in parliament made by Richard and Morgan.

1. The Proper Representation of Wales

It is instructive to begin by examining the issue of representation: what was it that Welsh M.P.s were supposed to be doing in the house of commons? Traditionally, the Welsh seats in parliament had been occupied by local notables, and whether tory or whig they were invariably presented to their constituents at election time in similar terms: they were to be returned because of their position at the apex of the local hierarchy. Wales, for legislative purposes, had no separate existence from England and the possibility of parliamentary redress of her legitimate grievances formed no part of the contemporary political debate. During the two decades prior to the Second Reform Act, however, a new view of what Wales was had been born and elaborated. The religious census of 1851 had demonstrated that nonconformists were apparently in a majority of 4 to 1 compared to anglicans; by 1861, the image of Wales as a 'nation of nonconformists' had become familiar in both religious and radical circles, categories which, in practice, overlapped considerably. In this context, both parts of the new tag became important. Not only were the people of Wales seen as giving their overwhelming loyalty to the nonconformist chapels, but the people had a collective identity, a nationality as clear and well-defined as that of the Scots and the Irish. Wales was a nation, and a nation of nonconformists.[20]

At the general election of 1868, although the issue of Irish disestablishment naturally dominated the campaign, an active debate took place as to what this 'nation' of nonconformists required of its representatives in parliament. As early as 1865, Henry Richard, in his *Letters on the Social and Political Condition of Wales*, had denigrated the existing M.P.s on the grounds that they were anglicised anglicans: their presence as the representatives of the Welsh-speaking, nonconformist nation of Wales was, he argued, 'utterly anomalous and unsatisfactory'.[21] As evidence of their unsuitability, he cited their votes in a series of divisions on subjects of interest to the nonconformists, and demonstrated that on all occasions a majority of Welsh M.P.s had voted against the concession under discussion.[22] He further instanced a recent debate in the house of commons when an English M.P. averred that the only reason the Welsh built so many chapels was that they got a healthy

---

[20] M. Cragoe, 'Welsh Electioneering and the Purpose of Parliament: From Radicalism to Nationalism Reconsidered', *Parliamentary History*, XVII (1998), 113–30.

[21] H. Richard, *Letters on the Social and Political Condition of the Principality of Wales* (1867), pp. 84–6

[22] *Ibid.*, pp. 75–6

rate of interest on the money they lent for the purpose: no Welsh member had stood up to defend his countrymen from the charge, said Richard.[23] What was needed, he argued, were men who would represent the nation of Wales and uphold her honour.

In the wake of the Second Reform Act, this theme, the proper representation of the nation in parliament, became a standard topic among the more radical Liberal candidates in Wales. A leading article in *Baner Ac Amserau Cymru*, for example, argued that it was a truth universally acknowledged by Liberals in the principality, 'that the professed principles & the votes of our members in parliament are a disgrace to us as a nation'.[24] In the following months, as the electoral contest got into full swing, correspondents of newspapers like *Y Faner* represented the candidates who had come forward in the Liberal cause as men who would defend the honour of the nation and represent its true interests: Henry Richard himself was greeted as 'a second Cobden' who would stand up for the rights of Wales 'as a nation' in the house of commons;[25] Watkin Williams's decision to stand for the Denbigh Boroughs prompted the editor to assure readers that 'He is a thorough Welshman, born and raised in our midst, who understands our language and is familiar with our national characteristics, and is full of real Welsh patriotism';[26] E. M. Richards, the former mayor of Swansea who stood for Cardiganshire, was hailed as 'a pure Welshman [and] a zealous patriot, risen from amongst the people'.[27] The radical candidate in Beaumaris, Morgan Lloyd, similarly, was characterized as someone who understood the character of the Welsh nation, would defend it against insults in parliament and protect the rights of the nonconformists.[28] And when Osborne Morgan made his late appearance as a candidate for Denbighshire, he was again greeted as 'a Liberal of the right sort', of Welsh blood and Welsh feeling.[29]

Ideas of patriotism and nationalism, and the way in which these affected the ways in which Welsh M.P.s should represent not only their constituencies in parliament, but also their nation, thus formed an important strand of discussion at the election. In attempting to judge how well the new M.P.s met the interests of their constituents, it is necessary first to identify what issues those pressing for the proper representation of Wales in parliament had in mind. As the election campaign got underway, a series of suggestions were made as to what Welsh M.P.s should stand for. Few of the demands were explicitly 'Welsh': some wished the Welsh M.P.s to push for the disestablishment of the Welsh Church as soon as that for Ireland had been effected; others urged that all candidates ought to be pressed on whether they felt there should be a Welsh university, supported by a government grant.[30] In the main, however, the 'shopping lists' were

---

[23] *Ibid.*, pp. 47–8; Hansard, *Parl. Debs*, 3rd. ser. CLXXXI, 1683–4 [7 Mar. 1866]; Garthorne Hardy was the guilty M.P. The story continued to rankle for some time: *Baner ac Amserau Cymru*, 27 Rhagfyr 1871, p. 4: 'Llythr Adda Jones'.

[24] *Baner ac Amserau Cymru*, 19 Awst 1868, pp. 3–4: 'Y Gwir Anrhydeddus H. A. Bruce'.

[25] *Ibid.*, 4 Ionawr 1868, p. 7: letter of 'Rhegn'r Yd', 'Cynnrychiolaeth Sir Ddinbych'.

[26] *Ibid.*, 20 Mehefin 1868, p. 4: editorial, 'Yr Etholiad Cyffredinol a Bwrdeisdrefi Dinbych'.

[27] *Ibid.*, 19 Awst 1868, pp. 8–9: editorial, 'Cynnrychiolaeth Sir Aberteifi'; he was spoken of in similar terms in private: Nat. Lib. Wales, Gee Mss, 8308D, f. 294: Henry Richard to Thomas Gee, 8 July 1868.

[28] *Baner ac Amserau Cymru*, 28 Hydref 1868, pp. 8–9: editorial, 'Cynnrychiolaeth Bwrdeisdrefi Mon'.

[29] *Ibid.*, 21 Tachwedd 1868, p. 4: editorial 'Brwydr Arall yn Sir Ddinbych'.

[30] *Ibid.*, 23 Medi 1868, p. 7: 1. of 'Hen Gardi'.

quite broadly constructed. That from one of *Y Faner's* regular correspondents was, per-haps, the most comprehensive, but even that was typical in its overwhelming concentration upon the disabilities of nonconformists. Alongside his demand that the Welsh M.P.s help secure the ballot and reform the game and the land transfer laws, he wished to see them assist in opening the universities to nonconformists and anglican burial grounds to nonconformist services; securing a free national system of education and an act allowing compulsory purchase of land for chapels; and finally, disestablishing and disendowing all 'religious palaces' in Britain.[31] The only issue missing from this list which occupied much attention during the 1868 campaign was the temperance-led demand for a change in the licensing laws.[32]

In turning to examine the activities of Morgan and Richard in the parliament of 1868–74, it is important to recognize the nature of the debate concerning nationhood that had preceded their return, and the kinds of expectations it had aroused in Welsh political and religious circles. What an increasing number of Welsh opinion-formers wanted was that Wales have her voice heard on the floor of the House. There was little call yet for separate legislation for the principality, but there were a number of issues that were deemed to be of 'national' interest to Wales and, in determining these, there was an increasing demand that the principality's representatives should have a say. In section two, it is the involvement of Morgan and Richard with those issues deemed of para-mount importance to a Wales defined as a 'nation of nonconformists' that must be examined.

2. *Richard and Morgan at Westminster*

There can be little doubt that Watkin Williams's motion to disestablish the Church in Wales was something of a fiasco. Public opinion within the principality was sharply divided as to the merits of the motion, and many, including Gohebydd, were angry at what they considered the self-publicising antics of a loose cannon among the Welsh Liberals which retarded the larger cause towards which they ought to be working.[33] To Henry Richard, it was the impact the motion would have on the prospects for 'Welsh' legislation that seemed important. He feared that Williams's proposal, coming so soon on the heels of Irish disestablishment, would signal to the tories that it was 'war to the knife' on religious issues, and persuade them to 'raise the banner of "No Compromise" in regard to every other question whatever'. The first casualties, he feared, would be the Burials Bill and the Sites for Public Worship Bill.[34]

In this section, these measures, the Burials Bill and the Sites for Public Worship Bill, will be examined in some detail. Both were precisely of that type which commentators

[31] *Ibid.*, 28 Hydref 1868: 1. of 'Eich Ewyrth o'r Cwm', 'Yr Etholiad Etto'.
[32] *Ibid.*, 17 Mehefin 1868, p. 14: letter of 'Etholwr Sirol', 'Yr Etholiad Agoshaol'. The monthly and quarterly meetings which, as the institutional face of dissent, exercised a great deal of influence within Wales, recommended that their adherents support only candidates who would promote political and religious freedom. *ibid.*, 1 Gorphenaf 1868, p. 5: 'Cymmanfoedd yr Annibynwir': a) Llanbrynmair; *ibid.*, 14 Hydref 1868, p. 10: 'Cyfarfod Chwarterol Annibynwyr Sir Aberteifi.
[33] *Ibid.*, 18 Awst 1869, pp. 3–4: 'Llythr y Gohebydd'.
[34] Nat. Lib. Wales, Gee MS 8308D, f. 297: Henry Richard to Thomas Gee, 17 Aug. 1869.

at the 1868 election had deemed of 'national' importance to Wales, and with which they wished to see M.P.s from the principality becoming involved. In Osborne Morgan, they found a member who not only supported these issues, but came to champion them. And with Henry Richard taking up the question of elementary education, there was a very real sense in which the quality of Welsh representation after the 1868 election accorded closely with what progressive opinion considered fitting for the Welsh 'nation'. The parliament of 1868–74 marked a real turning point in the representative history of the principality of Wales.

George Osborne Morgan inherited the burials issue on entering parliament. The fact that they were unable to perform their own burial services in anglican churchyards had been a major nonconformist grievance throughout the 1860s, and Morton Peto, M.P. for Finsbury and, later, Bristol, had introduced several bills on the subject during the 1860s.[35] When he retired in 1868, his mantle fell upon the shoulders of Osborne Morgan. Although the issue attracted a great deal of parliamentary support from Liberal M.P.s, the government were not able to give it official backing,[36] and so Morgan, in each year between 1870 and 1873, introduced a private member's bill which aimed to throw the graveyards open to the nonconformist services.[37]

Although the bill and its contents were familiar enough to the house of commons, Morgan's advocacy brought a new tone to the proceedings: the measure was now presented as being of particular relevance to the principality. During the second reading of the bill in 1870, for example, he related the story of the burial in the churchyard at Llandyssilio of the famous calvinistic methodist minister Rev. Henry Rees. The minister's coffin was apparently followed by 'a large cortege of poor country people'. When the procession arrived at Llandyssilio churchyard, however, as Morgan continued, 'the rector of the parish – standing no doubt on his strict rights – positively refused to allow any expression of feeling on the part of the vast multitude assembled, except the singing of a hymn selected by himself, and this being declined, the body was deposited in the grave amid that enforced silence'. 'It was impossible to describe the painful impression created by this incident', Morgan went on, 'not only in the neighbourhood where it occurred, but throughout the whole of Wales – no single circumstance which had occurred within the last ninety years had done more to . . . shake the already weakened and tottering fabric of the Church in Wales.'[38] Henry Richard also spoke to the bad effects of the current burial laws in the principality.

The Burials Bill, and the fact that it was now associated with the names of the new Welsh M.P.s, made a big impression in Wales. To some, the Burials campaign was in any case associated with the wider disestablishment movement since it diluted the autonomy of the established Church.[39] More generally, the combination of a piece of legislation of general benefit to nonconformists, justified in the house of commons as of particular value to the dissenters of Wales, was precisely what was understood as

---

[35] Peto was M.P. for Norwich (1847–54), Finsbury (1859–65) and Bristol (1865–8).

[36] B.L., Add. MS 44435, f. 3: G. O. Morgan to W. E. Gladstone, 2 Aug. 1872; Add. MS 44436, ff. 116–7: G. O. Morgan to W. E. Gladstone, 11 Dec. 1872.

[37] Wiggins, 'The Burial Act of 1880', is the best recent treatment of this topic.

[38] Hansard, *Parl. Debs*, 3rd. ser., 513 ff.: 23 Mar. 1870.

[39] *Baner ac Amserau Cymru*, 24 Chwefror 1872, p. 2: 'Llythr Adda Jones'.

legislation in which the Welsh 'nation' had a particular interest, and which its representatives had a duty to secure. Morgan's efforts accordingly received widespread attention in the Welsh press, and he himself was the subject of tremendously enthusiastic welcomes when he visited his Denbighshire constituents at the end of the session.[40]

Morgan had to wait until 1880 before the Burial Bill ultimately became law, but he enjoyed greater success with another measure in this, his first parliament. Morgan was at the forefront of a campaign to secure for congregations the right of compulsorily purchasing land upon which to erect a school or a place of worship. Although the Sites for Public Worship Bill would have extended that right to England and Wales alike, the tone of the Welsh members who took part in the debates on the proposal made it clear that it was, above all, a Welsh measure. Indeed, it was an issue which had attracted considerable attention during the election campaign of 1868, and Morgan himself had promised to raise it at the earliest opportunity if returned to parliament.

Morgan was as good as his word, and in 1870, he introduced the first Sites for Public Worship Bill. In preparing his case for the second reading of the bill, he sought help from Thomas Gee after hearing that a 'strong opposition' was planned: 'unless I am well fortified with "grievances"', he confided, 'I fear I shall hardly press the bill through parliament'.[41] That which came most readily to hand was a case in Carnarvonshire which Henry Richard had played up during the 1868 election. In a letter to the *Morning Star*, Richard revealed that about 80 nonconformists, tenants or employees of Lord Penrhyn who lived in the vicinity of Chwarel Goch, had asked, through the County Association, for land upon which to erect a chapel. The County Association deputed Rev. Robert Thomas of Bangor and Rev. Richard Parry of Llandudno (known by his bardic name, Gwalchmai) to approach the estate's agent. The agent met their request, however, by asking them whether they had attended a recent Liberation Society meeting in that area. The subject was apparently one upon which Lord Penrhyn felt 'very sore', and when the ministers answered that they had indeed been at the meeting, they were refused the site. Gwalchmai then published the correspondence which generated a wave of excited commentaries in the press, including Richard's own. Richard, in typical fashion, urged 'that some means must be found to impose a check upon the "fantastic tricks" of Welsh landlords, who are constantly taking tyrannical advantage of their monopoly of the land to wound and worry the Nonconformists in matters pertaining to religion and education'.[42] In his mind, at least, this was clearly a distinctively Welsh problem.[43]

---

[40] *Carnarvon and Denbigh Herald*, 28 Aug. 1869 [Wrexham], 25 Sept. 1869 (Rhosllanerchrugog); 2 Oct. 1869 [Denbigh].

[41] Nat. Lib. Wales, Gee MS, 8307D: G. O. Morgan to Thomas Gee, 12 July 1870.

[42] *Baner ac Amserau Cymru*, 24 Hydref 1868, p. 3: 'Politics in Wales – Carnarvonshire' by 'H. R.'; 7 Hydref 1868, pp. 3–4: 'Llythr Y Gohebydd': 'Tir i Godi Capelau'.

[43] *Ibid.*, 7 Hydref 1868, pp. 8–9: 'Bwrdeisdrefi Sir Ddinbych'. Another story emerged later in the campaign concerning the Conservative candidate in Denbigh Boroughs, Thomas Mainwaring. It appeared that Mainwaring had, several years earlier, refused a request for chapel land at Bryn Eglwys saying, 'there was a place of worship for them in the parish church, which is close to them, and I believe, is never close to being full.' In Beaumaris, too, Morgan Lloyd made much of the problem, *Ibid.*, 14 Tachwedd, 1868, pp. 1–2: 'Llythr y Gohebydd': 'Etholiad Aberdar'.

The detail of Morgan's bill was complicated. If a congregation could not find a site for a chapel or a school, they would, under the terms of the proposed legislation, be allowed to submit a petition signed by 50 people living within a three-mile radius of the place where they wished to build, to the enclosure commissioners. The commissioners would then conduct an enquiry, and if they came down on the side of the petitioners, they could order that a parcel of suitable land be conveyed to those wishing to erect a chapel or school. The petitioners then had five years within which to utilise the site; if, however, nothing was done to the site for any period of 12 months within this period, the site would revert to the original owner at the expiry of the five-year term. As with burials, Morgan was at pains to point out the special applicability of the measure to Wales. Introducing the second reading in April 1870, he observed: 'No doubt in England, where the land was held by many owners, there was no particular difficulty in obtaining sites; but in Wales, where the land was possessed by a few great proprietors, the congregations were at the mercy of those few persons.'[44] Whilst the numbers of cases in which land was refused even in Wales might be small, he continued, this should not deter parliament from supporting the measure, and he drew a telling parallel between the special needs of Wales and those of Ireland: 'how much of their legislation', he demanded, referring to Ireland, 'was founded on exceptional cases? What was the Irish Land Bill but a piece of exceptional legislation?'[45] If parliament could recognize and legislate for the special needs of the Irish nation, Morgan seemed to imply, it was surely fair that the grievances of the Welsh nation receive similar redress.

As in the burials debate, Morgan found ready support from Henry Richard. True to the temper of his article in the *Morning Star*, he regaled the House with a whole series of examples of Welsh congregations who had been denied the conscientious right of worshipping in their own chapels by the obstructionism of the landowning classes and the established Church.[46] Eventually, Morgan withdrew the measure, as the Education Act of 1870 contained clauses regarding the acquisition of sites for the building of schools which rendered half the bill redundant. Yet, once again, this was a measure which had been flagged at the election time as of especial interest to the Welsh 'nation', and Morgan's bringing it forward was greeted enthusiastically as evidence that Wales was at last being properly represented in parliament.[47] When it was reintroduced two years later, shorn of the offensive compulsory clauses, it had mutated into a measure which simply liberalized the terms under which land could be given for purposes such as the erection of chapels, and it passed through both Houses unopposed. Nevertheless, Gohebydd, really the guardian of the Welsh nation's politics in this period, devoted a flattering letter to it in *Y Faner* whilst the editor was likewise disposed to approve of both the measure and its champion, Osborne Morgan, in glowing terms.[48]

If Osborne Morgan attracted a good deal of favourable attention for his involvement with the Burials and Sites for Public Worship Bills, he was, ultimately, somewhat

    44 Hansard, *Parl. Debs*, 3rd. ser., 1382–90: 6 Apr. 1870.
    45 *Ibid.*, 1384: 6 Apr. 1870.
    46 *Ibid.*, 1392–94: 6 Apr. 1870.
    47 *Baner ac Amserau Cymru*, 13 Ebrill 1870, pp. 3–5: 'Llythr Y Gohebydd': 'Tir i Godi Capelau ac Ysgolion'.
    48 *Ibid.*, 9 Ebrill 1873, p. 3: Llythr y Gohebydd; 9 Awst 1873, p. 4: 'Mesur Tir i Adeiladu Addoldi'.

eclipsed by Henry Richard who devoted considerable energy to the problem of elementary education. Richard was a long-standing opponent of state-aided education, having written on the subject as long ago as 1848.[49] In the debates surrounding W. E. Forster's Education Bill of 1870, he restated his belief that:

> it was not right to take money received from the general taxation of the country, and apply it to purposes of religious instruction and worship . . . if they claimed the right to compel one man to pay for the support of another man's religion, and to enforce that, as they must, by penalties of law, they passed at once into the region of religious persecution.[50]

Religious instruction, he argued, should be left to the religious denominations. In pursuit of this, he introduced an important amendment to the bill, effectively seeking to undermine the controversial Cowper-Temple clause, which allowed some sectarian teaching in schools, but forbade the use of catechisms and formularies.[51]

Whilst the substance of Richard's amendment, which was couched in terms of broad nonconformist principles, is beyond the scope of this article, the reaction of the Welsh M.P.s and Welsh public opinion to his initiative is of considerable interest. Osborne Morgan, for example, played the 'Welsh' card in parliament. Offering the house of commons a very Welsh perspective on the issue at stake, he claimed, in a rather lumbering pun, that 'the British Schools in Wales . . . were really national schools, for what were called National Schools were so only in name'.[52] Inside Wales, similarly, Richard's actions were interpreted within a specifically Welsh context. In Caernarfon, as H. G. Williams has recorded, the Rev. Evan Williams of Pendref, 'roused an audience to a pitch of patriotic fervour' by calling upon 'the Welsh nation' to 'tell the government "We will not have their Bill" '.[53] The press, meanwhile, lauded Richard's campaign, and local meetings of the nonconformist bodies passed motions supporting his stand and urging their adherents to send petitions to parliament.[54] And though Richard was ultimately unsuccessful in restricting Board Schools to secular education, his activity on other aspects of the education question continued to impress contemporaries: he wrote to W. E. Forster about the 'Inspectors of Schools' to be appointed by the education department, demanding that some of the appointments go to nonconformists.

Public interest in the issue reached a climax with the calling together in Aberystwyth of a great public meeting to discuss the education question, alongside other policies deemed to be of particular interest to the Welsh 'nation'. The meeting was held shortly before the 1871–2 session, and aimed to assist co-ordination of action among Welsh M.P.s in subsequent moves to amend the 1870 act.[55] This

[49] H. Richard, *On the Progress and Efficacy of Voluntary Education, as Exemplified by Wales* (1848).

[50] Hansard, *Parl. Debs*, 3rd. ser., CCII, 498–9: 20 June 1870.

[51] J. Parry, *Democracy and Religion. Gladstone and the Liberal Party, 1867–1875* (Cambridge, 1986), pp. 304–5.

[52] Hansard, *Parl. Debs*, 3rd, ser., CCII, 668: 20 June 1870.

[53] H. G. Williams, 'The Forster Education Act and Welsh Politics, 1870–1874', *Welsh History Review*, XIV (1989), 254.

[54] *Baner ac Amserau Cymru*, 6 Gorphenhaf 1870: meeting of the Independents in Glamorgan.

[55] This paragraph is based upon the report in, *Carnarvon and Denbigh Herald*, 2 Dec. 1871: 'The Welsh Conference at Aberystwyth'.

meeting, a self-conscious calling together of delegates from all over Wales, to discuss with their M.P.s the stance to be taken on a great national question, was a major departure in the political life of Wales. At the meeting, both Henry Richard and Osborne Morgan spoke in terms which offered a glimpse of the way in which the dynamics of politics in the principality had changed since the 1868 election, and become decidedly more 'Welsh'. Richard assured the conference that its deliberations would be brought 'before Mr. Gladstone, to make an impression upon his mind as to what the feeling of Wales is in reference to these questions (loud applause)'. Osborne Morgan went further: what difference could a small band of Welsh M.P.s make in the house of commons, he asked: 'he believed half-a-dozen poor Welsh members, led by his hon. friend (Mr. H. Richard) there, would do a great deal in the House of Commons, when supported by truth and justice, and when those half-a-dozen Welsh members were backed by half-a-million of the liberals of Wales (applause)'. These were the kinds of stirring rhetorical pronouncements that had hitherto been lacking in Welsh politics: their application to the issue of education reflected the head of steam that had been built up by the new Welsh members in the wake of the 1868 election, and which infused discussion of issues of parallel interest to nonconformists, such as burials and sites for public worship.

In the event, the Burials Act was not passed until the next decade; the Sites for Public Worship Bill only made it to the statute book shorn of its compulsory clauses; whilst Henry Richard's secular education movements failed altogether. To this extent, it may seem that the Welsh M.P.s achieved little in the parliament of 1868–74. In all these measures, however, the rights and aspirations of nonconformists were of paramount concern. To those who argued that the Welsh 'nation' had not been represented properly in parliament, the leadership provided by the new Welsh members in such issues marked the start of a new era. And there were other areas of involvement which reflected the same imperatives. In 1869, on the thorny issue of licensing legislation, for example, Osborne Morgan spoke in favour of Sir Wilfrid Lawson's bill, and presented no fewer than 40 petitions from Denbighshire in its favour.[56] In the same session, he gave strong support to the University Tests Bill, urging that dissenters should be allowed to hold fellowships.[57] As the Rev. Thomas Levi remarked, the efforts of men like Morgan and Richard furnished 'striking proof that we now have members for Wales who understand our situation, who appreciate our needs, and who have their eyes open to watch out for our interests'.[58]

3. Conclusion

In the final speech on the motion to disestablish the Church in Wales in 1870, the veteran Conservative member for Pembrokeshire, Henry Scourfield, couched his opposition to the motion in a typically light-hearted terms:

---

[56] Nat. Lib. Wales, Gee MS, 8307D, f. 182: G. O. Morgan to Thomas Gee, 20 May 1869; Hansard, *Parl. Debs*, 3rd. ser., CXCVI 650–5: 12 May 1869.

[57] Nat. Lib. Wales, Gee MS 3307D, f. 178: G. O. Morgan to Thomas Gee, 16 Mar. 1869.

[58] *Baner ac Amserau Cymru*, 12 Hydref 1870, p. 13: letter of Revd Thomas Levi. Forster replied that the appointments lay with Lord de Grey and that he would pass Richard's letter on.

He had always objected to abstract Resolutions of this character. Since he had first obtained a seat in that House he had observed that it was used for two purposes – namely, as a machine for carrying on business, and as a chimney for letting off steam. He supposed it was under the latter aspect that the hon. and learned Member regarded it when he introduced his Motion; and he hoped that, having relieved his mind, he would not proceed any further.[59]

There is a sense in which, as noted in the introduction, the attitude of modern historians to the efforts of the Welsh Liberal M.P.s returned to Gladstone's first parliament reflects this view – that for all the hot air, the Welsh M.P.s lifted few balloons. It has been the argument of this paper, however, that there was more to the history of this parliament from the perspective of Wales than the current historiography allows.

If the 1868–74 cohort is viewed against the background of the debates concerning representation that took place during the 1868 election campaign, it seems clear that the concept of Wales as a 'nation' with its own specific needs was widely shared amongst the religious and radical *élites* in the principality at this time and that her M.P.s took this message with them to Westminster. What it is important to bear in mind, however, is the contemporary judgement as to what form the proper representation of national interests should take. Whereas, in the 1880s, during the period when there was a widespread demand for separate legislation for Wales, and even home rule,[60] the central demand in 1868 was that Wales have an equal share in the transaction of parliamentary business with the other 'nations' represented there, England, Scotland and Ireland.[61]

To this extent, there is no doubt that the activities of Henry Richard and George Osborne Morgan appeared very satisfactory to contemporaries. As *Y Faner's* south Wales correspondent argued in 1872, the presence in parliament of a Welshman like Henry Richard, sitting for a Welsh seat, bestowed great importance on the Welsh nation and raised it to an equal standing with Scotland or England.[62] Their very presence, indeed, vindicated the existence of Wales as a 'nation'. Their role was more than simply symbolic, however. They not only became involved in a wide range of different issues, but also used a wide variety of techniques in pursuit of their objectives. In Henry Scourfield's terms, they used parliament as an engine for business. They not only spoke in debates and cast their votes, but they also proposed motions, tabled amendments to existing bills, divided the House and introduced legislation of their own to effect the changes they sought. It was this sense of her representatives at last getting to grips with the machinery of the state, perhaps that, lay behind the comment of the editor of the *Carnarvon and Denbigh Herald*, in March 1870: after a week during which Henry Richard had introduced his amendment to Forster's Education Bill and Osborne Morgan had introduced the first of his Burial Bills he wrote, 'the reality of Welsh representation twice vindicated itself'.[63]

---

[59] Hansard, *Parl. Debs*, 3rd. ser., CCI, 1304.

[60] This is occasionally mentioned: i.e. *Baner ac Amserau Cymru*, 31 Ionawr 1874, p. 7: letter of 'Gwenffrwd', 'Bwrdeisdrefi Sir Fflint'.

[61] *Ibid.*, 4 Ion. 1871, p. 7: 'Mr Henry Richard, a Mr. Watkin Williams'; 24 Mawrth 1868, p. 4: 'Llythr y Gohebydd'; 21 Ebrill 1869, p. 3: 'Cymdeithasau Cyfeillgor'; *Owestry Advertiser*, 14 Apr. 1869: editorial.

[62] *Baner ac Amserau Cymru*, 24 Ion. 1872, p. 5: 'Oddi Wrth Ein Gohebydd o'r Deheudir'; 4 Chwefror 1874, p. 9: 'Bwrdeisdrefi y Deheudir'.

[63] *Carnarvon and Herald*, 2 Apr. 1870: editorial.

And, in contrast to the lukewarm reception accorded to the Liberal M.P.s who served in the 1868–74 parliament by modern historians, contemporaries were convinced that a secure platform had been laid for the achievement of even greater things in future years. The editor of the *Carnarvon and Denbigh Herald* considered that the previous five years had witnessed 'the partial removal of national grievances'.[64] Much, doubtless, remained to be done: nevertheless, it was clear that in 1868, the project was got underway.[65] Parliament, as Adda Jones, another *Y Faner* columnist wrote, 'knows that it contains Welsh members'.[66]

[64] *Ibid.*, 7 Feb. 1874: editorial.

[65] *Baner ac Amserau Cymru*, 14 Awst 1872, pp. 13–14: letter of 'Ap Creuddyn', 'Mr Love-Jones Parry, A.S., Cynnrychiolydd Sir Gaernarfon'.

[66] *Ibid.*, 16 Mawrth 1872: 'Llythr Adda Jones'.

Parliament, the Church of England, and the Prayer Book Crisis, 1927–8

G. I. T. MACHIN

From the time of the Henrician reformation the Church of England had been governed by the sovereign, and from the revolution of 1688 by the sovereign in parliament. The dominance of parliament in Church government had been emphasized by the failure to convene the convocations of the two provinces of the Church from 1717 to 1852. Even after the gradual revival of convocation, every change in the Church's government had to be embodied in a parliamentary statute.

By the later nineteenth century the governing role of parliament was becoming increasingly irksome to the Church, for at least four reasons. First, there had been a marked general tendency for the anglican component in the house of commons (and even, to a lesser extent, in the house of lords) to decrease. In the course of the nineteenth century Roman catholics, men of non-Christian religions, and declared agnostics and atheists had been admitted to parliament, joining the anglicans, members of the Church of Scotland, and protestant dissenters who were already allowed to occupy it. Protestant dissenters were much more numerous in the house of commons at the end of the nineteenth century than they were at the beginning. Secondly, the Church of England had become, on the whole, less erastian in attitude because of the growth of the tractarian, succeeded by that of the ritualist, movement. Ritualism made spiritual and liturgical claims which involved demands for more freedom from state regulation. Thirdly, as parliamentary business became more voluminous and complicated, the attempt to pass legislation for the Church was often marginalized and frustrated, measures to reform the Church being delayed or abandoned. Finally, the position of the Church of Scotland was an object of envy to anglican reformers. Although subject to parliament, the Scottish establishment had a good deal more freedom of religious self-government than the English one, and these self-regulating powers were confirmed as complete by a parliamentary measure (the Church of Scotland Act) of 1921. While similarly complete self-government was not widely pressed among anglicans, a more substantial degree of autonomy was desired by many of them. 'Parliament', said B. F. Westcott, bishop of Durham, in 1897, 'is not able to deal effectively in debate with questions of Church reform. It no longer represents Church feeling, has not the time for ecclesiastical legislation. The Church must obtain more power to govern itself, while remaining in partnership with the State.'[1]

---

[1] Quoted G. I. T. Machin, *Politics and the Churches in Great Britain, 1869 to 1921* (Oxford, 1987), p. 232.

In the first two decades of the twentieth century, some steps were taken to obtain a greater degree of self-government in the Church of England. In 1903 an unofficial Representative Church Council was formed, consisting of some 700 persons both clerical and lay, having no legislative power but being intended to 'present the mind of the Church' to the convocations and to parliament. In accordance with a resolution of this body in July 1913, a committee on Church and state was appointed early in the following year by the archbishops of Canterbury and York, in order to suggest means of obtaining a fuller expression of spiritual independence. The report of this committee in July 1916 said that recent experience had shown that parliament had 'neither time nor inclination nor knowledge for dealing with ecclesiastical affairs'. Two hundred and seventeen Church bills had been brought into the house of commons between 1880 and 1913, but only 33 had been passed. One had been defeated, and 183 had been dropped. 'The wheels of the ecclesiastical machine', said the report, 'creak and groan and sometimes refuse to move.'[2] The radical solution of disestablishment was supported by some members of the committee, but rejected by the body as a whole. The committee recommended that the Church be given more power of self-regulation, while remaining subject to a parliamentary veto on proposed legislation. In order to achieve greater self-government a Church body should be created with more power than the Representative Church Council.

An enthusiastic 'Life and Liberty' movement and a new Church Self-Government Association advocated the speedy adoption of these recommendations by parliament. In 1919 an 'enabling' act – officially entitled the National Assembly of the Church of England (Powers) Act – gave the Church the authority to establish a new National Assembly. Under the act, measures adopted by this assembly which it desired to place before parliament for legal enactment were to be considered by a new ecclesiastical committee of both Houses. The committee's membership of 30 was to be divided equally between Lords and Commons. The 15 members of the house of lords on the committee would be nominated by the lord chancellor, and the 15 members of the house of commons by the Speaker. If the ecclesiastical committee reported favourably on a measure, the latter would then have to be passed by a single division in each house before it could be submitted for the royal assent. This was an important change from the original intention on this matter, which was that, if a measure were approved by the ecclesiastical committee, it would be submitted for royal assent unless either house of parliament directed to the contrary within 40 days. It was now also provided that, even if the opinion of the ecclesiastical committee was against it, the measure could still be submitted for royal assent if both houses resolved in its favour.

These alterations gave more power to parliament than was originally intended to decide on ecclesiastical measures. Any such measure which received the royal assent would have the full force of an act of parliament.[3] The National Assembly could adopt resolutions on the government of the Church without submitting them to parliament, but these would be ordinances of the Church without being part of the law of the land.

---

[2] *Ibid.*, p. 317.
[3] G. K. A. Bell, *Randall Davidson, Archbishop of Canterbury* (2 vols., 1935), II, 973–9.

The enabling bill had a controversial passage through parliament.[4] Among its more prominent opponents were Viscount Haldane, who said that it tended to narrow the base of the Church of England from that of a national Church to that of a denomination; and Herbert Hensley Henson, bishop of Durham, who disliked the weakening of erastianism implicit in it and argued that it 'scotticized' the Church of England. Some nonconformist opinion claimed that the bill proposed to confer too much autonomous power on a Church which retained established status, and – unlike Henson at this stage – argued that disestablishment was the essential route to spiritual freedom. On account of current moves to alter the Book of Common Prayer in a ritualist direction, some anti-ritualist anglicans were concerned that an enabling act might allow controversial changes in the prayer book to slip through without parliamentary consideration and decision. But the archbishop of Canterbury, Randall Davidson, explicitly agreed in the Lords to a plea that 'it would be necessary for the permission of Parliament to be obtained in any circumstances before anything of that kind is done'.[5] This may have been his intention in 1919, but it was not borne out in the results of the prayer book crisis in 1928–9.

The provisions of the enabling act indeed proved controversial in the crisis of 1927–8. An important prayer book measure, adopted by large majorities in the National Assembly of the Church of England (created after the passage of the enabling bill), was debated in parliament and passed by the Lords but rejected by the Commons. This episode created a great deal of stir, not simply because parliament opposed the offi- cially declared wishes of the Church, but because it rejected them in relation to doctrinal issues of long-standing importance and dispute.

In this crisis it seemed that the state overcame the desires of the Church by using the crucial powers left to parliament by the enabling act. Contrasting reactions arose, both at the time and in later years, over the prayer book crisis. To A. J. P. Taylor the dispute was an 'echo of dead themes' in an England which had 'ceased to be, in any real sense, a Chris- tian nation'.[6] This seems a somewhat exaggerated opinion in view of the intensely living debates and widespread concern which were caused by the crisis; though the *Methodist Recorder* might have exaggerated in the opposite direction by saying, in December 1927, that 'even to-day there is no subject in which your Englishman takes more intelligent interest than he does in religion, nor any on which he has such deep convictions'.[7]

1

The reasons which produced the prayer book crisis had developed over much the same period as the reasons which produced the enabling bill. Since about 1880 there had been a marked growth of ritualist (or anglo-catholic) usage in the Church of England, and a great deal of dispute had ensued, particularly in the years 1895 to 1905 when 'the

---

[4] D. M. Thompson, 'The Politics of the Enabling Act, 1919', *Studies in Church History*, XII (1975), 383–92; A. Wilkinson, *The Church of England and the First World War* (1978), pp. 271–4.
[5] Bell, *Davidson*, II, 978.
[6] A. J. P. Taylor, *English History, 1914–45* (Oxford, 1965), p. 259.
[7] 22 Dec. 1927, p. 3.

crisis in the Church' was a description applied to aspects of this decade.[8] The turmoil had resulted, not in the suppression of ritualism by the bishops, which had been strongly demanded by many, but in an effort to extend a degree of toleration to ritualism by altering and expanding the provisions of the prayer book of 1662. By this means it was hoped to accommodate the more moderate ritualist practices within the law, while in return it was hoped that ritualists would accept liturgical discipline much more readily, and not insist on following practices which remained illegal.

In 1906 the report of a Royal Commission on Ecclesiastical Discipline recommended the adoption of 'the greater elasticity which a reasonable recognition of the comprehensiveness of the Church of England and of its present needs seems to demand'.[9] The extension of permitted practice should include confession, prayers for the dead, and (with reservations) the use of incense. But it should exclude the veneration of images; confession to or invocation of the Virgin Mary or the saints; and (a matter of central importance to the dispute in the 1920s) the reservation of the blessed sacrament under conditions which might lead to its adoration, and processions with the sacrament.[10] On the basis of these recommendations the convocations of Canterbury and York were instructed, in royal letters of business, to prepare appropriate revisions of the prayer book for the conduct of public worship, with a view to submitting them to parliament for legal enactment.

Largely because of the intricate and controversial nature of the subject, and delays caused by the First World War, the convocations did not complete their task until 1920.[11] A formal reply to the letters of business was then drawn up. On the suggestion of Randall Davidson, archbishop of Canterbury, it was decided by the home secretary (Edward Shortt) that the proposals in the reply should be submitted to the new National Assembly of the Church of England, in the hope that this body would recommend their enactment by parliament. The Church Assembly appointed a prayer book revision committee. This reported on the proposals, generally favourably but with some ominous expressions of dissent, in June 1922. A Revised Prayer Book permissive use measure, complete with an appended schedule, was drawn up and presented to the Church Assembly in October. The assembly gave general but not unanimous approval by April 1923, and submitted the measure and schedule to each of its constituent Houses in succession for detailed consideration – first the house of clergy, then the house of laity, and finally (in October 1925) the house of bishops. Both the house of clergy and the house of laity suggested many amendments for consideration by the house of bishops, and Archbishop Davidson said that he had received 800 memorials on aspects of change.[12]

[8] Machin, Politics and the Churches, pp. 234–55; O. Chadwick, The Victorian Church (2 vols., 1970), II, 311–12, 324.

[9] Quoted C. Garbett, Church and State in England (1950), p. 211.

[10] Bell, Davidson, I, 470–3. For the question of whether outdoor processions with the sacrament could be held by the Roman catholic church in Britain, see G. I. T. Machin, 'The Liberal Government and the Eucharistic Procession of 1908', Journal of Ecclesiastical History, XXXIV (1983), 559–83; Susan McGee, 'Carfin [Lanarkshire] and the Roman Catholic Relief Act of 1926', Innes Review, XVI (1965), 56–78.

[11] Bell, Davidson, II, 1335–8.

[12] This procedure was summarized and explained by Davidson to the jointly assembled convocations on 7 Feb. 1927; draft of speech (dated 28 Jan. 1927) in Lambeth Palace Library, Davidson Papers [hereafter D.P.], vol. 450, ff. 48, 60–5 (see also Bell, Davidson, II, 1328–30).

The amended measure was presented and explained by Davidson to a joint meeting of the convocations on 7 February 1927. The convocations had the opportunity to consider and comment on the final draft of the bishops' proposals, before formal presentation of the completed measure to the Church Assembly at the end of March. Davidson emphasized in his speech of 7 February that the Revised (or Alternative) Prayer Book, to be incorporated in the measure, would be permissive only. The 1662 prayer book would also be incorporated in the measure (with some minor changes in wording), and clergy who preferred to continue using this would be fully able to do so. Indeed the measure was a composite one, containing both books, the old and the revised. Moreover, most of the new forms in the revised book – such as permission to shorten the morning and evening prayers, and placing the use of the Athanasian creed on a voluntary basis – were expected to be uncontroversial.

Davidson admitted in his speech, however, that some of the forms it was proposed to allow 'cannot be called uncontroversial', and that these 'inevitably invited discussion'. These were an alternative order for holy communion, the use of which was subject to the permission of the diocesan bishop; and continuous reservation of consecrated bread and wine for the communion of the sick and dying but for no other purpose.[13] The firm reference to 'no other purpose' strongly implied that corporate acts of worship before the reserved sacrament, such as were practised by Roman catholics and which many anglo-catholics wanted, would be forbidden. But, as in the past, legal restrictions might not be adequate to prevent strongly desired practice; and reservation and its limits were already, as Davidson spoke, proving to be the most contentious issue in the prayer book dispute. Extreme evangelicals were against any reservation, while extreme anglo-catholics opposed any limits on reservation. Another matter which caused considerable, if less pronounced, perturbation was the fear that the permitted shortening of morning and evening prayer in the revised book might cause the omission of prayers for the king and the royal family.

After further revisions, the final version of the prayer book measure was submitted to the convocations on 29 and 30 March 1927, and large majorities in these bodies recommended that it be accepted by the National Church Assembly. The crucial debates in the assembly were on 5 and 6 July. Davidson recommended the measure as promising to provide adequate comprehensiveness and adequate discipline. In spite of strong attacks by extreme evangelicals and extreme anglo-catholics in the debate, the measure was accepted by an impressive overall majority of 517 to 133 (in the house of bishops the voting was 34 to 4 in favour, in the house of clergy 253 to 37, and in the house of laity 230 to 92).[14] Voting in diocesan conferences on the measure produced total figures of 8,415 in favour and 1,969 against.[15] The Church of England had thus spoken officially in overwhelming favour of the measure. It was now to be seen whether parliament would agree with the Church's decision.

---

[13] Bell, *Davidson*, II, 1330–4. This matter is dealt with in detail in I. Machin, 'Reservation under Pressure: Ritual in the Prayer Book Crisis, 1927–8', *Studies in Church History*, XXXV (1999).

[14] Bell, *Davidson*, II, 1339–40.

[15] Leaflet of Nov. 1927, in D.P., vol. 454, f. 62.

2

Apart from Davidson's promise in 1919 that the proposed changes would be submitted for parliamentary consideration, it was desired to give the revisions the full force of law – thus preventing them from being simply regulations of the Church which might be challenged in the law-courts as contravening the legal Book of Common Prayer. Amidst wide and intense public interest, divisions into supporters and opponents of the revised book occurred among both evangelicals and anglo-catholics.[16] Some opponents claimed that the Church of England would be disrupted if the measure passed.[17] In this controversial atmosphere the Revised or Alternative Prayer Book was deposited for consideration by parliament – thus acquiring yet a third cognomen, the 'Deposited Book'. In order to become law, the measure had, in accordance with the enabling act, first to be approved by the ecclesiastical committee of parliament, and then (after the abbreviated process of a single debate and a favourable division in each House) to receive resolutions from both houses of parliament that it should be submitted for royal assent.

On account of the parliamentary time available, it seemed that the measure could not be expected to come before the two houses until December 1927 at the earliest. The earl of Selborne, who supported the measure, was anxious that Davidson and the archbishop of York (Cosmo Gordon Lang) should explain the revisions at a meeting with members of the house of lords, before the latter became 'hopelessly prejudiced and pledged' on the subject.[18] In the event, Archbishop Lang addressed a meeting of M.P.s on the matter during the summer, and Davidson addressed a meeting of peers.[19] Members of the ecclesiastical committee began to prepare to judge the measure. C. G. Ammon, a Labour M.P. and a Wesleyan, who represented his party on the ecclesiastical committee, consulted the Revd J. Scott Lidgett, a leading minister in his denomination, about the course he might take. Lidgett informed Davidson that he had 'strongly advised' Ammon that 'he and his Party should support the Prayer Book measure', and that Ammon's opinion was 'confirmed by what I said to him'.[20]

In mid-July 1927 the legislative committee of the National Church Assembly – in one of the links which graphically demonstrated the dual role of Church and state in this matter – submitted the measure to the ecclesiastical committee of parliament. Along with the measure was presented a commentary and an explanation which had been prepared by a small committee of bishops.[21] The ecclesiastical committee appointed a sub-committee of four of its members to receive and consider objections to the measure, and the sub-committee was engaged on this task by late July.[22] The voluminous

---

[16] A great many examples of the differing opinions are in *ibid.*, vols. 450–4.

[17] *Ibid.*, 454, f. 115: W. H. Bridge (chairman, Northern Council of the Committee for the Maintenance of Truth and Faith) to Davidson, 29 Nov. 1927.

[18] *Ibid.*, 451, ff. 253–6: Selborne to Davidson, 30 Mar. 1927.

[19] *Ibid.*, 452, ff. 181–2: Waldron Smithers, M. P., to Lang, 12 July 1927; Bell, *Davidson*, II, 1340.

[20] D.P., 452, f. 171: Lidgett to Davidson, 11 July 1927.

[21] *Ibid.*, f. 25: Davidson to Selborne, 23 May 1927. The arrangements for drafting the accompanying report of the legislative committee are summarized in this letter.

[22] Lambeth Palace Lib., Minutes of Council of English Church Union, 1927, pp. 208–9: Edward Vigors, secretary of the ecclesiastical committee, to the secretary of the English Church Union, 28 July 1927; D.P., 453, ff. 36–7: Vigors to Davidson, 26 Aug. 1927; Parliamentary Papers [hereafter P.P.], 1927, 7. 1 (117 and 118), p. 496: Report of ecclesiastical committee of parliament on prayer-book measure, 22 Nov.1927.

objections received by the sub-committee were all made in writing. Archbishop Lang told Davidson on 19 October that he was worried that the large amount of work thus imposed on the sub-committee would delay the parliamentary decision on the measure. He wrote:

> it was impossible, without writing a huge treatise, to deal with the mass of somewhat irrelevant doctrinal objections which has been poured in upon the Sub-Committee. I very much hope that they will not think it their duty (which it clearly is not) to attempt to decide upon doctrinal matters of this kind. It will obviously take some time for the Sub-Committee to complete its own Report, and who knows how long the Ecclesiastical Committee itself will take and whether it may wish for some conference with the Legislative Committee [of the assembly].[23]

These were not unlike the complaints which had led to the enabling act. That act had left some scope for them still to be made. But events moved more quickly than Lang feared. When parliament commenced its session of 1927–8 on 8 November, the sub-committee had submitted its report to its superior body, the ecclesiastical committee. The report replied to the objections, doctrinal and constitutional, which the sub-committee had received, and included a letter from the bishop of Chelmsford (Guy Warman) rebutting the objections.[24] The ecclesiastical committee met on 16 November to decide on its general attitude to the prayer book measure. Following this, there was produced a draft report which was intended to be agreed on in final form at a further meeting of the committee on 22 November. After the meeting on 16 November it became known that the committee was favourable to the measure, and it was therefore arranged that resolutions to submit the measure for royal assent would be moved and debated in the house of lords on 12 and 13 December, and in the house of commons very shortly thereafter.[25]

The final form of the ecclesiastical committee's report was duly agreed at the meeting on 22 November. The report was immediately sent to the Church Assembly's legislative committee, which considered it at a meeting on the following day.[26] The Ecclesiastical Committee's report stated that:

> the Committee . . . would not recommend any interference with the decisions of the Church Assembly on matters so clearly lying within the province of that Assembly as the doctrines and ceremonial of the Church, unless persuaded that any proposed change of doctrine were of so vital a description as materially to alter the general character of the National Church recognised in the Act of Settlement [of 1701] and by the oath sworn by His Majesty at his Coronation, whereby His Majesty has promised to maintain the Protestant Reformed Religion established by law. . . Without entering into argument on doctrinal questions, but having considered all that has been laid before them and the expressed opinion of the Archbishops and

[23] D.P., 453, f. 235: Lang to Davidson, 19 Oct. 1927.
[24] The sub-committee's report is printed in full in Appendix II of the ecclesiastical committee's report of 22 Nov. 1927: P. P. 1927, 7. 1 (117 and 118), pp. 505–35.
[25] Note (headed 'Opinion') in Lambeth Palace Lib., Lang Papers [hereafter L.P.], Nov. 1927, f. 299.
[26] *Ibid.*

Bishops as the doctrinal position of the Church of England, the Committee take the view that no change of doctrine of constitutional importance is involved, that accordingly the 'constitutional rights of all His Majesty's subjects' [quoted from enabling act] are not in this respect prejudicially affected, and there is nothing to modify the purport of the Coronation Oath . . . it does not appear to the Committee that the Measure prejudicially affects the constitutional rights of His Majesty's subjects, and they are of opinion that it should proceed.[27]

The committee's report did consider one objection received by the sub-committee. This alleged that the prayer book measure was *ultra vires* because it had not met the condition, stated in article 14(1) of the enabling act, that the final measure should be debated and voted upon by each of the three houses of the Church Assembly sitting separately. The complaint was based on the opinion that 'the Measure now presented is not, owing to the extensive nature of the amendments made by the House of Bishops, the same Measure as that originally presented for the consideration of the Houses of Clergy and Laity'.[28] But the committee would not sustain this objection. Its report concluded that:

all the amendments made by the House of Bishops were 'relevant to the general purport of the Measure' as provided by the Standing Orders of the Church Assembly, and are not such as to make the Measure a new one. It is true that the Measure is altered in form, but it is comparatively little altered in substance. . . Certain modifications . . . in the direction of conferring greater liberty, are made in the rubrics, but these were almost without exception implicit in the Book as originally considered.[29]

3

The ecclesiastical committee may have believed that it had dealt with all the objections to the prayer book measure, but some of the objections had such force that they brought about defeat of the measure in the house of commons. Both Davidson and the marquess of Salisbury had imagined that the Lords would be less amenable to the measure than the Commons.[30] The Lords belied this prediction by agreeing to Davidson's motion to submit the measure for royal assent on 14 December, after debating it on three days, by the overwhelming majority of 288 to 41. [31] In the debate there were some able speeches both for and against the motion. Among the opponents were the octogenarian marquess of Lincolnshire, who (besides recalling his memories of the disturbed year of 1848) said he was one of the evangelical army 'resolutely resolved to stand by the old faith which we learned at our mother's knee';[32] and, from an opposite anglo-catholic viewpoint, Viscount Halifax, who asked how discipline could be

[27] P.P. 1927, 7. 1 (117 and 118), pp. 497–8 (part quoted in Bell, *Davidson*, II, 1342).

[28] *Ibid.*, p. 498.

[29] *Ibid.*

[30] D.P., 453, ff. 222–3: Salisbury to Davidson, 18 Oct. 1927; also *ibid.*, ff. 236–7: Davidson's memorandum, 19 Oct. 1927.

[31] Hansard, *Parl. Debs*, 5th ser., LXXIX, 771–990.

[32] *Ibid.*, 815.

applied under the revised book to 'the clergy who deny the right of any Bishop to forbid the reservation of the Blessed Sacrament in the parish church?' [33]

The Commons proved so much of a tougher proposition that they rejected the book. Among some M.P.s there had grown a determination to resist the measure, based mainly on the strong protestant reasons which had already been directed against it in meetings and petitions. An inter-party group of M.P.s was formed under the leadership of the home secretary, Sir William Joynson-Hicks (or 'Jix'), who played as large an opposing part among evangelical laity as did the octogenarian Bishop E. A. Knox among evangelical clergy. This group was marshalling forces by the end of November for a determined defence of Reformation principles in the lower house. *The Times* informed its readers on 1 December:

> In the House of Commons the opponents of the Measure have already begun their campaign, and the Home Secretary presided over a meeting last night, at which about 100 members were present, when there was a preliminary discussion on the course to be adopted during the debate. Four Whips were appointed . . . and the following members were elected as an executive committee: Sir William Joynson-Hicks [Conservative], Mr [Stephen] Walsh [Labour], Mr Hopkin Morris [Liberal], Sir Thomas Inskip [Conservative], Mr Rosslyn Mitchell [Labour], and Lord Curzon [Conservative].[34]

The reward of these preparations was reaped in the Commons debate on 15 December.[35] The debate was opened by W. C. Bridgeman, first lord of the admiralty, who moved that the measure be submitted for royal assent but disappointed supporters by his caution and diffidence. He was followed by Joynson-Hicks, a veteran and foremost evangelical anglican. 'Jix' vigorously commenced an anti-Roman line in the debate, especially in opposition to the sacramental reservation permitted in the measure, which gradually killed the hopes of Archbishop Davidson (who was watching from the gallery) that the measure would succeed. 'Before ten minutes had passed', noted Bishop George Bell in his detailed account, 'he [Joynson-Hicks] had kindled the first sparks of the fire which was to consume the new Book, the fire of the fear of Rome'.[36] W. R. Inge, dean of St Paul's, a lukewarm supporter of the measure who was a spectator at the debate, thought that 'Jix' spoke 'better than he had ever spoken before', that he was ably seconded by Rosslyn Mitchell (Labour M.P. for Paisley) who 'fulminated like an old Covenanter', and that 'these two speeches did most to determine the result'.[37] Mitchell, a Scottish United Free Churchman, said that the proposals on reservation in the revised book would encourage acceptance of transubstantiation, and claimed that:

> In one generation, with that Deposited Book, you can swing over all the children of England from the Protestant Reformed Faith to the Roman Catholic Faith. . . . I do not believe that the Church of England can permanently endure to be

[33] *Ibid.*, 844.

[34] *The Times*, 1 Dec. 1927, p. 16.

[35] Hansard, *Parl. Debs*, 5th ser., CCXI, 2531–655.

[36] Bell, *Davidson*, II, 1345.

[37] A. Fox, *Dean Inge* (1960), p. 216. For the speeches of Joynson-Hicks and Mitchell, see Hansard, *Parl. Debs*, 5th ser., CCXI, 2540–50, 2560–7.

half-Reformist and half-Romanist. Either it will be one thing, or the other . . . I, for one, confirmed, convinced and determined in my Protestantism . . . can do nothing but vote against the Measure.[38]

Other opposing speeches on similar lines were made by Sir John Simon (Liberal), Stephen Walsh (Labour), Sir Douglas Hogg (Conservative), and Sir Thomas Inskip (Conservative).[39] Against the force of the opposition, the ten members who spoke for the motion failed to persuade that House to vote in favour.[40] Apart from Bridgeman, the speakers in favour comprised Stanley Baldwin (the prime minister), the countess of Iveagh, Viscount Wolmer, Lord Hugh Cecil, John Buchan, Sir Henry Slesser (an anglo-catholic), and Major J. W. Hills (all of whom were Conservatives); and C. G. Ammon and the Revd Herbert Dunnico (both Labour and both nonconformists). Lord Hugh Cecil, a high churchman (perhaps falling short of being an anglo-catholic), who was expected to be the strongest speaker for the motion, addressed the House at length but rather discursively and not as effectively as had been hoped.[41] In the view of Bishop William Temple, a supporter of the measure, the best speech in favour was made by Dunnico, a Baptist minister (M.P. for Consett, Co. Durham), who said he had no reason to object to the reservation provisions for anglicans in the revised book.[42]

Two speakers for the measure, J. W. Hills and John Buchan (the novelist, later Lord Tweedsmuir), emphasized that they saw the enabling act as having been passed in order to allow the Church to regulate itself by such means as the Revised Prayer Book. Hills asked:

When . . . you come to a point of doctrine, a point of internal government, a point even of those very deep and great mysteries [i.e. reservation] which have been referred to, they are points which this House delegated to the opinion of the Church itself. Otherwise, I do not believe this House would have passed the Act of 1919 at all. If all these points of doctrine are to be brought here every time and discussed and re-discussed, why did we profess to give the Church those powers?[43]

Similarly Buchan, a Scottish United Free Churchman, said: 'Surely it is not the duty of this House to take away from the Church of England the right of self-government which was granted to it, except upon the most solemn constitutional grounds'.[44]

However, a majority of the House did not agree that the measure was sufficiently harmless to allow through. In the division the motion was lost by 238 votes to 205.[45] The Conservatives split almost evenly on the motion; twice as many Labour M.P.s voted against as voted in favour; and nearly all the Liberals who voted were against the motion.[46]

[38] Hansard, Parl. Debs, 5th ser., CCXI, 2566–7.

[39] Ibid., 2571–8, 2603–7, 2620–5, 2637–48.

[40] See the comments on the debate in British Weekly, 22 Dec. 1927, pp. 305–6; and J. G. Lockhart, Cosmo Gordon Lang (1949), pp. 305–6.

[41] Hansard, Parl. Debs, 5th ser., CCXI, 2578–92.

[42] Ibid., 2625–9; F. A. Iremonger, William Temple, Archbishop of Canterbury. His life and letters (1948), p. 352.

[43] Hansard, Parl. Debs, 5th ser., CCXI, 2607.

[44] Ibid., 2615–16, 2620.

[45] Ibid., 2651–6: Division list.

[46] The Christian World, 22 Dec. 1927, p. 1.

Joynson-Hicks had appealed to nonconformist M.P.s to vote (as they were of course entitled to do if they wished), in the expectation that most of them would oppose the measure. The Roman Catholics in both Houses decided not to participate in the debates and divisions, but some nonconformists and members of the Church of Scotland took part in them. By no means all of these opposed the measure. But in the Commons division the majority against the motion was accounted for by non-anglican votes and by most of the M.P.s for Scottish and Welsh constituencies who did not abstain. Thirty-three of the M.P.s for Scottish constituencies voted against, and only six in favour, though 31 abstained. Eighteen of the M.P.s for Welsh constituencies voted against, and only two in favour, though 14 abstained. A reversal of these votes for and against would easily have carried the motion. The dean of Lincoln (Very Revd T. E. Fry) pointed out in a letter in *The Times* that among the members for English constituencies there was a majority of 21 for the measure.[47] The discrepancy between this figure and the result of the division revived long-standing protests against a partly non-anglican parliament having the right to legislate or not to legislate for the Church of England.

Lord Selborne had suggested to Davidson that Lloyd George might be induced to persuade Welsh Liberal M.P.s to abstain.[48] But if such an attempt was made it did not succeed, for Lloyd George voted against the measure himself. The vote which caused the greatest remark, however, was the one given against the motion by a Parsee, Sapurji Saklatvala, Communist M.P. for Battersea North.

4

A variety of options faced the surprised and deflated archbishops and Church Assembly after the rejection of their measure. They could accept the Commons verdict as final, simply abandoning the revised book and writing off the labours of 20 years. They could reflect for a considerable time, perhaps until the next Lambeth Conference of anglican bishops (planned for 1930), before deciding on further action. They could seek disestablishment, or a solution involving self-government within establishment similar to that obtained by the Church of Scotland in 1921, in order to free themselves of parliamentary authority in their spiritual concerns. They could, as advised by the earl of Birkenhead, Lord Hugh Cecil and others, put the revised book into operation as a Church ordinance in spite of parliament's refusal to make it the law of the land.[49] Finally, in view of the small majority against the book in the Commons and the large majority for it in the Lords, they could immediately alter the book and re-submit it to parliament in the hope of obtaining the compliance of the lower house.

The last course was taken, but without success. Some alterations to the revised book were made. These strengthened and made more explicit the restrictions on reservation;

[47] *The Times*, 20 Dec. 1927, p. 16.

[48] D.P., 453, ff. 295–7: Selborne to Davidson, 27 Oct. 1927.

[49] Letter of Birkenhead in *The Times*, 20 Dec. 1927, p. 15 (reprinted in *Church Times*, 23 Dec. 1927, pp. 749–50); D.P., 454, ff. 205–16: memorandum by Lord Hugh Cecil, enclosed in Cecil to Davidson, 18 Dec. 1927; *ibid.*, f. 203: P. V. Smith to Davidson, 17 Dec. 1927.

included in the alternative order of communion the 'Black Rubric' which forbade, as normal practice in church, adoration of the consecrated elements; and removed the provision which might have encouraged the omission of prayers for the king. But the tightening of the restrictions on reservation lost the acquiescence of some anglo-catholics in the measure, without being sufficient to increase evangelical support for it. The majorities for the re-revised book in the convocations and the National Church Assembly were smaller than they had been for the first book. In the assembly the overall vote in favour of the revised measure, on 27 April 1928, was 396 to 153, showing a drop of 121 in the number in favour, and an increase of 20 in the number against, compared with the figures in the preceding July.[50] The measure was then submitted to the ecclesiastical committee, which issued a report dated 16 May which concluded:

> They [the committee] have again carefully considered the present revised Measure in the light of what has since taken place, and of the representations now received; they see no reason to depart from the conclusion at which they then arrived, and they desire to report in the same sense.[51]

The measure then went to the Commons. Hopes of its passing that House were not very high after the disappointing vote in the assembly. After debates on 13 and 14 June – again concerned largely with reservation, and involving some of the same speakers as before – there was a second rejection by 266 to 220, a rather larger majority than in December.[52] The M.P.s for Scotland and Wales could be seen again as causing the defeat of the measure, 52 of them voting against.[53]

The rejection of the prayer book measure in December 1927, repeated in June 1928, can be regarded as an exertion of state authority over the Church, a rebuttal by the house of commons of an important official demand of the Church. It was indeed a rebuttal, thrown into clear relief by the large majorities in the Church Assembly in support of the demand, and by the crucial voting of M.P.s for Scotland and Wales (largely non-anglican) on an English and anglican issue. But parliament's refusal was permitted under the terms of the enabling act. There had, moreover, been considerable objection within the Church to the measure, as well as in the state. 'It was not a case of a unanimous Church versus a hostile State', wrote the bishop of Winchester (Theodore Woods) to Davidson. 'The State was moved to its action by prominent members of the Church.'[54] Almost certainly, acceptance of the book by the Commons would not have ended the liturgical indiscipline in the Church of England. The measure had attempted

---

[50] Bell, *Davidson*, II, 1347–51; Lockhart, *Lang*, pp. 307–8; Garbett, *Church and State in England*, pp. 214–15; D.P., 455, ff. 7–11: memorandum of conversations at Canterbury, 3 and 4 Jan. 1928, on submitting a new revised prayer book; *ibid.*, ff. 65–6: leaflet on *Prayer Book Measure, 1928*, dated 21 Jan. 1928; *ibid.*, ff. 172–3: leaflet issued by archbishop of Canterbury, headed 'not to be published before March 19th.', Mar. 1928; *Chronicle of the Convocation of Canterbury* (1853–), VII, 7, pp. 1–5, 31–41, 69–115 (debates of 28 and 29 Mar. 1928).

[51] P.P. 1928 (80), VII, 400 (full report, pp. 395–410).

[52] Hansard, *Parl. Debs*, 5th ser., CCXVIII, 218, 1003–39, 1197–1324.

[53] An analysis in *The Christian World*, 21 June 1928, p. 1, compared this division with that of 15 Dec. 1927. Cf. H. Hensley Henson, *Retrospect of an Unimportant Life* (3 vols., 1942–50), II, 198; E. R. Norman, *Church and Society in England, 1770–1970* (Oxford, 1976), pp. 341–2.

[54] D.P., 455, f. 101: Woods to Davidson, 23 June 1928.

to secure a compromise solution to a problem which was hardly susceptible to compromise. The proposed solution did not meet the desire of a sizeable section of anglican clergy for unrestricted reservation of the sacrament and its use for purposes of congregational worship. At the same time the proposals rejected the desire of some evangelicals to prevent reservation altogether. Both the more pronounced anglo-catholics and the more pronounced evangelical anglicans did not see their wishes realized in the measure. So it is likely that protest and disobedience would have continued, even if the revised prayer book had been given the sanction of law.

5

After both the first and the second rejections of the book, churchmen considered whether they should attempt to revise their relations with the state, perhaps even to demand disestablishment. It was suggested that the constitutional system provided for in the enabling act had failed to operate in 1927–8 because of the frustration of the Church's aim by the house of commons – an assertion of secular authority over spiritual. But the enabling act had given no guarantee, and indeed had not intended, that the Church of England's legislative desires, even if sanctioned by the ecclesiastical committee, would be necessarily accepted by parliament.[55] The machinery provided in 1919 had worked perfectly, as regards its intended limits, in 1927–8, and this was generally accepted. Whatever the statements of some supporters of the measure in the Commons, parliament's interpretation of the enabling act was not regarded as incorrect by the Church, which left it unchallenged. The Church was left to find other means of meeting the difficulty caused by the rejection of its measure. Archbishop Davidson had anticipated this situation when he wrote in July 1927: 'after the emphatic verdict of the Assembly the Parliamentary rejection of the Measure, *though constitutionally legitimate*, would inevitably produce within the Church a situation of the gravest difficulty'.[56] His own attempt at a solution was not to try and reduce state authority over the Church. It was rather to enable the operation, as a Church decision, of the liturgical provisions in the revised book of 1928, hoping that this course would not be challenged in the law-courts.

Among the constitutional initiatives suggested from the time of the first rejection, but not adopted, was a proposal by Lord Hugh Cecil for a measure 'to transfer doctrinal and liturgical matters from Parliament to Convocation and the King in Council'.[57] Davidson felt that he could not 'accept as wise' this suggestion, or some related ones made by Cecil.[58] The Revd Patrick Carnegie Simpson, a Scotsman who was currently a leading member of the Presbyterian Church of England and a professor at Westminster College, Cambridge, urged that the Church of England should now claim spiritual independence from the state, but not necessarily through disestablishment. Presumably

---

[55] A leading article in *The Times* (16 Dec. 1927, p. 15) argued, however, that the system established in 1919 had been given a severe blow by the rejection of the measure.

[56] D.P., 452, f. 302: memorandum by Davidson, 30 July 1927 (my italics).

[57] L.P., 57, ff. 368–9: Cecil to Archbishop Lang, 23 Dec. 1927.

[58] *Ibid.*, f. 384: Davidson to Lang, 29 Dec. 1927.

he favoured a measure similar to the Church of Scotland Act of 1921.[59] A motion was in fact proposed in the lower house of the convocation of Canterbury on 11 July 1928, by Prebendary R. M. Woolley, for the introduction into parliament by Davidson of 'a Bill so amending the Enabling Act as to procure for the Church of England the same measure of freedom as is enjoyed by the Established Religion in Scotland'. Woolley said that he did not support any moves for disestablishment, but argued that the enabling act should be amended 'in such a way as to make it what Churchmen thought at first that it was going to be, and so enabling the Church to be free in spiritual matters': 'They had been told that control by the State was the price they had to pay for being Established; but they all knew that that was not in accordance with the facts. They had only to look across the border and see an Established religion in Scotland.'[60] But Woolley's motion found no support, despite the fact that the Church Self-Government Association was seeking his kind of solution. One speaker in the debate on his motion, Canon T. A. Lacey, said that he would prefer 'a drastic measure of Disestablishment' to an attempt at self-government along with establishment.[61]

Winston Churchill had said in the Commons debate of 14 June that rejection of the measure (which he reluctantly supported) would 'inaugurate a period of chaos which could only be corrected by disestablishment'.[62] The most vocal anglican proposer of disestablishment (more vocal than any nonconformist supporter of it at this point) was Bishop Hensley Henson.[63] He provided a rare, and practically unsupported, voice of direct challenge to state control on account of the measure's rejection, seeking unlimited freedom for the Church to govern itself. He began to show that he favoured disestablishment in his diary entry of 16 December 1927, when regretfully noting the defeat on the previous night of the measure which he had strongly supported. He then wrote:

> The Episcopate can hardly sink so low as to accept its policy from a majority in the House of Commons. . . . Perhaps the best . . . course would be for the Primate to give notice that he would introduce a measure for Disestablishment. . . . Perhaps this humiliating defeat may turn out to be a blessing in disguise, for it has brought Disestablishment into prominence on a clear-cut and adequate issue.[64]

Advocacy of disestablishment was an entirely new course for Henson. But he was no stranger to sharp changes of direction, which held no fears for him. 'Ought I not to complete a life of tergiversation by adding this loyalty also to the holocaust?', he asked himself in his diary in December 1927, when he was about to jettison his hitherto unquestioned attachment to the Church establishment principle.[65] He proceeded to

---

[59] *British Weekly*, 21 June 1928, p. 250: article by Simpson on 'The Second Rejection'. Cf. P. Carnegie Simpson, *The Church and the State* (1929).

[60] *Chronicle of the Convocation of Canterbury*, VII, 8, p. 192: 11 July 1928.

[61] *Ibid.*, p. 193.

[62] Hansard, *Parl. Debs*, 5th ser., CCXVIII, 1270.

[63] Some current nonconformist views on disestablishment were shown in *Primitive Methodist Leader*, 15 Dec. 1927, p. 820; *Baptist Times*, 21 June 1928, pp. 449–50; *Methodist Times*, 15 Dec. 1927, p. 15, 21 June 1928, p. 13.

[64] Henson, *Retrospect*, II, 166–72: Henson's journal, 16, 18, and 23 Dec. 1927.

[65] *Ibid.*, II, 172.

urge his new cause in speeches and publications.[66] He was not quite alone amongst anglicans in proposing disestablishment as a consequence of the parliamentary rejections. J. H. Greig, bishop of Guildford, wrote to Davidson that the union of Church and state could hardly last after the second rejection by the Commons: '[Parliament] is no place in which the true doctrine and best use of the Blessed Sacrament can be rightly debated; or [in which] the doctrines and worship of a spiritual body [can] be added to or cut down or restated, by the same processes and in the same atmosphere as a money bill is shaped and manipulated.'[67] But, as the initial shocks created by the parliamentary rejections died down, Henson found himself with almost no support. He admitted as early as March 1928 that 'the raising of the Disestablishment issue is extraordinarily unpopular in every quarter'.[68] In response to the ecclesiastical unease arising from the rejections, the archbishops appointed a commission on the relations of Church and state in 1930. But its report in 1935 did not recommend a policy of disestablishment, and very few of its proposals led to actual change.[69] Lord Hugh Cecil had written to Archbishop Lang in January 1928: 'Disestablishment will only come when the people generally want it, which they don't at present.'[70]

The Church of England, therefore, would not challenge the state by urging disestablishment. Instead, it adopted a solution for 'the present emergency'. This was provisional in nature but has remained basically in being until the present time. The important extensions which have since been adopted have been in keeping with the tenor of this solution, which was reached by episcopal decision in 1929.

At the beginning of July 1928 the bishops unanimously agreed to a statement by Davidson that the Church must 'retain its inalienable right, in loyalty to our Lord and Saviour Jesus Christ, to formulate its Faith in Him and to arrange the expression of that Holy Faith in its forms of worship'.[71] The adoption of this statement commenced an independent line of action which was unpalatable to defenders of erastian tradition, such as members of the National Church League. The executive committee of this body declared on 24 October 1928 that:

> The Bishops, as the principal executive officers of the Church, should, it is submitted, set an example of obedience to the Constitutional authority that is over them, and should exhort the clergy to the like Obedience; whereas they appear to be compromising the clergy by seeking their support in action which falls little, if at all, short of rebellion against lawful authority.[72]

[66] H. H. Henson, *Disestablishment. The Charge Delivered at the Second Quadrennial Visitation of his Diocese, Together with an Introduction* (1929); H. H. Henson. *Church and State in England* (1930). See O. Chadwick, *Hensley Henson. A Study of Friction between Church and State* (Oxford, 1983), pp. 204–7; E. R. Norman, *Church and Society*, pp. 343–5; N. P. Williams, *The Bishop of Durham and Disestablishment* (1929), p. 24.

[67] D.P., 455, f. 263: Greig to Davidson, 15 June 1928.

[68] Henson, *Retrospect*, II, 188: Henson's journal, 9 Mar. 1928.

[69] Norman, *Church and Society*, p. 342; R. C. D. Jasper, *George Bell, Bishop of Chichester* (1967), pp. 183–95.

[70] L.P., 58, f. 37: 24 Jan. 1928.

[71] Quoted in Bell, *Davidson*, II, 1351; A. Hastings, *A History of English Christianity, 1920–85* (1986), p. 207; D.P., 456, ff. 139–40: notes by Davidson for his speech to the National Church Assembly, 28 June 1928; *ibid.*, f. 147: Davidson to the prolocutor of the convocation of Canterbury, 30 June 1928.

[72] D.P., 456, f. 258: declaration, as sent to Davidson.

At the end of the year, the 1928 Prayer Book was published as a service book for optional use in the Church. In July 1929 the bishops resolved to be guided by the 1928 book when giving liturgical counsel and directions to clergy who were dissatisfied with the 1662 book, and 'to endeavour to secure that the practices which are consistent neither with the Book of 1662 nor with the Book of 1928 shall cease'.[73] This referred, of course, to practices of an extreme anglo-catholic nature.

This resolution, however, failed to terminate indiscipline in the conduct of worship in the Church. When the bishop of London, A. F. Winnington-Ingram, tried to impose on his clergy the restrictions on reservation in the 1928 book, 21 incumbents refused to stop holding services with the blessed sacrament. These, however, were only a small portion of the 149 incumbents in the diocese who practised reservation; the remainder presumably accepted the episcopal directions.[74] Liturgical diversity had become too entrenched to be completely checked. Later, the policy adopted from the 1970s onwards was to increase the opportunities for diversity by licensing alternative services. Parliamentary sanction was obtained for some of these innovations, which indicated that the legislature shifted about 50 years later from the position taken by the Commons in 1927 and 1928.

The revised book of 1928 was adopted as an alternative guideline to the 1662 book even though parliament had not granted to the revised book the authority of civil law. The long-awaited attempt to achieve more discipline in the public worship of the Church of England, by means of making some concessions to ritualist desires, had not succeeded in winning the consent of the more extreme anglo-catholics and had aroused strong opposition from the more extreme evangelicals. It was the latter, led by Bishop E. A. Knox and others outside parliament, and by Joynson-Hicks, Rosslyn Mitchell and others inside, which mainly had destroyed the attempt to win parliamentary authorization for a Revised Prayer Book in 1927–8. Thereafter, the Church did not seek complete religious freedom through disestablishment, but initiated a compromise solution. This was untidy and was not intended to be permanent, but it proved fairly effective. In accordance with this compromise, the Church used the Revised Book, as an alternative to the 1662 book, without legal authorization. This practice could have been challenged in the law-courts – a move which might have resulted (as Archbishop Garbett wrote) in a judgement against the Church, precipitating 'a crisis . . . between obedience to the State and loyalty to the Church'.[75] Such a crisis did not occur, however, because a challenge was not made in the courts.

The bishops, in their search for greater peace and discipline within the Church, were placed in a continual dilemma over their relations with the state. The Church was unable to obtain immediate internal peace through the disputed settlement of 1929.[76]

---

[73] Bell, *Davidson*, II, 1358–9. Cf. Lockhart, *Lang*, pp. 309, 338–40; Garbett, *Church and State*, pp. 217–19.

[74] W. S. F. Pickering, *Anglo-Catholicism. A Study in Religious Ambiguity* (1991), p. 62. Cf. Jasper, *Bell*, pp. 165–76.

[75] Garbett, *Church and State*, p. 220.

[76] See Jasper, *Bell*, pp. 165–200.

Liturgical peace only came later, not through more restriction but through greater diversity. After the 1928 rejection, the Church retained its link with the state but later followed the example of its 1929 resolution by adopting more self-regulation, with parliamentary sanction on the more crucial matters.[77]

[77] On these matters see P. A. Welsby, *A History of the Church of England, 1945–80* (Oxford, 1986), pp. 217–26, 239–42.

The 1944 Education Act: A Church–State Perspective

S.J.D. GREEN

It is easy to forget that it was once 'customary to genuflect whenever the Butler [Education] Act was mentioned.'[1] Winston Churchill, legendary early opponent of change yet lesser known champion of the eventual legislation, hailed it as the 'greatest measure' of education reform 'passed in the history of this country'.[2] Even those less inclined to hyperbole tended to agree. James Chuter Ede, tireless proponent of progress, noted testily that this fine outcome was 'more the result of the coalition', that is, of Labour's support for Butler's plans, than of the prime minister's speedy enlightenment; yet he insisted that the act had gone 'a long way to unify the educational system of the country', and in so doing had given the 'whole service . . . a fresh start on improved lines'.[3] For a generation subsequently the majority of informed commentators and critics concurred; a few with Churchill's fine words, most with the more measured assent of Ede.[4] The occasional champion can still be found.[5]

But the prevailing orthodoxy is hostile. Variously berated for its failures to deal with the 'real problem[s]' of economic modernization, social justice or even administrative efficiency, the act is now widely condemned as a missed opportunity. Ostentatiously raising the school-leaving age to 15, it put off the much more important question of the virtual absence of higher education for all but a tiny minority. Ostensibly extending the possibility of educational opportunity for all, it only made universal an impoverished version of liberal studies at the expense of widespread technical instruction the nation so badly needed.[6] Worst of all, it left the structures of educational provision essentially unchanged. This view has been summarized with exemplary clarity by Dr Adrian Wooldridge who insists that the 1944 Education Act was

---

[1] Noel Annan, *Our Age. Portrait of a Generation* (1990), p. 362.

[2] *Labour and the Wartime Coalition. From the Diaries of James Chuter Ede*, ed. Kevin Jeffreys (1987), p. 210: 15 Mar. 1945.

[3] *Ibid.*, pp. 210 and 202: 15 Mar. 1945 and 31 Dec. 1944.

[4] Annan, *Our Age*, pp. 362–3; Marjorie Cruikshank, *Church and State in English Education. 1870 to the Present Day* (1964), p. 169; P.H.J.H. Gosden, *Education in the Second World War. A Study in Policy and Administration* (1976), pp. 431–3; H.C. Dent, *1870–1970. A Century of Growth in English Education* (1970), p. 116; Adrian Hastings, *A History of English Christianity, 1920–1985* (1986), ch.29.

[5] See, for instance, David Eccles, 'Education Act', in *A Rabanthology*, ed. Mollie Butler (York, 1995), pp. 23–6; or, more soberly, Keith Middlemas, *Power, Competition and the State. Vol. 1, Britain in Search of Balance, 1940–1961* (Basingstoke, 1986), p. 366.

[6] A.H. Halsey, A.F. Heath and J.M. Ridge, *Origins and Destinations. Family, Class and Education in Modern Britain* (Oxford, 1980), ch. 2; Corelli Barnett, *The Lost Victory. British Dreams, British Realities, 1945–1950* (1995), esp. pp. 288–91; Adrian Wooldridge, *Measuring the Mind. Education and Psychology in England, c. 1860–1990* (Cambridge, 1994), esp. pp. 251–60.

the work of a quintessentially Tory politician who reformed in order to preserve, pandering to a litany of cherished conservative beliefs – of traditional religion, the virtue of variety and decentralisation, the value of hierarchy and privilege – and left the balance of power in the educational world unaltered, with the LEAs retaining their autonomy and the churches preserving their accumulated powers.[7]

Yet it is a commonplace that the rage of hindsight often reveals more about the preoccupations of the present rather than the concerns of the past. More pointedly, its all too assured disillusion can also conflate, thereby to confuse, those concerns. Certainly, few contemporaries would have bracketed the continued autonomy of local education authorities with the statutory preservation of accumulated ecclesiastical powers in the post-war English educational system. Most would have regarded the two – for good or ill – as polar opposite outcomes of likely legislative reform; in effect, that more of one must have entailed less of the other. That they in fact flourished, together, enhanced and renewed for a generation after 1944 was, accordingly, a conscious and creative achievement of pedagogical balance, not a lazy concession to administrative or political convenience.

One might go further. No aspect of the 1944 Educational Act was more remarkable, that is, more unexpected and more far-reaching, than the preservation of accumulated Church powers which characterized its final provisions. Yet if this simple fact has often been noted, its causes have rarely been uncovered and its implications still less frequently explored. Opinion seems to have divided between those who deem that survival to have been inevitable and those who regard it as an accident.[8] Contemporary observers would have been surprised by such interpretative neglect. Whether in celebration or remorse, most would have shared the view of Canon W.T. Brown, special advisor to the Wakefield Divisional Association of Church Schools, that 'the most important contribution of the new Education Act is in its provisions dealing with voluntary schools and religious education'; similarly with his judgement that those 'provisions . . . are more generous' for the Church 'than seemed likely even three or four years ago'.[9]

For, whatever else it was, the 1944 Education Act was a measure of avowedly Christian stewardship: advanced by a Christian minister, passed by a Christian parliament, directed towards the goal of creating a truly Christian population. Put less politely, it enacted compulsory Christian education for the first time in all maintained schools. H.C. Dent, then headmaster of Westminster City School observed that, for all the official guff about a principle newly established that 'pupils are to be educated in accordance with the wishes of their parents', the actual outcome was a law which quite specifically 'denies the aid of the state to those groups of educationalists who might wish, with the approval of parents, to provide a purely secular education'.[10]

---

[7] Wooldridge, *Measuring the Mind*, pp. 259–60.

[8] For the inevitable, James Murphy, *Church, State and Schools in Britain, 1800–1970* (1971), pp. 114–15; and the accidental, Anthony Howard, *Rab. The Life of R.A. Butler* (1987), p. 127.

[9] W.J. Brown, *The Church and the Education Act* (Dewsbury, 1944), pp. 4 and 16.

[10] Lambeth Palace Library, William Temple Papers, vol. 21, f. 72 [hereafter cited as LPL/WTP]: H.C. Dent to Temple, 18 Sept. 1943.

Moreover, it was a protestant act. That is, it was conceived with the interests, prejudices and sensibilities of anglicans and nonconformists in mind. As Butler put it: 'I warned the Catholics that this particular settlement was not their pigeon.'[11] To be sure, the new regime provided for an equitable subsidy of Roman catholic so-called 'aided' schools.[12] But even that was just one-half of what the hierarchy had demanded.[13] And the 'agreed syllabus' for religious instruction in the re-named 'controlled schools' frightened the bishops into believing that the peculiar charms of their faith would eventually be 'crowded out of the state system.'[14] By December 1943 they had come to 'dislike . . . the whole trend of opinion which the Bill represented' and, in particular, 'the threat to family life and the liberty of the individual' which it implied.[15] Their problem was that the protestant majority in England and Wales simply did not see things that way; still less its representatives in parliament.[16]

Which is far from saying that the protestant majority saw the provisions of the Education Act in the same way. The act may indeed have arisen out of previously unresolved 'difficulties between the Nonconformists and the Anglicans'.[17] But what emerged was not a settlement of those disagreements. The act 'did not satisfy' the Free Churches.[18] Rather they acquiesced in it to the general good of 'positive advance in educational reconstruction'; all the while insisting that, for instance, the 'grant[ing] of large sums of public money towards the improvement of Denominational School Buildings without any extension of public control' openly 'clashes with the principle of democratic government'; similarly, they denounced the 'injustice' of leaving the question of single school areas so visibly 'unsolved'.[19] Put another way, 1944 was an anglican triumph; a reassertion not simply of the Christian principle in English and Welsh education, nor merely of the priority of protestantism in official thinking but of the peculiar privileges, both assumed and specified, of the Church of England in these vital aspects of national life.

1

That was what was so unexpected, by Canon Brown and many others, in 1940. For in scarcely any aspect of its existence was the priority and privilege of the Church of England so precariously placed just before the outbreak of the Second World War. A curious combination of ecclesiastical benevolence, denominational disputaciousness

[11] Trinity College, Cambridge, Butler Papers, G15/86/87 [hereafter cited as TCC/BP]: R.A. Butler 'Political Diary', 9 Sept. 1943.

[12] Cruikshank, *Church and State*, pp. 143–4, 154–9, 161–8.

[13] TCC/BP, G15/37: R.A. Butler, 'Note', 25 May 1943.

[14] TCC/BP, G15/85: Butler, 'Political Diary', 9 Sept. 1943.

[15] TCC/BP, G15/177: Butler 'Diary',? Dec. 1943.

[16] *Ibid.*

[17] TCC/BP, G15/86: Butler 'Political Diary', 9 Sept. 1943.

[18] LPL/WTP, 21/191: R.D. Whitehorn, moderator Free Church Federal Council, unpublished letter to *The Times*, 11 Nov. 1943.

[19] Free Church Federal Council, *A Statement on the Educational Proposals Published in the Board of Education's White Paper on 'Educational Reconstruction'* (1943), p. 1. More generally, see the remarks in Stephen Koss, *Nonconformity in Modern British Politics* (1975), p. 222.

and administrative accident had made the Church one of the principal providers of public education during the nineteenth century. But statutory intervention from 1870 onwards and especially after 1902 had seriously weakened this role.[20] The obligation of voluntary societies to provide for and keep their own buildings, particularly as interpreted subsequently to the 1921 Education Act, led to a precipitous decline – of something like 20 per cent – in the number of non-provided schools, and a still more marked decline – around one-third – in the average attendance of pupils at those schools, up to 1938. By the outbreak of the war, many had come to conclude that 'it was only a question of time when nearly all non-provided schools, other than Roman catholic, would cease to exist'.[21]

Such a shift of material and manpower resources reflected an equally significant alteration in the balance of educational influence between Church and state; or more accurately, between the churches and the local educational authorities.[22] And it was accompanied by a more nebulous but equally unmistakeable inversion in the respective social prestige of the clerical and teaching professions. Whether or not the 'fool of the family' really was now going into the Church, teaching was attracting more intelligent, and correspondingly more ambitious, recruits. As Sir Frederick Mandler, general secretary of the National Union of Teachers, put it in 1942: 'Times have changed since 1870 . . . the clerical profession can no longer claim any particular intellectual advantage over the teaching profession.'[23] In that way, what Temple described as the erstwhile 'natural tendency' for an incumbent 'to regard the schoolmaster as part of his parochial staff' was becoming harder and harder to sustain.[24]

The result was not a new equilibrium. Rather, it was increasingly bitter tension. What Temple deemed the 'unhappy prejudice in the minds of teachers . . . that their position in Church schools is one of less dignity than in other schools' remained, all too forcefully.[25] And it had its reasons. Nearly 10,000 headships remained out of reach to teachers who did not profess the doctrine of the Church of England. Moreover, in those schools the provision of religious education entailed the subjection of the teachers to virtual religious tests. Even the lessons themselves were set for prescribed times of the school day. For many teachers these were intolerable intrusions into professional integrity.[26] And the opportunity seemed ripe to put them right. Mandler again: 'If ever teachers were in a good bargaining position they are in one today.'[27]

One reason for Mandler's confidence in this respect was his belief that all impartial, and indeed much otherwise committed opinion, now sided with the teachers against the clergy in these maters. As he put it: '[E]very Minister of Education, every administrator, every teacher, every intelligent churchman and every honest politician knows

[20] Cruikshank, *Church and State*, chs. 2–6; Murphy, *Church, State and Schools*, ch. 7; Corelli Barnett, *The Collapse of British Power* (1972), pp. 103–6.

[21] Brown, *The Church and the Education Act*, p. 6.

[22] William Temple, *Our Trust and Our Task. Being the Presidential Address to the Annual Meeting of the National Society, on 3 June 1942* (1942), p. 6.

[23] Sir Frederick Mandler, *Religious Instruction Controversy* (1942), p. 9.

[24] Temple, *Our Trust*, p. 6.

[25] *Ibid.*, p. 7.

[26] Mandler, *Religious Instruction Controversy*, p. 9.

[27] *Ibid.*, p. 3.

quite well that the dual system lies like a tank trap across the highway to educational advance . . . a weird, outmoded . . . dichotomy which [causes] administrative impotence and [prevents] real equality of opportunity for . . . ordinary children.'[28] Some churchmen saw his point of view. Writing to Temple, the Reverend Canon Tissington Tatlow, of the Institute of Christian Education, felt bound to point out that, for board of education officials, L.E.A. directors, H.M.I.s and teachers anyway, 'church schools . . . always seem to mean . . . one thing and that is bad schools [moreover] places where . . . too many . . . children must go . . . and thus be educationally handicapped for life because it is not possible for the Educational Authority to remove the bad school and replace it by a good one'.[29]

The inadequacy of such schools was variously defined. And if for some it was as much a question of contestable administrative efficiency and all too precious professional pride, for others it was increasingly a matter of science; more specifically, of educational theory. This took the view that failure to divide pupils at 11, four times more likely in the case of Church than of council schools, constituted in itself a form of educational deprivation.[30] Similarly, it condemned the lack of space for 'indoor . . . physical training', again altogether more characteristic of non-provided than of provided schools, as 'likely to injure . . . a very large number of children'.[31] Certainly, it was in these respects that the Church's particular prominence on the list of so-called 'black-listed schools' presented by Butler to Temple as a matter of lamentable and undoubted fact was to prove so influential.[32]

This was why church schools, generally, and the dual system in particular had so few friends by the summer of 1942. Temple ruefully calculated the opposition as 'combin[ing] nearly all forces except the Roman Catholics and that . . . not very great . . . part of the [anglican] laity which cares'.[33] Mandler made bitter reference to the support of 'reactionary . . . groups . . . in the House of Commons'.[34] But no one presumed that its defenders formed anything like an interested majority. One thing alone, in fact, seemed to stand between the dual system and oblivion in the summer of 1942. Canon Brown called it 'public opinion'.[35] This was the perception, widespread from 1940 onwards, that England was in danger of becoming an irreligious country. More: that the cause of this calamity lay in the poor quality of contemporary religious education.

It began with a leader in *The Times*. Its author noted amongst the 'incidental results of the evacuation scheme' the disturbing 'discovery that large numbers of town children are being brought up with no religious knowledge at all'. He then cited the example of the country parson who had found that, within his makeshift class of 12-year-olds, 19 of the 31 did not know who it was who had been 'born on Christmas Day'.[36] What was almost certainly the principal cause of this ignorance – the spectacular decline in Sunday

[28] *Ibid.*, p. 2.
[29] LPL/WTP, 19/138: The Reverend Canon Tissington Tatlow to Temple, 24 June 1942.
[30] LPL/WTP, 20/49: Sir Maurice Holmes to Temple, 14 Nov. 1942.
[31] LPL/WTP, 20/47: Canon A.R. Wilkinson-Browne to Temple, 14 Nov. 1942.
[32] TCC/BP, G15/84: Butler, 'Political Diary', 9 Sept. 1943.
[33] LPL/WTP, 20/101: Temple to Mr Gibbins, 20 Nov. 1942.
[34] Mandler, *Religious Instruction Controversy*, p. 1.
[35] Brown, *The Church and the Education Act*, p. 6.
[36] 'Religious Education', *The Times*, 17 Feb. 1940.

school enrolment, of the region of 50 per cent, between the wars – eluded him.[37] What he latched on to was the grim fact that 'in some of the schools provided by the state there is no religious teaching'. This pointed, he argued, for 'a country professedly Christian' to address the need for a complete 'recast[ing] of the state scheme of education'.[38]

These sentiments were repeated virtually verbatim in the anonymous 'Preface' to *Crockford's Clerical Directory*, in 1941.[39] More importantly, they became the basis of the famous 'Five Points' outlined by the two English primates in *The Times* on 13 February 1941. There, Lang and Temple urged a pedagogical revolution which would provide for an 'effective Christian education', made available for the first time to 'all children' in 'every school', taught only by those teachers willing and competent to undertake the task. And one other thing: that the 'timetable be so arranged as to provide for an act of worship on the part of the whole school at the beginning of the school day'.[40] But nothing much happened as a result, not at least until one day in the summer of 1941, when the prime minister summoned R.A. Butler, the under-secretary of state for foreign affairs, to see him for a short chat.

Butler relates the rest:

> [Churchill] saw me after his afternoon nap. [He] was audibly purring. He said 'You have been in the House 15 years and it is time you were promoted'. I [replied] that I had only been there for 12 years but he waved this aside. He continued: 'I want you to go to the Board of Education. I think you can leave your mark there . . . it is true that you will be outside the main stream of the war but you will be independent . . . Besides you will be in the war. You will move poor children from here to there' and he lifted up imaginary children from one side of his writing pad to the other. 'This will be difficult', he concluded. I then said that I had always looked forward to going to the Board of Education if I was given the chance. At this he looked ever so slightly surprised, which showed that he felt in war a central job such as the one I am leaving is the most important. [But] he seemed genuinely pleased that I had shown so much pleasure and seemed to think the whole appointment quite suitable.[41]

2

There would have been no wartime education act but for Richard Austen Butler. He wanted it. Against considerable odds, he fought for it. And, much in the manner and to the ends for which he had worked, he secured it.[42] True, he did not originate the plan

---

[37] On this decline and its wider effects, see Christie Davies, 'Moralisation and Demoralisation: A Moral Explanation for Changes in Crime, Disorder and Social Problems', in *The Loss of Virtue. Moral Confusion and Social Disorder in Britain and America*, ed. Digby Anderson (1992), pp. 1–13.

[38] 'Religious Education'.

[39] Anon., 'Preface', *Crockford's Clerical Directory, 1941* (1941), pp. xiii–xiv.

[40] 'True Christian Education – Archbishop's Appeal', *The Times*, 13 Feb. 1941.

[41] TCC/BP, 513/158: R.A. Butler, 'Note', ? Aug. 1941; repeated in Lord Butler, *The Art of the Possible* (1972), p. 50; also, more accurately, in Howard, *Rab*, pp. 109–10.

[42] On which, see Kevin Jeffreys, 'R.A. Butler, The Board of Education and the 1944 Education Act', *History*, LXIX (1984), 415–31; a definitive refutation of 'revisionism' in this respect, also the remarks in Chris Patten, 'R.A. Butler: What We Missed', in *A Rabanthology*, ed. Butler, pp. 93–118, esp. p. 105.

either for educational reorganisation or for a general extension of educational opportunity; these can be traced back at least as far as the Hadow report of 1926.[43] More importantly, he laboured under circumstances in which the sheer range and frequent incompatibility of the competing interests involved ensured that no measure actually undertaken could ever have accorded with the intelligible wishes of any wholly rational person; unprincipled compromise, in that sense, was a prerequisite of action.[44] But the eventual result accorded more closely with Butler's vision and was more clearly the product of Butler's efforts than of any other involved party. He was not bluffing when he responded so enthusiastically to Churchill's lukewarm offer. He really did believe that 'education' was one of the 'two [major] problems' of contemporary British government 'most needing solution'. The other was India.[45]

But what did Butler mean by 'needing solution'? To some degree, he meant what every other informed observer insisted upon. He meant a better education service: more efficiently organized, more consciously directed to the maximum development of every pupil's potential, more carefully geared to the requirements of a modern society. Here, he could deliver bromides with the best of them: 'we are determined to make England a better place. A start might well be made in education . . . mak[ing] entrances more easy for those who need the chance . . . recruit[ing] a wider range of leaders for the egalitarian England of tomorrow.'[46]

But that was not all he meant. For Butler's position at that time, whether within the government or the Conservative party, was both peculiar and precarious. Indeed, it would scarcely be an exaggeration to observe that, alone among senior politicians, he had some reason to fear either a Labour or a Conservative victory after the war. No ally, or even admirer, of Churchill, he had tried harder than most to prevent the 'great . . . adventurer's' accession to the premiership.[47] He also toiled under the considerable burden of Anthony Eden's enmity. Indeed, there is every reason to believe that it was the foreign secretary, rather than the prime minister, who engineered Butler's removal to the board of education. His new deputy, James Chuter Ede, certainly thought so.[48] Unless he could make his mark, quickly, in the coalition government, Butler faced the prospect of being marginalized in future Conservative administrations; certainly, in any government led by Anthony Eden, his senior by only five years. Out of immediate control of his superiors, he figured that he just might be able to make that indelible impression which could make him politically significant for a further generation to come.

Yet Butler's motives were far from wholly personal. He hoped to do something for the coalition government, and by implication, for the Conservative party. In the wake of the publication of the Beveridge report on *Social Insurance and Allied Services*, in 1942, this became an increasingly insistent aspect of the official impetus to educational reform. Butler actually submitted a paper to cabinet precisely on those terms as early as August

[43] On Hadow, see Wooldridge, *Measuring the Mind*, pp. 224 ff; and on contemporary reactions to it, note the remarks of Eustace Percy, *Some Memories* (1958), pp. 101–2.

[44] See the remarks in Murphy, *Church, State and Schools*, pp. 113–15.

[45] TCC/BP, G15/4: R.A. Butler, 'Note', 8 May 1941.

[46] R.A. Butler, *A Future to Work For* (1942), p. 1.

[47] John Colville, *The Fringes of Power. Downing Street Diaries, 1939–1955* (1985), p. 122: 10 May 1940.

[48] *Labour and the Wartime Coalition*, ed. Jeffreys, p. 39: 12 Jan. 1942.

1942 arguing for 'educational benefits' that might be obtained for as little as '£100 millions a year' as 'an alternative' to the 'possibility of Beveridge at a projected £650 millions'.[49] Indeed he eventually won the support of his Conservative colleagues because, in the words of Lord President Anderson, they were 'not yet ready for Beveridge', fearing amongst other things that it might possibly have a deleterious 'effect . . . on national character'.[50] Conversely, it was in its guise as cynical variant to the prospect of wider social change that the education measure provoked its most determined opposition within the war cabinet. This was not from Churchill at all.[51] It was from Morrison, who as late as February 1944 argued that no 'Education Bill should go forward' precisely and solely because 'a Tory minister would be in charge of it'.[52]

But this was far from the whole truth. For Butler was also an unusually thoughtful and committed churchman. He wanted to do something for the good of the Church, and religious faith more generally. Even Selborne, one of his most persistent critics within the government, had no hesitation in identifying him as 'a very keen Christian as well as a keen educational reformer'; also, pointedly as one who 'recognises that no education is worth having unless it is based on religion'.[53] More to the point, Butler believed that the 1902 Education Act had inflicted 'infinite damage' on both the Conservative Party and the Church and he was determined to rectify its deleterious effects on both.[54] Yet his motives in this respect were never purely tactical. He argued for the importance of 'instilling the citizen of the future with a [proper] code of Christian ethics'. And, he considered, given the recent 'surge . . . of . . . frankly materialist opinion' which the war had unleashed, that it was now clearly imperative 'to rally our forces' so that 'old faiths' could again be made 'vivid to the [next] generation'. Otherwise, 'our civilisation', as he put it, will 'take a turn for the worse'.[55] Hence his insistence, made in all seriousness and with complete sincerity, that there was 'no more important feature of the government's proposals for educational reconstruction than those which made provision for religious teaching'.[56]

However, if these were traditional tory views, they pointed towards a distinct change in tory stewardship of the social order. For nothing perhaps so defined Butler amongst tory politicians of the time as in his profound reaction to the events of May and June 1940. This sense was picked up very quickly by his then P.P.S. Chips Channon, who noted in his diary as early as October 1940 that Butler was a man 'obsessed by the post-war new order', who thought that 'our whole system will be drastically modified'.[57]

[49] TCC/BP, G15/88: Butler, 'Political Diary', 9 Sept. 1943.
[50] *Labour and the Wartime Coalition*, ed. Jeffreys, p. 92: 7 Aug. 1942.
[51] TCC/BP, G13/160: copy of p.m.'s Minute, M/895/1: 13 Sept. 1941; but note G13/161: Holmes to Rab, 16 Sept. 1941, 'I do not think we need be unduly cast down . . . demand [for] a measure of educational reform . . . will be irresistible.'
[52] *Labour and the Wartime Coalition*, ed. Jeffreys, p. 169: 10 Feb. 1944.
[53] LPL/WTP, 19/319: Selborne to Temple, 14 Sept. 1942.
[54] TCC/BP, G15/88: Butler, 'Political Diary', 9 Sept. 1943.
[55] R.A. Butler, *Address Delivered on 30 March 1943 To The Third Annual Congress of the Free Church Council* (Cambridge, 1943), p. 2.
[56] *The Times*, 31 Aug. 1943.
[57] *Chips. The Diaries of Sir Henry Channon*, ed. Robert Rhodes James (1967), p. 268: 7 Oct. 1940, corroborated by Paul Addison, *The Road to 1945. British Politics and the Second World War* (1975), p. 172.

And it was powerfully echoed in his own observation that 'one of the objectives' of the 'religious settlement' in educational reconstruction was 'to relieve English politics of the squire and parson monopoly in rural areas'; not, he hastened to add 'because I, as a Conservative wish to remove it, but because economic circumstances and the decline in the influence of the Anglican Church have already removed it'.[58]

What, then, was to be done? Put simply: the welfare state was to be brought to the aid of the traditional institutions of British society. At its most basic, this involved 'the codificat[ion] of existing practice'. It also meant that degree of formalization in such practice which might allow 'improve[ment] for future use'.[59] In the context of educational reconstruction, this entailed shoring up the dual system of educational administration with the use of public money. The problem was that, in the summer of 1941, there was absolutely no basis in public sentiment, whether at the level of interest or of argument, to secure the necessary consensus so to proceed. Butler's challenge – and what became his towering achievement – was to create it.

In this task, he acquired by peculiar good fortune an ally in Archbishop Temple, from January 1942 onwards.[60] His luck in this respect was less a function of Lang's unexpected retirement than Temple's wholly unanticipated sympathy and guile. It is difficult in retrospect to appreciate just how unexpected these qualities were. Contemporary Conservatives were appalled by Temple's appointment to Canterbury, Butler included.[61] They hated him for his socialism; and Chips Channon at least, not merely for his politics but also on account of his corpulence.[62] So great was their distaste and distrust in Temple's ability ever to represent faithfully the thinking of the 'conservative wing of the Church' that Butler soon found that despite his preference for dealing with one man from each of the relevant religious constituencies he was compelled in the case of the most important – the Church of England – to hold simultaneous discussions with the archbishop of York and the bishops of London, Durham and Chichester for fear of arousing the 'indignation of certain Conservative MPs that any Temple solution should prevail'.[63]

Inconvenient as this must initially have been, it soon proved a huge advantage for Butler. For whilst many Conservatives would vouch for nothing unless it had also the signatures of Garbett and Fisher on it, Temple's long history of ecumenical involvement appealed to the nonconformists whilst his equally colourful background in radical politics assuaged the fears of many on the Labour benches.[64] At the same time, he proved in most of the crucial respects which concerned Butler to be altogether closer to the president's ways of thinking than the sceptical tory had ever

[58] TCC/BP, G15/88: Butler, 'Political Diary', 9 Sept. 1943.

[59] TCC/BP, G15/37: R.A. Butler, 'Note', 25 May 1943.

[60] On Temple's appointment, see Iremonger, *Temple*, pp. 474 ff; on tory reactions to it, see Angus Calder, *The People's War* (1965), pp. 558–9.

[61] TCC/BP, G14/23: R.A. Butler, 'Note', 21 Jan. 1942.

[62] *Chips*, ed. Rhodes James, pp. 337, 352, 368, 396: 27 Sept. 1942, 8 Mar. 1943, 22 June 1943, 26 Oct. 1944.

[63] TCC/BP, G15/176: R.A. Butler, 'Diary', ? Dec. 1943.

[64] On which, see F.A. Iremonger, *William Temple, Archbishop of Canterbury. His Life and Letters* (Oxford, 1948), esp. chs. 24 and 21. On Labour, see, *Labour and the Wartime Coalition*, ed. Jeffreys, 'Introduction', pp. 1–16; and more generally, R.S. Barker, *Education and Politics. A Study of the Labour Party* (Oxford, 1970), pp. 75–80.

envisaged. That revelation – for such it surely was – was embodied in a note which Butler sent to Temple on 5 February 1943, drawing the archbishop for the very first time into his confidence as he warned him that the draft measure of reform might see the light around Easter of that year: 'You have taken so wise and courageous a line in educational reform [that] I think you are entitled to know what is in the mind of the government. But I am not informing anyone else.'[65]

Temple's 'line' was simple. He wished to preserve the dual system. Given that, supporting coalition policy was not always easy. As late as April 1942, Temple believed that the government had as its 'object' nothing less than the 'end of the Dual System'.[66] And even when it did not appear antagonistic its purposes were by no means easy to follow. Temple initially 'disliked . . . Butler's method of dealing with each of us separately', of in effect inviting each side to cancel out the other's suggestions, whilst 'he tried to reach a result in his own mind'.[67] But eventually he came to see its merits. Against his expectations, 'that method of flying kites [of] seeing groups separately [and] watching their reactions to one another's proposals' actually did 'wonders in carrying us so far towards an agreement' by December 1942.[68] But how, exactly?

3

There were three main components to Butler's legislative strategy: first, he insisted upon the primacy of the religious question in all substantive deliberation about government education policy; secondly, he argued for the voluntary principle in every significant question of institutional transfer; finally, he stood for Christian progress at all times as part of the price of achieving political balance.

The first may seem obvious. It was not so. Religion, as any number of educational psychologists would happily have testified in the summer of 1941, was not the only substantive matter confronting national educational policy. Indeed, for many, it was a relatively minor issue, far less important than questions concerning the school-leaving age, payment of fees in state-maintained grammar schools, or even the availability of advanced technical instruction.[69] Even Conservatives had other problems on their minds. Not the least of these was the future of the public schools, seemingly endangered by the precipitous decline in enrolments over the previous generation. So much so that when the possibility of going to the board of education was first mooted, Butler was specifically implored by Ambassador Winant not to resolve the religious question but 'to keep the public schools [to] try . . . to . . . cheapen them [or] at any rate to pour more people into them'.[70]

[65] LPL/WTP, 20/202: Butler to Temple, 5 Feb. 1943.
[66] LPL/WTP, 19/15: Temple to Canon Alfred Woodward, 20 Apr. 1942.
[67] LPL/WTP, 20/95: Temple to Earl Grey, 30 Nov. 1942.
[68] TCC/BP, G14/160: Temple to Butler, 26 Dec. 1942.
[69] Wooldridge, *Measuring the Mind*, pp. 224 ff; also Adrian Wooldridge, 'The English State and Educational Theory', in *The Boundaries of the State in Modern Britain*, ed. S.J.D. Green and R.C. Whiting (Cambridge, 1996), pp. 231–57, esp. 238–40.
[70] TCC/BP, G13/4: R.A. Butler, 'Note', 8 May 1941.

This was a concern Butler fully shared. However, he chose to deal with it by ignoring it; or rather, by hiving it off to a separate body, the Fleming committee.[71] This was an act of salutary neglect. For the establishment of such a body with wide-ranging powers of review enabled Butler effectively to disaggregate the problem of the public schools from the question of war-time educational reorganization, concentrating administrative attention upon the maintained sector: and therefore, inevitably upon the question of the dual system. This cunning manoeuvre was carried out formally at the lord president's committee on 18 December 1942. Only the old-Haileyburian Attlee expressed real 'disappoint[ment]' that 'we had left [out] the public schools'. Only Morrison expressed 'doubts' about 'educational reform' as a whole.[72] Churchill, by then, had been 'considerably mollified' by the apparent 'approval' of 'High Church Tories' such as Stuart, Wilmer and the various Cecils.[73]

Moreover, in so directing common concerns towards the particular problem of the dual system, Butler was able to bring out into the open an underlying truth which few previously had acknowledged. This was that the so-called 'religious controversy' was only in part a dispute between the principal Christian denominations within the realm. To almost as great a degree, it was a symbol of tension between religious denominationalism in general and the relevant secular authorities in particular; more bluntly still, between the Church of England and the local educational authorities, or at village level between clergymen and teachers. Only in what were known as the 'single-school areas', loosely speaking, rural communities served only by an anglican school, was it ever really reducible to an 'oppressive churchy atmosphere' irritating to nonconformist parents.[74]

This was partly because the overwhelming majority of non-provided protestant schools in pre-war England were in fact anglican establishments. By 1938 there were barely more than 300 nonconformist schools left in England and Wales, catering for fewer than 40,000 pupils. For the purposes of public administration they scarcely existed.[75] But it was mainly because the question of the future of the large and rising number of Roman catholic schools – there were nearly 1,300 of these serving more than 300,000 pupils around the same time – was largely theoretical.[76] Put another way, it was virtually secure. No one perceived this so keenly, nor resented it so greatly, as the ubiquitous Mandler who complained, as early as 1942, that 'people keep talking as though the problem of Catholic schools was not there and [that] a settlement of the religious difficulty can be secured which leaves the Roman Catholic schools outside its scope'.[77]

But there was worse. For if official silence on the catholic question fuelled Mandler's suspicion that 'there is no present intention on the part of the churches to transfer their schools to the local authorities', it suggested to Butler a way in which that defiant

[71] Butler, *The Art of the Possible*, pp. 119–20; Howard, *Rab*, pp. 121–3; and especially the remarks in Addison, *The Road to 1945*, p. 239.
[72] *Labour and the Wartime Coalition*, ed. Jeffreys, pp. 14–15: 18 Dec. 1942.
[73] *Ibid.*, p. 103: 4 Nov. 1942.
[74] Cruikshank, *Church and State*, pp. 139–40.
[75] Brown, *The Church and the Education Act*, p. 6.
[76] *Ibid.*
[77] Mandler, *Religious Instruction Controversy*, p. 3.

intransigence might actually be brought within the bounds of a plausible, indeed of a plausibly progressive, public policy. The fact that those schools tended to be 'planted in areas where Roman Catholics abound' and funded by a peculiarly catholic 'form of taxation' ensured that no war-time British government would seriously attempt to sequester them.[78] In which case, fairness as well as prejudice suggested that protestant schools should be similarly treated. This is what Butler meant when he declared that 'To apply compulsion for the sake of unification of administration would neither be equitable nor in accordance with out national traditions.'[79]

In this way, the voluntary principle was born. No non-provided school which could reach a certain minimum standard of physical ambience and intellectual attainment would be compelled to transfer its physical plant and human resources over to local authority control; similarly no school would be prevented from doing so. But the ethic of consent did not imply the virtue of the *status quo*. On this, the president was clear. It was essential that education take 'first place in any plans for reconstruction that are brought in'. And the fundamental basis for 'educational change' was 'administrative reorganisation'.[80] Accordingly, those bodies which could not be compelled to hand over their schools might be 'encourage[d]' to do so.[81] And what better way to encourage them than to offer a financial inducement to the churches to transfer their schools, voluntarily, to local authority control?

Hence the crucial meeting between Butler and Temple on 1 May 1942. There, for the first time, Butler outlined the basis of what would become the final settlement. First, he conceded 'practically the whole of the Archbishop's Five Points'; specifically, the daily act of corporate worship, religious instruction in all schools performed by willing and competent teachers according to an agreed syllabus and subject to national inspection, and finally religious knowledge as an 'optional subject' in the course of teachers' certificate. Then, he outlined the projected terms for what would eventually become the division amongst non-provided sectors into: 'Category A', or 'controlled' schools, i.e. those eligible for 100 per cent of maintenance costs in return for local authority control of management and appointment of teachers; and crucially, 'Category B' or 'aided schools', that is, those eligible for just 50 per cent of maintenance costs from public funds but able, in return for furnishing the rest of the money from private sources, to retain their traditional denominational purposes, a majority of 'foundation managers' on their governing bodies and ecclesiastical control of appointments, both to headships and assistant posts.[82]

The difficulty for Butler lay in justifying the use of public resources in this way, especially as no increase in public control seemed thereby assured. Of course, anglican mainstream thinking, represented by the National Society, argued that since, 'Church people have contributed since 1870 to the maintenance of state schools [otherwise] unsatisfactory to them through rates and taxes . . . it was not unreasonable to hope that . . .

[78] LPL/WTP, 20/6: Temple to the Reverend H.K. Traviskis, 18 Sept. 1942.
[79] *The Times*, 16 Apr. 1942.
[80] LPL/WTP, 19/5/6: Butler to Temple, 1 Apr. 1942.
[81] LPL/WTP, 19/7: Board of Education, 'The Dual System and the Archbishops' Five Points: outline of a Scheme', n.d. unpub. memo., p. 1.
[82] LPL/WTP, 19/18: Temple, 'Interview with the President of the Board of Education', 1 May 1942.

public money [might] now be made available to bring their premises in line with modern standards.'[83] This persuaded no one else. Only a little more convincing was a later memo, from the same source, which suggested that 'The justification for such a grant lies in the fact that the cost of these [renovatory] services will, under the new order of education, be at least double what it was at the time of the settlement of 1902.'[84]

That was still clutching at straws. Butler preferred not to leave himself so vulnerable. Better to insinuate that what was projected was in effect, if not for apparent purposes, a measure for enhanced public control of educational services. Accordingly, over the next few months, Butler was happy to let it become known, or at least widely understood, that the creation of 'Category B', that is 'aided school' status had been inspired by the peculiar needs, and demands, of the Roman catholic authorities. Hence it was also widely presumed that all, or at least the overwhelming majority, of Church schools would opt for controlled status, thereby assuaging nonconformist opinion on one of its principal sticking points: the appointment of the headmaster by the local authority, thereby allowing 'nonconformist children to thrive in a non-churchy atmosphere'.[85] This was certainly the view of *The Times* which predicted a figure of 'seven out of eight', as early as October 1942.[86] It was equally the opinion of Chuter Ede who rather more forcefully insisted that 'we must have the surrender of 8,000 Church schools (i.e. eight out of nine) to make the job worthwhile'.[87] Perhaps that is why Anthony Howard, in his official *Life* of Butler, asserts that the 'eventual total' of aided schools was 'foreseen neither by Butler nor by Temple'.[88]

Yet it is perfectly clear that, whatever he had in mind about the special requirements of the Roman catholic hierarchy – and generally his thoughts were unsympathetic – Butler made this offer specifically to Temple and in relation to the Church of England. Secondly, it can be established from the contemporary record that both he and Temple harboured from the very beginning a very different interpretation of what extent of such a transfer would make it 'worth his while to proceed with the proposal'. Even in May 1942, Butler had a figure of no more than 'something like two-thirds (i.e. around 5,500) of present Non-Provided schools'.[89] By 1944, this had become a matter of 'achiev[ing] the right balance' in which it was now quite 'wrong . . . to attempt to interpret this balance in terms of numbers or percentages'.[90] That was probably just as well, for as early as November 1942, Temple had confidently predicted that 'on the new basis' the Church 'ought to keep at least half of our schools'.[91] It very nearly did.[92]

---

[83] LPL/WTP, 19/125: anon., 'Draft Memorandum of the National Society in Regard to the Dual System', 1942, p. 1.

[84] LPL/WTP, 338: anon., 'Memorandum of the National Society (Further Revisions)', 30 Sept. 1942, p. 1.

[85] TCC/BP, G15/37: Butler, 'Note', 25 May 1943.

[86] *The Times*, 29 Oct. 1942; for Temple's rebuttal, see LPC/WTP, 20/33: Temple to Browne-Wilkinson, 16 Nov. 1942.

[87] B.L., Add. MS 59697, Ede Diaries, p. 14: 15 Sept. 1943.

[88] Howard, *Rab*, p. 127.

[89] LPL/WTP, 22/53: Temple 'Interview', 1 May 1942.

[90] LPL/WTP, 22/53: Butler to Temple, 13 May 1944.

[91] LPL/WTP, 20/35: Temple to Eastaugh, 13 Nov. 1942.

[92] Compare Howard, *Rab*, p. 127, which posits a figure of around one-third with J.W.C. Wand, *Anglicanism. In History and Today* (1961), p. 173, which cites 3,434 'aided' and 4,411 'controlled' schools, as of 1961.

In this way, the voluntary principle became under Butler's guidance and with Temple's connivance almost as much a means for obscuring wider purposes as of achieving common consent to them; or rather, a means of effecting consensus through the vehicle of obfuscation. Nor was that pliable application of principle limited to the question of institutional transfer. Quizzed by Temple on the almost equally sensitive issue about whether so-called 'unreserved' teachers might 'volunteer' to provide occasional denominational instruction in controlled schools, should they be willing and capable, Butler replied as follows:

> The Bill will not preclude an unreserved teacher from volunteering to give instruction if she is willing and able . . . If I were to say this explicitly in the Bill I am quite certain that there would be an outcry from the Free Churches and the teachers . . . who would resist it accordingly. So long as the point is implicit and not explicit – as is my intention – I have no doubt that you will find teachers volunteering for the job.[93]

The point of all this, however, was not the pursuit of deviousness for its own sake. Nor was it merely to preserve the dual system intact. Rather, it was to improve the performance of Christian schools, similarly to improve the performance of Christianity in schools, in England and Wales. Of the former, Butler said this:

> I would not have ventured into the minefield of religious controversy except for the sole reason that non-provided schools need more public money if necessary general educational advance is to be secured. [Accordingly,] changes in the system of their control must be made. [Thus,] what is strictly necessary for this purpose must be done . . . but it would be foolish in the extreme . . . to attempt . . . a reversal of our long-established religious education policy.[94]

Of the latter, Butler believed that:

> now is the [right] time to secure . . . a permanent and acceptable place for the teaching of religion in our primary and secondary schools . . . for out of the crucible of common suffering . . . has come a certain unity [of feeling] which provides [an] opportunity for a statesman . . . in war-time . . . to resolve one of the main problems affecting the spiritual well-being of our children.[95]

His aim was Christian progress. Beyond Church schools, the mechanism was the agreed syllabus. This was to be the preferred method of instruction both in 'controlled' and 'provided' schools from 1944 onwards. Its essence was that synthesis of denominationally uncontested, common, Christianity which could be taught by competent teachers to children of any religious persuasion, bar Roman catholics and Jews. Yet it resisted precisely that reduction of religious knowledge to academic criteria which the teachers had demanded. Mandler had called for a 'national syllabus', drawn up by 'national representatives of the churches, the local authorities and the teachers', and imparted only by professional teachers unrestricted by religious tests.[96] He got joy in

---

[93] LPL/WTP, 20/349: Butler to Temple, 6 May 1943.
[94] LPL/WTP, 20/198: Butler to Temple, 2 Feb. 1943.
[95] Butler, *Address To The Free Church Council*, pp. 1–2.
[96] Mandler, *Religious Instruction Controversy*, p. 9.

neither respect. Agreements remained local and reserved teachers remained the norm in controlled schools after 1944.[97] The Assistant Masters Association decried any 'statutory provision' for a daily act of collective worship as both 'unnecessary [and] undesirable'. Their pleas were ignored.[98]

At the same time, Butler refused to countenance any concession to denominational sectarianism in religious instruction as implied either in the bishop of Oxford's scheme for pluralistic denominational instruction or in Bishop Bell's advocacy of the so-called Scottish system.[99] In his own words: 'It is not part of the function of the state to train children in the dogmas of the various religious denominations so as to attach them to the worshipping communities for which the denominations stand'. Similarly: 'The Scottish solution . . . tends to so wholesale a dependence of teachers' appointments and professional advancement on personal religious adherence . . . as would not only be repugnant to the great body of teachers in this country, but would also be unacceptable to most LEA's too.'[100]

4

Butler's legislative strategy proved outstandingly successful. No finer testimony to its success need be sought than the striking similarity between the act that was passed in May 1944 and the bill that was introduced into parliament in December 1943; or for that matter, between the bill and the white paper on 'educational reconstruction', published in July 1943.[101] In this respect, the very concentration of educational reform on religious matters proved a bonus because it rendered the 'controversial parts of the bill' in a curious sense 'non-political'; not so much because they truly lacked a political dimension but rather because, as Butler caustically remarked of his colleagues, 'whereas . . . it has been very difficult to obtain agreement between the parties on matters which involve property or the pocket . . . on religious questions there is a feeling that it is [all] an out-of-date wrangle'. Yet this was not Butler's own view of the matter. As he observed, in the very next sentence of these notes, 'this is a further example of how political interest is shifting from the soul of man to his economic position, which all seems very unhealthy'.[102]

Nor was this the whole story. To be sure, the voluntary mechanism allied to the agreed principles was supposed to neutralize serious opposition from the various protestant factions in parliament. None the less, very little was actually left to chance. Nonconformist opposition to the bill, which at least found voice in the eloquence of Sir Geoffrey Shakespeare, was pre-empted by a methodist *Statement on the Education Bill*, 'regretting' its various defects whilst eventually commending its 'excellent qualities to

---

[97] Murphy, *Church, State and Schools*, ch. 7; Cruikshank, *Church and State*, ch. 6.

[98] Incorporated Association of Assistant Masters in Secondary Schools, *Memorandum on The Education Bill* (1944), pp. 4–5.

[99] On the 'Scottish system', see Cruikshank, *Church and State*, pp. 158 ff.

[100] LPL/WTP, 20/198: Butler to Temple, 2 Feb. 1943.

[101] See the remarks in Cruikshank, *Church and State*, pp. 161–9, esp. at p. 164; also those in Addison, *The Road to 1945*, at p. 172.

[102] TCC/BP, G15/84, Butler: 'Political Diary', 9 Sept. 1943.

the nation'.[103] Similarly, the creaking giant of high tory anglicanism was continually assuaged through the carefully primed interventions of Henry Brooke.[104] The one famous reversal, over Mrs Thelma Cazalet Keir and the salary scales of female teachers, was the product more of a rare lapse of front-bench foresight than an early example of back-bench feminism.[105]

Yet precisely because the strategy was successful, it is easy to lose sight of what the eventual goal actually was. Howard, in his official *Life*, calls it an 'essentially Erastian' measure.[106] This is an almost exact inversion of the truth. Moreover, in its gross misconception of official priorities, it feeds those shrewder judges of the act who have criticised its bias towards traditional curricula and privileged diversity. Hence it is important to insist upon the force of contemporary purposes; above all, those purposes as interpreted through Butler's mind. After all, utilitarian ends in education were a long way removed from the preoccupations of one who stressed that 'the forces of materialism . . . can only be kept in their proper place . . . if we make a decided advance on the [educational] front'.[107] Similarly, ideas of educational justice made only so much sense to a man who believed that 'contacts in all the major cities of England show me' that it was precisely such a traditional, diverse and Christian educational system 'that the British public want if only it is dressed up in the [garb] of non-privilege and social equality'.[108]

What Butler was trying to do in 1944 was to draw Church and state together in pursuit of Christian education. In this analysis, 1870 and 1902 had pulled them apart, disastrously and needlessly. Disastrously because they had left Church schools to fend for themselves in an increasingly hostile environment, burdening them with ever more intolerable costs; needlessly, because they had cast provided schools in the caricature of creeping secularism when in fact, as many churchmen privately admitted, perfectly decent Christian instruction could be, and often was, imparted within them.[109] The Butler Act was an attempt to 'codify' this existing practice by bridging the formal gap which previous legislation had gratuitously forged.

Its method was ingenious. Instead of abolishing the 'dual system', which would have inflamed clerical opinion as it pandered to teachers' prejudices, or of formalising doctrinal division along the Scottish lines which would have had precisely the opposite effect, it sought reform not so much in preservation as through complication. Indeed, Bishop Bell, during the course of a somewhat mischievous analysis of the white paper, argued that its principal achievement would be to transform the 'Dual System . . . into

---

[103] Leslie Church, Edwin Finch and A.W. Harrison, *Methodist Statement on the Education Bill, 27 January 1944* (1944), p. 1.

[104] LPL/WTP, 21/223: A.R. Woodard to Temple, 9 Dec. 1943; also 21/225: Willink to Temple, 10 Dec. 1943; this correspondence reveals the clear plan to use Brook in precisely this fashion, and Butler's prior approval of it.

[105] Recounted in Thelma Cazalet Keir, *From the Wings* (1967), pp. 143–5; ignored in Butler's *Memoirs*, but related by Howard, in *Rab*, at p. 136. Its contemporary significance may be judged from the fact that it was the *only* aspect of the education measure to be noted in Alexander Cadogan's diary; see *The Diaries of Sir Alexander Cadogan, 1938–1945*, ed. David Dilks, (1971), p. 615.

[106] Howard, *Rab*, p. 135.

[107] LPL/WTP, 19/27: Butler to Temple, 8 May 1942.

[108] TCL/BP, G14/107: Butler to Lieutenant-Colonel J.M. Alport, 2 May 1945.

[109] LPL/WTP, 19/138: Tatlow to Temple, 24 June 1942.

. . . a Triple System'.[110] But this was to pay Butler a curious compliment. For in the president's mind, and so too increasingly in Temple's, complication was the road to assimilation. As Temple put it,'state subsidy', tempered by increased public control and bracketed with sound Christian teaching in all schools, not only might 'save [the Church] a very good deal [of money] but at the same time [would] get it into the position of cooperative colleague with the government and the LEA's and so immensely extend our influence'.[111]

If it is now customary to deride the secular purposes of the act, it is well nigh axiomatic to presume the failure of its religious aspirations. Butler himself came to such a view by the time of the publication of his autobiography in 1972.[112] But as ever with the 'old oriental', timing was a crucial part of this judgement.[113] Such pessimism was entirely absent, indeed was contradicted by the very positive remarks which characterised his 'foreword' to the then standard account of the 1944 act, published by Marjorie Cruikshank, in 1964.[114] And with reason. For pleasant surprise at the outcome was not an uncommon view amongst committed churchmen as late as the early 1960's. It certainly informed Bishop Wand's analysis of what he called the 'generous aid [then] offered by the state to the church' during the course of his influential study of *Anglicanism*, published in 1961.[115] More widely, it provided ballast to the far from idiosyncratic view that England, an ostensibly Christian country before the war, became – if anything – a rather more observationally Christian country afterwards. How else to explain the 'religious revival' of the 1950's?[116]

[110] LPL/WTP, 21/80: George Bell, bishop of Chichester, 'The Dual System: White Paper Plan', unpub. memo, ? Sept. 1943.
[111] LPL/WTP, 19/366: Temple to Glenday, 13 Oct. 1942.
[112] Butler, *The Art of the Possible*, p. 124.
[113] *Chips*, ed. Rhodes James, p. 178: 23 Nov. 1938.
[114] R.A. Butler, 'Foreword', to Cruikshank, *Church and State*, p. vii.
[115] Wand, *Anglicanism*, pp. 172–3.
[116] On which, see Hastings, *A History of English Christianity*, pp. 422–35; I hope to return to this, underexplored, theme at a later stage.

Sir Makepeace Watermaster and the March of Christian People: An Interaction of Fiction, Fact and Politics*

CLYDE BINFIELD

'We've got God driving for us . . . They can't stop progress, Sir Makepeace, and they can't stop the march of Christian people.'[1]

It is a Spring Sunday somewhere on the South Devon coast, a 'swirling, sopping doom-laden midmorning . . . Old leaves, old pine needles and old confetti stick to the wet church steps as the humble flow of worshippers files in for its weekly dose of perdition or salvation, though I never saw that much to choose between the two of them.'[2] So gathers a congregation to be described with a scene-painter's allusive accuracy: time, place, colour, climate, the whole capturing an unfashionable range of social nuance as a preparation for impending drama. The scenery is in place. The chorus is assembling. A plot has been set in motion.

> . . . something is up. There's a buzz around . . . You can read it everywhere: in the portentous rolling tread of the brown-suited deacon, in the fluttering and exhaling of the hatted women who arrive in a rush imagining they are late, then sit blushing through their white face-powder because they are early. Everyone agog, everyone on tiptoe and a first-class turn out . . . A few of them have come by car – such wonders of the day as Lanchesters and Singers – others by trolleybus, and some have walked; and God's sea rain has given them beards of cold inside their cheap fox stoles, and God's sea wind is cutting through the threadbare serge of their Sunday best. Yet there is not one of them, however he has come, who does not brave the weather a second longer to pause and goggle at the notice-board and confirm with his own eyes what the bush telegraph has been telling him these several days. Two posters are fixed to it, both smeared by rain, both to the passer-by as dreary as cups of cold tea. Yet to those who know the code they transmit an electrifying signal. The first in orange proclaims the five-thousand-pound appeal mounted by the Baptist Women's League to provide a reading room – though all of them know that no

---

* I am indebted for help in the preparation of this paper to Mr John Creasey (Dr Williams' Library), the late Revd Walter Dickinson, Mrs E. Dickinson, Professor M.R.D. Foot, Mrs Diana Gray, Mr John Gratton, the Revd Dr L.C. Green, Mr David Haig, Miss. K Head, Mr John le Carré, Mrs Susan Mills (Angus Library, Regent's Park College, Oxford), Dr J. P. Parry, Mr Barrie Smith, Mrs K. Spackman (Dorset Library Services), Dr J.H. Thompson, The Revd Dr and Mrs John Travell, Miss Jean Wilson. Extracts from *A Perfect Spy* are reproduced by kind permission of John le Carré and Hodder and Stoughton Limited, the publishers.

[1] John le Carré, *A Perfect Spy* (1986), p. 39.
[2] *Ibid.*, p. 26.

book will ever be read in it, that it will be a place to set out home-made cakes and photographs of leprous children in the Congo. A plywood thermometer . . . is fastened to the railings revealing that the first thousand has already been achieved. The second notice, green, declares that today's address will be given by the Minister, all welcome. But this information has been corrected. A rigid bulletin has been pinned over it, typed in full like a legal warning, with the comically misplaced capital letters that in these parts signal omens:

> *Due to unforeseen Circumstances, Sir Makepeace Watermaster Justice of the Peace and Liberal Member of Parliament for this Constituency, will provide today's Message. Appeal Committee please to Remain behind Afterwards for an Extraordinary meeting.*

Makepeace Watermaster himself! And they know why![3]

The congregation settles down. Lady and Miss Watermaster, sisters-in-law, though in age they are mother and daughter or aunt and niece, 'have arrived early. They sit shoulder to shoulder in the pew for notables beneath the pulpit'.[4] And behind them,

far behind, by chance as far as the great long aisle allows, at the very back of the church, in their chosen pew directly beside the closed doors, sits the flower of our young men, their neckties pulled up and outward from their stiff collars, their slicked hair parted in a razor slash. These are the Night School Boys, as they are affectionately known, our Tabernacle's apostles of tomorrow, our white hopes, our future ministers of religion, our doctors, missionaries and philanthropists, our future Highest in the Land, who will one day go out into the world and Save it as it has never been Saved before. It is they who by their zeal have acquired the duties customarily entrusted to older men: the distributing of hymn books and special notices, the taking of collection money and the hanging up of overcoats. It is they who once a week, by bicycle, motorcycle and kindly parents' motorcars, distribute our church magazine to every god-fearing front door, including that of Sir Makepeace Watermaster himself, whose cook has standing orders that a piece of cake and a glass of lemon barley be always waiting for the bringer; they who collect the few shillings of rent from the church's poor cottages, who pilot the pleasure boats on Brinkley Mere at children's outings, host the Band of Hope's Christmas bunfights and put fire into Christian Endeavour action week. And it is they who have taken upon themselves as a direct commission from Jesus the burden of the Women's League Appeal, target Five thousand pounds, at a time when two hundred would maintain a family for a year. Not a door bell they have not offered to clean, flowerbed to weed and dig for Jesus. Day after day the young troops have marched out, to return, reeking of peppermint, long after their parents are asleep. Sir Makepeace has sung their praises, so has our Minister. No sabbath is complete without a reminder to Our Father regarding their devotion. And bravely the red line on the plywood thermometer at the church gates has climbed through the fifties, the hundreds to the first thousand, where for a while now, for all their efforts it has seemed to stick. Not that they have

---

[3] *Ibid.*, pp. 26–7.
[4] *Ibid.*, p. 28.

lost momentum, far from it. Failure is not in their thoughts. No need for Makepeace Watermaster to remind them of Bruce's spider, though he often does. The Night School Boys are 'crackerjack', as our saying goes. The Night School Boys are Christ's own vanguard and they will be the Highest in the Land.

There are five of them . . .[5]

And it is chiefly to them that Sir Makepeace directs his Address, 'extolling youth's ideals, likening them to stars . . . Stars as our destiny. Stars that guide Wise Men across deserts to the very Cradle of Truth. Stars to lighten the darkness of our despair, yea even in the pit of Sin. Stars of every shape, for every occasion. Shining above us like God's very light.'[6] So to the inevitable peroration, final and preposterous, no Watermaster sermon complete without it:

> 'Ideals, my young brethren! Ideals, my beloved brethren all, are to be likened unto those splendid stars above us' – I see him lift his sad, starless eyes to the pine roof – 'we cannot reach them. Millions of miles separate us from them' – I see him hold out his drooping arms as if to catch a falling sinner – 'But oh my brethren, how greatly do we profit from their presence!'[7]

But what Sir Makepeace has profited from is the enterprise of his father, old Goodman Watermaster, 'a Welshman, a preaching, singing, widowed, miserable potteryman', who came to Devon, 'sampled the clay, sniffed the sea air' and built three potteries in two years as well as the baptist church.[8] The Watermasters are men of a type. Goodman imported cheap labour to man his potteries, first from Wales and then, 'cheaper still and lower', from Ireland. He 'hired them with his tied cottages, starved them with his rotten wages and beat the fear of Hell into them from his pulpit, before himself being taken off to Paradise, witness the unassuming monument to him six thousand feet high which stood in the pottery forecourt until . . . the whole lot was ripped down to make way for a bungalow estate and good riddance'.[9] His son has transferred such responsibilities to public life, for he is 'the greatest preacher and Liberal ever born, and one of the Highest in the Land', literally so, six-foot-six, big feet, long head, 'moist little rosebud ears', 'little baby eyes', 'improbably tiny lips', 'ridiculously tiny backside',

> tall as one of his own factory chimneys, and as tapered. Rubbery, with weak pinched shoulders and a wide bendy waist. One jointless arm tipped out at us like a railway signal, one baggy hand flopping on the end of it. And the wet, elastic little mouth that should have been a woman's, too small even to feed him by, stretching and contracting as it labours to deliver the indignant vowels.[10]

Sir Makepeace is the member for Purgatory – the place is never named – a 'wooded hollow of clefts and chines and dripping laurels . . with red windswept beaches always out of season and creaking swings and sodden sandpits that were closed to enjoyment on

[5] *Ibid.*, pp. 30–1.
[6] *Ibid.*, pp. 31–2.
[7] *Ibid.*, p. 32.
[8] *Ibid.*, pp. 27–8.
[9] *Ibid.*, p. 28.
[10] *Ibid.*, pp. 27, 28, 32, 33, 38, 40.

the sabbath . . Purgatory was Makepeace Watermaster's great sad house, The Glades', with its nannies, 'smiles . . . alight with pious optimism, uniformed like wardresses', its 'great dark orchard', with a summerhouse in it, and its dark drawing room. Purgatory 'served bread and margarine instead of buttered toast. When we sang, we droned "There is a Green Hill Far Away". ' Purgatory 'was the Tabernacle. . . . and Makepeace Watermaster's frightful sermons; and Mr. Philpott's sermons; and sermons from every aunt, cousin and neighbourhood philosopher . . .'. Purgatory 'stultified its young and dragged them down, its prohibition of everything exciting that they cared about: from Sunday newspapers to Popery, from psychology to art, from flimsy underwear to high spirits to low spirits, from love to laughter and back again, I don't think there was a corner of the human state where its disapproval did not fall.'[11]

1

There are not many late twentieth-century best-selling novels in which evangelical nonconformity has been so searchingly or so prominently portrayed as in John le Carré's *A Perfect Spy*. The portrait is hardly loving, but it is, for its immediate purposes, accurate, the work of an insider. The accuracy may be that of caricature, but it is born of sharp observation. The nuances are deftly caught: of denominational outreach and aspiration (the Belgian Congo was a Baptist Missionary Society heartland); of attitude ('Baptists do not kneel before God . . . They squat'); of class ('A deacon in his brown suit hobbles with an artisan's mysterious discomfort towards the vestry').[12] The mode is autobiographical, and it rings true though, as is proper in a novel, the autobiography is shaped, and its context is consequently quite expertly distorted, into a many-layered story of deceit and betrayal.

And integral to the novel, for it precipitates each layer of betrayal, is the Christian, or at least the ecclesiastical, dimension; each stage of the narrator's career, and each church with which he toys, is to be defected from. On the face of it, the narrator, Magnus Pym, is embarked on a career of conventional upward mobility. A nonconformist formation is channelled into an anglican boarding school followed by exposure to Europe. But the conventional world of good school and ancient university is thwarted by the social ambiguities of that formative nonconformity and distorted by the peculiar dishonesty which comes when nonconformity loses its evangelical motor while retaining its evangelical rhetoric. For the narrator's father is a confidence trickster of near genius and the narrator's journey into adulthood is determined by his relationship with his father and punctuated steadily by religion's outward form. Thus school chapel leads to the carefully plotted thought of entering the Church ('By the end of the week he is promised to a boys' camp in Hereford, a pan-denominational retreat in Shropshire, a Trade Unionists' pilgrimage in Wakefield and a Celebration of Witness in Derby').[13] Later come Europe's English churches – one of them in Bern's 'diplomatic fairyland', 'with its ironback diplomatic families, ancient Britons and dubious anglophiles', and its counter-

[11] *Ibid.*, pp. 28, 29, 41, 81.
[12] *Ibid.*, pp. 29, 34.
[13] *Ibid.*, p. 147.

part in Vienna, 30 years later, ' "just the sexiest little church you ever saw" ', according to an American 'diplomat' with a presbyterian wife, with its 'usual band of upwardly mobile Christians led by the British Ambassadress and the American Minister's wife . . . and a heavy contingent of Dutch, Norwegians and also-rans from the German Embassy next door'.[14] Graz and marriage come between Bern and Vienna, and Roman catholicism vies with anglicanism. At Graz the narrator, a national serviceman now, takes instruction with Rome in view; his superior officer is a convert, years later to be found retired in 'one of those half urbanized Georgian settlements on the edge of Bath where English Catholics of a certain standing have elected to gather in their exile . . . [his] household in permanent and benevolent disorder, pervaded by the gentle thrill of religious persecution'.[15] The marriage, however, is anglican, to a stockbroker's daughter in a 'great church famed for its permanence and previous successes', served by priests 'of upper-class humility', with a frugal reception for 'the crowned heads of suburbia' in a 'tomblike Bayswater hotel'.[16]

Thus is a congenital betrayer's 50 years'-worth of life threaded into his country's ecclesiastical fabric. For most readers that fabric's baptist weave will be incidental. In fact it is fundamental to an understanding of the whole. It explains the honesty of the story-telling, most truly shown when the last layer of deception has been peeled away and a perfect spy has been revealed. It informs the rhythm of its language, most truly appreciated by those who have the lay preacher's ear for cadence and timbre.

2

Here, in short, is a personal memoir of Christian endeavour transmuted – if not fore-ordained – into malformation and decay. When the story opens the narrator has been conceived but he is yet to be born. The focus is on his father, Richard Thomas Pym, a blue-eyed boy 'still dreaming of his first Bentley', leader of the night school five, captain of the tabernacle football team, treasurer of the Young Liberals, and son of 'the beloved TP, who fought in the Great War trenches before he became our mayor, and passed away these seven years ago, though it seems like yesterday, and what a preacher he was before his Maker took him back!' A shotgun wedding in a new register office off the western bypass ('just where you turn left for Northolt aerodrome'), turns Rick Pym into Makepeace Watermaster's brother-in-law; and since the night school boys' circle includes a budding accountant, a goat-headed solicitor, and 'a small punchy fighter with the townie's nimbleness and twinkle', who is a Freemason, there are all the makings in painful parody of such a network as had for generations sustained countless small-town chapels.[17]

But this is dissent in dissolution, malformed, introverted and decadent. Sir Makepeace epitomises it, large-framed and small-featured. So does his wife, 'known as Lady Nell', with her liver-coloured spectacles and her habit 'of flicking her greying

[14] *Ibid.*, pp. 191–2, 271, 326.
[15] *Ibid.*, p. 368.
[16] *Ibid.*, p. 409.
[17] *Ibid.*, pp. 31, 33, 34, 39, 41, 43–4.

head without warning as if she were shaking off flies'. Nell Watermaster is 'not yet fifty but already she is hunched and shrivelled like a witch', while her sister-in-law Dorothy, 'rightly called Dot', is a 'tiny earnest statue', an 'immaculate speck', an 'unreal, empty woman permanently in flight'. Too much was unmentionable at The Glades, which was 'why Lady Nell drank and why Sir Makepeace was so ill-at-ease with himself, and why his damp little eyes were so tormented, and his mouth unequal to his appetites, and why he was able to castigate sin with such passionate familiarity . . . And why it was that Dorothy had taken herself to sleep, far from Lady Nell's room and further still from Makepeace's'.[18]

And there is more than a flavour of Lloyd George: the Welshness of Watermaster and of Philpott the minister; R.T. Pym's habit of going to fancy dress parties as Lloyd George. Such celticism is extended by Pym's Irish mother, sitting 'with a widow's majesty at home in Airdale Road behind drawn curtains under the tinted giant photograph of TP in mayoral regalia'.[19]

There are confirming flavours of dissolution: the hint of uniformed youth, the cynical exploitation of proliferating networks, the incipient frauds bringing famous dissenting scandals irresistibly to mind, the exculpatory rhetoric, all focused on the night school boys, Christ's own vanguard. They

> process down the aisle and in a practiced drill movement fan out to their appointed posts. Rick, smart as paint today and every Sunday, proffers the collecting plate . . . his blue eyes glistening with divine intelligence. . . . The Boys line up before the Lord's Table, the Minister accepts the offerings, says a perfunctory blessing . . .[20]

As for the networks, there is mention of Balham's of Brinkley, coachbuilders, 'some of the finest Liberals in the county. Christians to a man', ripe for exploitation.[21] As for the gathering frauds, there are – shades of the Liberator scandal of 40 years earlier – the Magnus Star Equitable Insurance Co. Ltd., share capital £2,000, to provide life insurance to the 'Needy, Disabled and Elderly' and, a wartime decade later, dealings with a moribund friendly society sitting on a fortune in the midlands:

> The Chairman of the Society, name of Higgs – destiny has decreed that all conspirators bear monosyllables – turns out to be a lifelong Baptist. So is Rick; he could never have got where he is today without it. The fortune derives from a family trust watched over by a country solicitor named Crabbe, who went off to the war the moment it became available, leaving the trust to watch over itself as it thought best. As a Baptist Higgs can fiddle no funds without Crabbe to cover him.[22]

[18] *Ibid.*, pp. 28, 29, 30.
[19] *Ibid.*, p. 34.
[20] *Ibid.*, p. 33.
[21] *Ibid.*, p. 39.
[22] *Ibid.*, pp. 44, 133–4. Higgs was a famous Baptist building name; Higgses had built the Metropolitan Tabernacle to rehouse Spurgeon's congregation. The Liberator Scandal of 1892 is described in D. Kynaston, *The City of London. Vol. II, Golden Years, 1890–1914* (1995), pp. 65–6. Its promoter, Jabez Spencer Balfour (1843–1910), of baptist and congregational stock, was first mayor of Croydon and Liberal M.P. Tamworth (1880–5) and Burnley (1889–92). He served 11 years of a 14-year sentence to penal servitude, 1895–1906.

And as for the rhetoric, all can be defended in 'a mounting bombardment of passionate, grammatically unnerving pseudo-Biblical phrases'.[23] Here is a fluently politicized society warped into an obstinate introversion, masterfully patronized by the sitting member: 'elsewhere in the world, Hitler is winding himself up to set fire to the universe, in America and Europe the miseries of the Depression are spreading like an incurable plague . . . But the congregation doesn't presume to hold opinions on these impenetrable aspects of God's purpose. Theirs is the dissenting church and their temporal overlord is Sir Makepeace Watermaster', his mastery caught in the amber of yellowed press-cuttings:

> Makepeace accused nobody outright, Makepeace framed no charge. This is the land of innuendo; straight speaking is for sinners. 'M.P. sounds a Stern Warning against Youthful Covetousness, Greed' . . . 'Perils of young Ambition splendidly Highlighted'. In Makepeace's imposing person, the anonymous writer declares, 'are met the poet's Celtic grace, the statesman's eloquence, the lawgiver's Iron sense of Justice'. The congregation was 'spellbound unto the Meekest of its Members'.

Thus were 'the cadences of Makepeace's rhetoric . . . every Welsh note of it . . . rammed home with a botched stab of the lugubrious Watermaster forefinger'.[24] And thus, in the fulness of time, were the world's heroes diminished in the narrator's imagination into the monsters of The Glades: 'De Gaulle, with his tilted pineapple head, was too much like Uncle Makepeace, while Roosevelt, with his stick and wheelchair, was clearly Aunt Nell in disguise'.[25]

3

The novel describes two stages of Liberal and dissenting decay. If the Liberal enthusiasms of the south west reached their nadir in the 1930s, those of East Anglia reach theirs a generation later in the 'unlit post-war years before television replaced the Temperance Hall and communications were such that a man's character could be born again by removing it a hundred and fifty miles north-east of London'. Purgatory's perpetual autumn has given way to winter. 'Snow lies over the fens and marshes and freezes Quixote's windmills to a standstill against the cindery Flemish sky . . . steepled towns dangle from the sea's horizon, the Brueghel faces of our electorate are . . . . pink with zeal'. For this is the setting of an East Anglian by-election. 'A village, then a church spire glide towards them . . . The frosted air smells of cow dung and the sea. Before them rises the archaic Temperance Hall'.[26] The constituency, Gulworth North, is a composite, an ancient fishing and weaving town. Here, where once Colmans, Cozens-Hardys, Jewsons and Tilletts, Barretts and Shakespeares, had held an undisputed Free Church sway, there has been no Liberal candidate since the war. The traditionary radicalism has been transmuted into socialism.

[23] le Carré, *A Perfect Spy*, p 37
[24] *Ibid.*, pp. 27, 31.
[25] *Ibid.*, p. 100.
[26] *Ibid.*, pp. 273, 280.

The Labour candidate is a Glasgow schoolmaster; 'Got a red beard. Small bloke'. The tory 'is everything a Tory candidate should be with knobs on. A landed pukka sahib who toils one day a week in the City, rides to hounds, gives beads to the natives and wants to bring back the thumb-screw for first offenders. His wife opens garden fetes with her teeth'. Those descriptions are furnished by one of the night school boys, for there is a third candidate, the Liberal Richard Thomas Pym, described in a Sunday newspaper as 'a philanthropist and property broker' and on his posters as 'Pym, the People's Man'.[27]

The campaign proves to be 'a drama tour of the theatre of the politically absurd', 'never a by-election like it'. The Liberal headquarters are in Mrs Searle's Temperance Rest, a rundown corner house whence spread Liberal rumours about 'the Tory candidate's support of Sir Oswald Mosley and the Labour candidate's over-addiction to his pupils'. Into this world are wheeled 'witless cricketers and titled owners of hotel chains and other so-called Liberal personalities', among them 'the great Bertie Tregenza, the Radio Bird Man, a lifelong Liberal'. (Can we discern here a parallel with the patter-perfect, smoothly-packaged type of real-life Liberalism, perpetually poised for renaissance, represented by men like Peter Bessell, M.P., lay-preacher and lecturer?)[28] Professional presentation fools the chapel values of the novel. That is why on Sunday 'Our Candidate . . . contents himself with pious appearances at the best attended Baptist churches, where he is disposed to preach on simplicity and service', and why his election address features 'his childhood Mentor and Friend, Sir Makepeace Watermaster, M.P., the World Famous Liberal and Christian Employer . . . a man of God-fearing Family, an Abstainer, an orator . . . who went to his grave preaching Man's Moral right to Property, free Trading and a fair Crack of the Whip for Women'.[29] That tone is revived in the candidate's eve-of-poll speech in Gulworth's town hall, the thunder of his piety rising into the wagon roof, the rhythm of his rhetoric forsaking the sermon for an 'address' or a 'message', pressing for decision:

> Now comes the good news. You can hear it from the faith in his voice . . . Gulworth North will undergo a Renaissance beyond its dreams. Its moribund herring trade shall rise from its bed and walk. Its decaying textile industry shall bring forth milk and honey. Its farms shall be freed of Socialist bureaucracy and become the envy of the world. Its crumbling railways and canals shall be miraculously cut loose from the toils of the Industrial Revolution. Its streets shall run with liquidity. Its aged shall have their savings protected against Confiscation by the State, its menfolk shall be spared the ignominies of conscription. Pay-As-You-Earn taxation shall go.

Then, 'on a note of ever-mounting humility', he reaches his peroration:

> People will say to you, and they've said it to me – they've stopped me in the street – touched my arm . . . they say, 'What is Liberalism except a package of ideals? We can't eat ideals . . .', they say. 'Ideals don't buy us a cup of tea or a nice touch of English lamb

---

[27] *Ibid.*, pp. 269, 279.

[28] *Ibid.*, pp. 273, 274, 275, 279, 290. 'The God-Thumpers – the Masons . . . the Old Nellies. The teetotallers are a cakewalk, so's the anti-betting league . . .'. For Peter Bessell, see L. Chester, M. Linklater and D. May, *Jeremy Thorpe. A Secret Life* (1979), ch. 4.

[29] le Carré, *A Perfect Spy*, pp. 280, 286.

chop . . . We can't put our ideals in the collection box. We can't pay for our son's education with ideals . . . So what's the point . . .', they say to me, 'in this modern world of
ours, of a party of ideals?' The voice drops. The hand, till now so agitated, reached out
palm downward to cup the head of an invisible child. 'And I say to them, good people
of Gulworth, and I say to you too!' The same hand flies upward and points to Heaven
as Pym in his sickly apprehension sees the ghost of Makepeace Watermaster leap from
its pulpit and fill the Town Hall with a dismal glow. 'I say this. Ideals are like the stars.
We cannot reach them, but we profit by their presence!'[30]

As things turned out, Gulworth's Liberals profited not at all, although the chapel vote
bore up remarkably well. Their candidate, philanthropist and property broker, gaolbird
too, filed for bankruptcy on 29 March, 1951, as did his 83 associated companies.[31]

4

This study began 20 years earlier with the Pyms, Watermasters, and their fellow baptists,
on a Sunday morning somewhere on the south Devon coast. It began in 1931, with a
fiction. But that fiction has a grounding in fact. *A Perfect Spy* is semi-autobiographical.[32]
There are contemporary parallels for the Pyms, the Watermasters, and Purgatory,
though they cannot be definitive since the novelist's discipline is not the historian's and
the autobiographer's is different again. 'John le Carré' may come so close to David
Cornwell (his real name) as at times to be indistinguishable, but he has a relationship to
explore – that of his narrator with his father – for which the context lies in the
shadowlands of a parliamentary democracy, exploiting the uncertainties and ambiguities of its political nation. Even so some of those ambiguities can be detached from the
shadows to illuminate the decline of a distinctive segment of that nation and its parliament. Sir Makepeace Watermaster, J.P., M.P., pottery manufacturer, of The Glades,
and Richard Thomas Pym, his shotgun brother-in-law, and Magnus Pym, the narrator
and Rick's son, can be glimpsed through John le Carré's distorting mirror and identified, and Purgatory can be located. South Devon turns out to be east Dorset and
Purgatory is Poole, or rather, Parkstone, 'the English Mentone' (so called 'on account
of its charming scenery and genial climate').[33] Its baptists are in fact congregationalists,
or rather they are both, for the baptist Parkstone Tabernacle had been built in 1891,
seating 800, while the congregational church, seating between 550 and 750, 'attractive,
substantial, and capacious, worthy of fashionable Parkstone, and a credit to the denomination', had been rebuilt in 1893, with George Williams, 'the well-known founder and
president of the Young Men's Christian Association', to preside at its midsummer
opening's evening meeting.[34] By 1931 the Tabernacle had 213 members and the

[30] *Ibid.*, pp. 274, 276.
[31] *Ibid.*, pp. 302, 304. The Labour vote was 17,970; the Conservative 15,711; the Liberal 6,404.
[32] *The Independent on Sunday*, 1 Aug. 1993, p. 4.
[33] W. Densham and J. Ogle, *The Story of the Congregational Churches of Dorset, From their Foundation to
the Present Time* (Bournemouth, 1899), p. 175.
[34] *Ibid.*, pp 178–9. The links are suggestive. George Williams' (1821–1905) wife was the niece of a
retired missionary couple who had returned from India to settle in Parkstone; Williams, a London
wholesale draper, had left congregationalism for evangelical anglicanism.

congregationalists had 230.[35] They were both forces in Parkstone. But were they the spirit of Purgatory? The English Mentone had chines like Purgatory, and Poole had its pottery, but neither was dominated by Watermasters though the real Sir Makepeace was certainly prominent in his town, his county, his party, and his denomination, as were the real T.P., Alderman Pym, at least in his town and his church, and the real Lady Nell, at least among women.

The real Sir Makepeace was Alec Ewart Glassey, J.P. and briefly M.P., but esquire, not knight, of The Homestead, Parkstone, an Edwardian house, large but not ostentatious, in church-garden-party-sized grounds, with tennis courts. Glassey was a man of apparently ample means who no longer needed to work for his living and had moved to Dorset after the Great War. He had a wife and three daughters, two of whom went to Wentworth, the school at Boscombe founded in 1899 as Bournemouth Collegiate School for Girls. Wentworth's attraction as a 'School for the Daughters of Gentlemen', was that it particularly catered for the daughters of nonconformist gentlemen. Like Bournemouth, Parkstone, and The Homestead, Wentworth was new yet established, an encouraging essay in alternative tradition. Glassey fitted that tradition like a glove. He was a man of Watermaster build, six feet four, large head, huge jaw, smallish mouth and eyes, but fine looking in a way that Watermaster was not. He was also a lay preacher whom most congregations found entirely acceptable though his sermons seemed appallingly long and his lectures quite unendurable to the small nephew, issue of an unfortunate marriage and reliant on him for what was in conventional terms a good, indeed expensive, education, who stayed frequently at The Homestead in the 1930s and disliked the experience intensely.[36]

The similarities between fiction and reality may not end there, but they are already enough to be etched on both sides of that small boy's family. The Glasseys of The Homestead were congregationalists. Their church was Parkstone congregational church. The Cornwells of Bay View were baptists. They went to Parkstone Tabernacle. Baptists and congregationalists share polity but differed in accent. And 'accent' is the word. The formative accent of *A Perfect Spy* is Baptist. That against which its author chiefly reacted was congregationalist. Alec Glassey, whose profession depended on it and who had a national role within his sights, spoke a beautifully modulated English, accent-free and musical. The Cornwells, by contrast, 'all spoke with a regional accent', and Ronald Cornwell, who married Olive Glassey, has been described by his son as 'a small time guy . . . who got himself together, learned the language, the manners as best he could.'[37]

---

[35] Parkstone Tabernacle had 213 members; 152 in its Sunday school; 21 Sunday school teachers and 7 lay preachers; the congregationalists, with 230 members, had a Sunday school of 138, 21 teachers and 4 lay preachers: *Baptist Hand Book* (1932), p. 78; *Congregational Year Book* (1932), p. 267.

[36] For Glassey (1887–1970), see M. Stenton and S. Lees, *Who's Who of British Members of Parliament, III, 1919–1945* (Brighton 1979), p. 129, and *Who's Who* (1948), p. 1051. See also *Christian World*, 23 Feb. 1939 and 15 May 1941. His portrait forms the frontispiece to *Congregational Year Book* (1941). For Wentworth see Teresa Carlysle, *Wentworth College. A History* (Bournemouth 1997). That Mrs Peggy Wentworth was the cause of Rick Pym's collapse at Gulworth North is doubtless fortuitous.

[37] He added, as if to underline the parallels between Ronald Cornwell and Rick Pym: 'He came over as a somewhat more refined Robert Maxwell, as if he had learned his English at the Berlitz.' (*The Independent on Sunday*, 1 Aug. 1993, p. 4) There are numerous testimonies to Glassey's quality of voice. See below n. 58.

Accent is packaging. It is none the less suggestive. This study is largely about packaging and what it suggests in its later stages about the regionally significant yet nationwide aspirations of an alternative culture lodged within the political nation: protestant nonconformity. In this light the Cornwells and Glasseys merit closer inspection than the Pyms and Watermasters.

Alderman Pym, 'the beloved TP', with his good war and his Irish initials and wife, had died in the 1920s, leaving a stained-glass image of honourable bonhomie to which his son clung until his own death 60 years later night-portering in a run-down office block in Cheapside.[38] Such relationships as those between T.P. and Rick, Rick and Magnus, are the music of good fiction. Alderman Cornwell, known no less by his initials (A.E.F), was longer lived. He died in 1946. In private life he played bowls; in public life he was councillor, alderman, sheriff and mayor of Poole.[39] By profession an engineer (T.P. had been a timber merchant) and by religious profession a baptist, it was the latter which called for obituaries hinting at larger things. For his was an active church membership: superintendent of the York Road mission for at least 25 years, lay pastor at King's Road, Swanage, from its formation in 1908 and latterly honorary pastor,[40] secretary of the Parkstone Tabernacle at the time of his death, a personal member of the national Baptist Union from 1928 and treasurer of the Southern Baptist Association from 1931. The association's memorial resolution was at once conventional and revealing, at least for those knowing enough to break the code. The alderman was one of four commemorated laymen in 1946; two of the others were J.P.s. Here was no honorary treasurer[41] but an active citizen whose financial concerns were pastorally informed.[42]

Two factors give point to this memorial. The first is that his son Ronald's conviction for fraud, his first public (and chronic) disgrace, coincided with the alderman's prime as an association officer. R.T.A. Cornwell was a more than passable real-life Rick Pym. The second is Alderman Cornwell's relationship with the Tabernacle's minister. William Henry Higgins was no Welshman, and he may or may not have been Purgatory's Mr Philpott, but he was certainly a dissenting warhorse, serving in the west and east midlands before mellowing on the south coast. Parkstone was his last pastorate; he arrived in 1927 and stayed on after his retirement in 1935.[43] His first pastorate had been in Coventry. There he had been a passive resister, committed to Warwick gaol in March 1904 because of his opposition to Balfour's Education Act and his refusal to pay 'a rate . . . levied . . . through the influence of the secret societies at work throughout the

---

[38] le Carré, *A Perfect Spy*, pp. 33, 34, 437; 'T.P.' were the initials synonymous with the Irish nationalist M.P., Thomas Power ('Tay Pay') O'Connor (1848–1929), M.P. for Galway then Liverpool Scotland 1880–1929.

[39] For A.E.F. Cornwell (1876–1946) see *The Baptist Who's Who* [1933–4], p. 39, and *Southern Baptist Association Year Book 1946–1947*, pp. 8, 9, 25.

[40] In 1931 King's Road, Swanage, sat 80 and had 17 church members and 17 Sunday scholars. *Baptist Hand Book* (1932), p. 78. It closed in 1953.

[41] 'In matters of finance he was meticulous, scrupulously and jealously safeguarding as a sacred trust the monies that came to him. The "Spending" of the Association was ever a matter of conscience.' In short, his son's antithesis. *Southern Baptist Association Year Book 1946–1947* p. 25.

[42] Thus, 'The small Church had a great attraction for him'; and 'he sought and succeeded in interpreting the Christian ethic' – with the added reflection, 'his was a truly Christian home'. *Ibid.*

[43] For William Henry Higgins (1864–1951), see *Baptist Hand Book* (1952), pp. 328–9.

length and breadth of the Land'.[44] That martyrdom, referred to obliquely if at all in his official obituary ('His courage and integrity were flawless. He never feared the face of man'), was not repeated. The warhorse turned workhorse, freeing successive churches of debt, Parkstone among them, and holding the Southern Association's 75 churches together as its secretary during Cornwell's first five years as treasurer, and then as president two years after Cornwell. The alderman's theme was 'Our Ample and Guaranteed Possessions'. Higgins's was 'The Word of God and our Church Polity'.[45]

Higgins and Cornwell were brotherly veterans of nonconformity's brief, bright Edwardian afternoon. Glassey's generation too basked in its later rays. Cornwell was Bridgwater born, Higgins was Birmingham. Glassey was a Yorkshireman, though no short 'a' ever betrayed him. His formation, in fact, was quite unlike Makepeace Watermaster's. Less obviously representative of a type, it was truer to life. Far from being a Welsh manufacturer like old Goodman Watermaster, who exploited his cheap immigrant labour and satisfied his ancestral conscience by building a baptist chapel, Glassey's father, William, was a midland born and trained congregational minister who died of pneumonia and overwork in his early 40s. His career had been exemplary: an early vocation, a 'big awkward lad's' training at J.B. Paton's Nottingham Institute, specifically aimed at men whose calling ran ahead of their education, and then an early marriage and four pastorates in 20 years, one of them an assistantship, all of them in Yorkshire, two of them with moderately-sized churches in sturdily self-contained communities. Attendances grew, activities prospered, opportunities beckoned: membership of the board of guardians, a workhouse chaplaincy, the secretaryship of the local London Missionary Society auxiliary, chairmanship of the local Free Church Council and of the Huddersfield and Heckmondwike district of the powerful Yorkshire Congregational Union; and an early death because 'flu turned into pneumonia when he left his sickroom to conduct a funeral in poor weather. He left a widow and four children, of whom Alec, the eldest, was 18, and Olive was a few weeks. His own funeral was a demonstration of civic and ecclesiastical solidarity. 'There had not been such a funeral at Earlsheaton within the memory of man.'[46]

Alec Glassey was a credit to his father's memory. Penistone Grammar, a Pennine school with a sound academic reputation (William Glassey's penultimate pastorate had been in Penistone), was followed by Sheffield, business, and early marriage. Elizabeth Glassey and her children settled in Pitsmoor, an acceptable Sheffield suburb, more red-brick than stone and not yet swamped by council housing, rising Barnsley-wards above the heavy metal works of the ugliest city in Europe. Pitsmoor was attractive to clerks, Alec now among them, teachers, middle managers, and an encouraging swathe of manufacturers. It has since gone down in the world. There were two flourishing congregational churches close to hand, Wicker and Burngreave, both now long closed. And there were the Longbottoms.

---

[44] See C. Binfield, *Pastors and People. The Biography of a Baptist Church. Queen's Road, Coventry* (Coventry 1984), p. 132.

[45] W. Fancutt, *The Southern Baptist Association and Its Churches* (Andover, [c. 1974]), p. ix.

[46] For William Glassey (1863–1906) see *Congregational Year Book* (1907), pp. 155–6. The Earlsheaton church, on the edge of Dewsbury, paid for the funeral and raised a memorial fund for the bereaved family of £580 (approx £30,000 in 1999 terms). In 1906 its membership was 165, with a Sunday school of 364 and 46 teachers. *Ibid.*, p. 321.

The Longbottoms, William, George, Charles, and Harry, their wives, sisters, and daughters, were an increasingly well-circumstanced family of coal merchants, colliery agents, and congregationalists. By 1921 Longbottom and Co. Ltd (telegraphic address 'Longbottom, Sheffield') had seven depots and were agents for at least five large colliery companies in south Yorkshire, Derbyshire, and Nottinghamshire.[47] Their houses, mostly in Pitsmoor but increasingly further afield, had names like Oakleigh (or Oak Lea) and The Hollies. Their chapel was Burngreave, a vigorous cause in red romanesque, half as large again as Earlsheaton, propelled into social service and settlement work by Thomas Tucker Broad, its minister from 1893.[48] Broad, a man of William Glassey's generation, was set in the Silvester Horne mould: he became M.P. for Clay Cross at the coupon election.[49] The Longbottom connexion extended from the 1880s to the Great War, thus encompassing Burngreave's prime, Broad's prime, and their own rise to affluence. The Longbottom men contributed to its good causes, most notably its jubilee fund, and to their city's go-ahead Congregational Association. Between 1897 and 1917, three of them represented their church at national and county union assemblies, a commitment which entailed attendance at four slabs of meetings, each lasting for several days. Representative congregationalists were deeply politicized. In due course Burngreave acquired a stained glass window and an organ in Longbottom memory. The Longbottom women were correspondingly active in the chapel's sewing meeting, women's meeting, young women's missionary band, and Sunday school.[50] Mary Hannah ('Miss Longbottom'), who had been matron of the local workhouse, was their pace-setter, representing her church at both county and national level for a longer period than any of the male Longbottoms.[51] Her niece, Mary Eleanor, was set to emulate her.

Mary Eleanor Longbottom (always Mary, never Nell), was a little, managing woman, recalled in later life as difficult and manipulative (the word 'dauntless' comes to mind), more in the public eye than Nell Watermaster can ever have been. She was the daughter of George Longbottom of Oakleigh, across the Barnsley Road from T.T. Broad's manse. Hers was the bustling, conscientiously networked, naturally political, community which the Glasseys joined. Elizabeth Glassey found herself sitting on the women's meeting committee and representing Burngreave at the Sheffield Gospel Temperance Association. Alec found himself secretary of Burngreave's Congregational Guild and leader of its Young People's Own.

[47] Advertisement, *Sheffield Congregational Year Book* (1921), p. 123.

[48] In 1910, the year of Alec Glassey's marriage, Burngreave, erected in 1868, had 233 members and a Sunday school of 300. *Congregational Year Book* (1911), p. 352.

[49] For Thomas Tucker Broad (1863–1935), Liberal M.P. Clay Cross 1918–22, candidate Leyton East 1923, see Stenton and Lees, *Who's Who of British Members of Parliament, III, 1919–1945* p. 42. For C.S. Horne (1865–1914), minister of Whitefield's Tabernacle London, who was also Liberal M.P. Ipswich 1906–14, see *Dictionary of National Biography. Missing Persons*, ed. C.S. Nicholls (Oxford, 1993).

[50] For Longbottom congregationalism see especially *Sheffield Congregational Year Books* (1904–13), *passim*; the records of Burngreave congregational church are now lodged with Sheffield City Archives, although some remain with Central United Reformed Church, Sheffield. I am particularly indebted for help here to Miss K. Head.

[51] Mary Hannah Longbottom (d. 1917) 'was a most valuable worker, not only in the Church at Burngreave, but in the Association and the Missionary Auxiliary'. *Sheffield Congregational Year Book* (1918), unpaginated. The Fir Vale Workhouse, off Barnsley Road, is now the Northern General Hospital.

There is a story, though the dates fail to match the remembered details, that Mary Longbottom left an enviably eligible prospect for the handsomely penniless, and younger, Alec Glassey.[52] Certainly their marriage was in the chapel mainstream. She was secretary of the Sheffield Congregational Association's Young Women's Missionary Band and he was secretary of its male equivalent. Those were strategic positions, whence talent could be scouted and sensible friendships cemented. Sheffield congregationalism was not wealthy but it was long established, surprisingly influential and, apparently, expanding. For several generations it had played a formative role in Sheffield Liberalism. Its activities offered considerable opportunities for go-ahead young men and women.

Mary Eleanor Longbottom and Alec Ewart Glassey were married in September 1908. They moved from Pitsmoor's Firshill Road to Abbeydale's Fossdale Road, similar houses but a quite different side of Sheffield.[53] There was a change of occupation too. The young clerk became an elocution teacher.

That profession has largely vanished. Views have changed on accent and articulation. In 1910 voice and appearance told. They were indispensable counters in the English pastime of placing people, and people in Mary Longbottom's and Alec Glassey's position could not afford to ignore them. For at least the first three decades of the century, and in some places for longer, the requirements of chapel bazaars and conversaziones, and the multiplicity of social events needing to be at once uplifting, educational, enjoyable, and profitable, provided presentable young men and women with an alluring opportunity midway between the stage, the pulpit, and the party platform. The 1911 *Congregational Year Book* carried a full page advertisement on Glassey's behalf. It was admirably angled ('the son of the late Rev. W. Glassey, of Dewsbury'). He was available for week-end engagements for preaching and recitals. He offered The Sky Pilot, Black Rock, The Prospector, among selections from all leading authors. He was young (a studio photograph was included), businesslike (syllabus, terms, dates etc were available), up-to-date (there was a telephone number), and experienced (there were testimonials from Hove – 'One seldom has the opportunity to be present at such a magnificent recital' – and Bromley – 'Humour and pathos, declamation and entreaty, rusticity and refinement, all had their place and were beautifully pourtrayed [*sic*]'). He was also fundamentally serious. 'He has rendered valuable service to the Colonial Missionary Society by the recital of Ralph Connor's stories, and has charmed his audience by the beautiful modulation of his voice and descriptive acting of the parts', wrote the society's secretary, Dr Burford Hooke.[54] It would be hard to imagine a better preparation for the work of a party agent or, indeed, a better way of becoming nationally known among one's natural constituency. Sheffield provided the opportunity and the springboard.

---

[52] She is said to have broken off her engagement to the owner of Skipper Sardines in favour of Glassey who was three and a half years her junior. But the owner of Skipper Sardines, (Sir) Angus Watson (b. 1874) of Newcastle was by then married to a childhood sweetheart. He was, however, a congregationalist and a Liberal, chairman of the Congregational Union in 1935–6. See A. Watson, *My Life. An Autobiography*, (1937).

[53] 'Charnwood', 33 Fossdale Road, surrounded by Abbeydale, Coverdale, Bannerdale, Swaledale, Dovedale, and Edgedale Roads, might furnish the conspiracy theorists with a prototype for Purgatory's Airdale Road, where lived 'T.P.'s' widow.

[54] *Congregational Year Book* (1911), p. 20, advertisement section.

The accent vanished and timbre took over. Longbottom's coal provided the necessary financial cushion. War provided the decisive break.

Glassey's was an active war. He commanded a trench mortar battery in France and was mentioned in despatches. He did not return to Sheffield. An up-and-coming congregational architect, Mansell Jenkinson, who was a fellow graduate of the Young Men's Missionary Band, now serving in the Artists' Rifles and newly married to a baptist from Leicester, took over the house in Fossdale Road in Spring 1916[55], and in January 1920 Alec and Mary Glassey transferred their church membership from Sheffield to Parkstone. Theirs were now southern lives. Alec had become a leisured gentleman; he looked and sounded the part to perfection and his homestead proved it. His public life was now divided between politics and the voluntary sector. On the broader front there were the local bench, Bournemouth Y.M.C.A., the Brotherhood Movement and, later in life and spurred on by his wife whose special interest it became, there was the N.S.P.C.C. On the denominational front there was the London Missionary Society's easily forgotten sister, the Colonial (later the Commonwealth) Missionary Society, with its particular focus on the Caribbean. This too was a special interest of Mary Glassey's. In Sheffield Alec had recited for it. From Parkstone he twice served as its national chairman. Sheffield's Congregational Association was now replaced by Dorset's Congregational Association, of which he thrice became chairman. Here too Mary Glassey complemented her husband. In 1933 she was the Dorset Congregational Association's first woman chairman. Since Women's Guilds were her forte (shades of her sisters, mother, and aunts at Burngreave), 1933 was remembered as a 'time of uplift' for Dorset's Guilds,[56] and by 1940 she had been co-opted to the council of the national Congregational Union as well as to its Women's Guild committee. As petite as her husband was commanding, fiercely teetotal, well turned-out (her expensive-looking fur coats have been recalled by one who knew – and liked – her), and generally careful of appearances – the name Longbottom had long been an agony to her, for hers was the generation which never referred to a 'bottom', only a 'base' – Mrs Glassey becomes less and less like Lady Watermaster.

If this was the small change of public life, it was none the less the small change indispensable to serious political ambition, especially for Liberals. Mary Glassey was a Liberal of purest essence, undeviatingly Gladstonian. Alec would have been more of a trimmer. Together they conscientiously played their party's traditionary networks. Dorset had an old dissenting tradition, well represented among its rural middle classes. Alec Glassey became president of the East Dorset Liberal Association and a vice-president of the Western Liberal Federation. He stood for East Dorset in 1924 and sat for East Dorset from May 1929 to October 1931. Within a year of his arrival at Westminster he was his party's English whip (1930–1) and in September 1931 he became a junior lord of the treasury. It was a rapid rise, none like it since the M.P. for Stroud, the congregational barrister H.S.P. Winterbotham, had been given minor office by Gladstone in 1871.[57]

---

[55] John Mansell Jenkinson (1883–1965) founded a sizeable architectural practice and was a prominent Sheffield congregationalist. His wife belonged to the baptist branch of a Leicester timber and engineering family, the Gimsons, notable for their Arts and Crafts links. Thus are cousinhoods consolidated.

[56] L. Brown, *The Story of the Dorset Congregational Association* (Bridport, 1971), p. 85.

He was thus in his early 40s, almost his father's age when felled by pneumonia, when his political ambitions peaked and fell, shortly after Olive Glassey and Dot Watermaster fell for Ronald Cornwell and Rick Pym, and Sir Makepeace Watermaster (whose age, though nowhere given, must have had a good ten years' edge on Glassey) confronted Purgatory's night school boys and their march of Christian people to join the highest in the land.

Alec Glassey's brief place among the highest was deftly captured in a book of parliamentary portraits, James Johnson's *A Hundred Commoners*.[58] Glassey was one of the 100. He was one of 59 Liberal M.P.s, 32 of them nonconformists, who had been returned on 23.4 per cent of the vote.[59] It was not too difficult for a determined man to shine in so reduced, yet not hopeless, a context, but it was Glassey's maiden speech which marked him out for inclusion among Johnson's commoners. It was the reciter's reward and Johnson nicely displayed its strengths and weaknesses. He rhapsodized over such a voice as a man would die for, 'deep, strong, melodious', apparently effortless, quite perfect. 'Mr. Glassey, the moment that he opened his mouth, filled with pleasing and satisfying sound ears that are always expectant but often disappointed'. Johnson analyzed the style; he skipped over the content:

> Mr. Glassey does not cultivate the plain, unadorned style so common today in Parliament. He has a certain genre of beautiful expression, and he is not afraid of using images and pictures, of threading purple into his speeches. That, also, is a welcome quality, if it is not too conspicuous . . . He recites poetry supremely well . . . but a long poetical quotation may easily sink a speech. That Mr. Glassey finished his maiden speech with a fourteen or sixteen line quotation and yet did not entirely risk both it and himself is a proof that he has unusual elocutionary powers as well as an unusual personality. But he must be careful to avoid such a thing in the future.

There was an easy explanation for both strengths and weaknesses, with a word of warning:

> He is an ardent Free Churchman, and one guesses that he belongs to that class of public speakers who have learned the rudiments of their art in the pulpit and have spoken much more in it than on the platform . . . He is an ethical politician, and when he pleads for a moral cause, such as disarmament, his sincerity is manifest . . . yet it would be well for him to avoid the sermonic style . . . habitual Parliamentary usefulness is procurable only along another line of speech.

Would he achieve it? Would what had been forged in Penistone Grammar and tempered in Burngreave, Hove, and Bromley, be transmuted in Westminster? 'He has the intelligence and the speaking aptitude, probably also the speaker's sense of atmosphere, which makes it easy to accommodate one's natural characteristics to the special requirements of Parliament'. What he did not have was time. Glassey's political footwork was not deft

---

[57] For Henry Selfe-Page Winterbotham (1837–73), Liberal M.P. Stroud 1867–73, under-secretary of state, home office, 1871–3, see *D.N.B.*

[58] J. Johnson, *A Hundred Commoners* (1931), pp. 292–4. The subsequent quotations are taken from this.

[59] S. Koss, *Nonconformity in Modern British Politics* (1975), p. 182.

enough. The family were on good terms with Lloyd George, who stayed at The Homestead and for whom the youngest Glassey girl made the statutory apple pie bed; but in parliament Glassey was a Samuelite, which explains the minor coalition office, and the further evidence is that he was on the way to becoming a Simonite. His defeat in 1931 put paid to any of that. It was felt in east Dorset, and not least in Parkstone, that their member preferred Westminster to constituency duties. The Parkstone deacon credited with securing Glassey's selection is also credited with engineering his defeat.[60] It is such a story as lends itself best to the embroideries of fiction.[61]

There remained congregationalism. Glassey had a gift for fund-raising. In the early 1920s, and still in his early 30s, he raised £3,000 as Dorset's contribution to the Congregational Forward Movement.[62] This was intended to augment low ministerial stipends, foreshadowing Alderman Cornwell's similar though more local concern for baptist ministerial sustentation funds. Twenty years later Glassey repeated his campaign on a national scale as chief commissioner between 1942 and 1957 for congregationalism's reconstruction fund for damaged or destroyed churches. 'And Alec Glassey will always be remembered for his clarion call, like Nehemiah of old, to "arise and build".'[63] There is certainly a Watermasterish sound to that, for he had already been recognized as among the highest in the Congregational land when he became chairman of the Congregational Union of England and Wales in May 1941, his denomination's supreme representative honour. He could claim, he said, 'the distinction of being the first ordinary man to occupy the chair'.[64]

Glassey's later years are inevitably to be seen as years of decline, perhaps disintegration. He still came across as a man to be liked, 'tall, attractive, unassuming and charming', in contrast to his wife, who was admired for other qualities; but his eye for good-looking women aroused comment and there were rumours about his drinking habits. The denomination's leadership began to distance itself. He wrote, and he and Mary paid for, *1662 and All That*, a Dorset commemoration of the tercentenary of the great ejectment. He retired from the bench. He died in June 1970, lonely and blind, his eyes, like Makepeace Watermaster's, literally starless. Congregationalism's highest in

---

[60] This was H. W. Hicks (1880–1947), headmaster of Branksome Heath, Parkstone, a future secretary of the Dorset Congregational Association and Dorset commissioner for the denominational reconstruction fund of which Glassey became chief commissioner. See below, n. 63.

[61] There is indeed a now forgotten classic which charts the career of a fictional younger anglican contemporary of Glassey's, Augustus Stryver of Bury St Edmunds, who becomes a Roman catholic in the year he comes out as a National Liberal: R. Fulford, *The Right Honourable Gentleman. A Satire* (1945).

[62] Brown, *Dorset Congregational Association*, p. 79.

[63] *Ibid.*, p. 89. And from 1953–7 he combined this with the co-treasurership of the Congregational Union of England and Wales. Many found his public utterances memorable. His description, and the gestures which accompanied it, of the cabbage smells from the British Restaurant lodged in the Memorial Hall (congregationalism's headquarters in the City) has remained in one memory 50 years after it was first heard at a May assembly in Westminster Chapel.

[64] *Christian World*, 15 May 1941. Two years earlier, 23 Feb. 1939, he had been *Christian World*'s 'Portrait of the Week'; Mary Glassey was 'Portrait of the Week' for 13 June 1940. Glassey's year as chairman allowed for some useful networking. A preaching engagement in Worksop (where the Charles Longbottoms now lived) led to the removal of its young minister, Walter Dickinson, to Parkstone, where he spent the rest of his life.

the land were not at his funeral. The Homestead now has several lesser homesteads built in its garden-party grounds.

5

As an account of the world and mentality of espionage, *A Perfect Spy* has an inescapable political dimension, yet neither that nor the more surprising ecclesiastical dimension of 'this most beguiling of spy stories' is caught in the publisher's dust-jacket *précis*, nor were they caught in the novel's adaptation for television. These two dimensions, however, are integral to the plot and to each other. For *A Perfect Spy* is also a novel of relationships – the narrator with his true self, and the narrator with his father, as well as with his friends, his wives, his class, his country. All save the first two relationships are hollow and each is hollow because of what had formed those first relationships. And here we come to their prime cement – evangelical dissent.

Two things are foundational for evangelical dissenters. The first is their fallen-ness. The second is their relationship with their Saviour. If the second has no substance, then the first is the more terrible. That is what makes *A Perfect Spy* both credible and powerful for those who know the dissenting tradition. The betrayals may hurt. They cannot surprise.

There is also a third foundation. Dissent is a political condition. Dissenters are disso-ciated from established ways in church, politics, and society, however much they are also brought into being and defined by those ways. *A Perfect Spy* illuminates a late stage in the relationship between what until recently had been two remarkable success stories – Liberalism and the nonconformist conscience; and the quality of the illumination is explained once it is realized that this novel is a *roman à clef*.

The relationship between a political nation's establishment and dissent, secular or religious, is bound to be problematic. Success is inimical to dissent, although not neces-sarily to the alternative values which dissent represents. Integrity is bound to be compromised. That is cruelly explored and exploited in the world of the Watermasters and the Pyms, but it has its natural, less dramatic, parallels in the world of the Cornwells, Glasseys, Longbottoms, their fellow deacons and their ministers. These parallels can be the more suggestively drawn because Alec Glassey, Congregationalism's first 'ordinary' layman to be Union chairman, was representative not exceptional. Fiction may be strengthened by his weaknesses. History needs to be sensitive to his strengths.

There is a further element to both worlds, a political and moral underside which is certainly destructive of integrity although it is supposedly necessary for stability and consequently to be regarded as a form of public service, namely the engagement with espionage. This, in both fact and fiction, can only be glimpsed through a decidedly distorting mirror.

Magnus Pym's observation of life in the 1930s and 1940s at The Glades and in Purgatory's Tabernacle distils and perhaps explains the qualities of a perfect spy. He becomes head of station in Vienna. It is not surprising to find that espionage recruits from the once dissenting and still parliamentary classes, slithering on the quicksands of class and exploiting the ambiguities of their position, conjoining them with the real establishment. Pym, who is after all the public-school-educated nephew of a famous Liberal M.P. and the son of a notorious Liberal candidate, is asked if he too might like to enter parliament, 'where he can keep an eye on some of these fellow-travelling MPs'; but when he is also asked if he has any particular preference as to party, he has the grace to reply, 'I'd rather prefer it not to be the Liberals, if it's all the same to you'.[65] And Pym the baptist who has toyed with both Rome and Canterbury eventually marries into the real thing, the 'Church and spy Establishment' with spy connexions back to William the Conqueror and a Saxon church on the family estate, its 'Colonel the Reverend High Anglican vicar barking out his fire orders and rattling the incense like a mess-gong'.[66]

Pym's creator, John le Carré, worked as David Cornwell (and therefore Alec Glassey's nephew) for the foreign service between 1959 and 1964. In the words of an early publisher's blurb, he was 'educated at an English public school . . . entered the civil service [sic] . . . writes novels as an antidote to the *déformation professionelle* of a service which he much admires . . . His interests are foreign travel, book illustration and politics'.[67]

Neither Magnus Pym nor John le Carré is unique. Others of dissenting stock could be cited as having taken this way of reconciling what *A Perfect Spy's* dust-jacket called 'the conflicting elements' of a 'very English heritage'. To give one: H.S.P. Winterbotham's great-nephew, F.W. Winterbotham, Charterhouse, Christ Church and pedigree stock breeding notwithstanding, was brought up in Stroud congregationalism before service with the air staff and foreign office from 1929. Although he chiefly owed his subsequent fame to his part in 'Ultra' as misremembered in his memoirs, Winterbotham was of real significance in setting up the special liaison units to be inconspicuously found in each headquarters.

With such in mind we return with Magnus Pym, head of station in Vienna and in his 50s, to the south Devon coast, not to Purgatory but to Farleigh Abbot, a resort not far from it though its topography suggests Penzance, not in Spring 1931 but in Autumn 1984. It is still Sunday, 'the small hours of a blustery October Morning', 'a black and gusty day . . . as sabbaths in these parts mostly are'. Here too, across 'from a granite workhouse with Public Library engraved over a funereal door', there is a 'hideous Baptist church that told you God was no fun either', its 'graceless tower' 'posturing against the racing clouds':[68]

> This was granny-land. This was Sunday, when aunts rode to church with collection-coins inside their gloves . . . Pym gazed down fondly on chimney pots, churches, dunes and slate roofs that looked as though they were waiting to be lifted up to Heaven by their topknots . . . a hymn tune issued from the house, together with a smell of roast chicken, blue bag, carbolic soap and godliness. . . In her kitchen, the wife of the Baptist minister, wearing her lovat dressing gown, is unpegging her son's football gear from the washing line in preparation for today's match. Pym draws back swiftly. He has

---

[65] le Carré, *A Perfect Spy*, p. 411.
[66] *Ibid.*, pp. 435, 270.
[67] Description in *Call For the Dead* (Penguin edn., 1964). The outline of John le Carré's (David John Moore Cornwell) early career in *Who's Who*, from Sherborne School to Bern University, certainly runs parallel to Magnus Pym's.
[68] le Carré, *A Perfect Spy*, pp. 7, 455.

caught a glint of steel in the manse gateway, but it is only the minister's bicycle still chained to the trunk of a monkey-puzzle tree as a precaution against unchristian covetousness.[69]

And Magnus Pym's cover is about to be blown.

---

[69] *Ibid.*, p. 24.

Index